RACE, MULTICULTURALISM, AND THE MEDIA

CLINT C. WILSON II
FÉLIX GUTIÉRREZ

RACE, MULTICULTURALISM, AND THE MEDIA

FROM MASS TO CLASS COMMUNICATION

SECOND EDITION

PUBLISHED IN THE FIRST EDITION AS
MINORITIES AND THE MEDIA

SAGE Publications
International Educational and Professional Publisher
Thousand Oaks   London   New Delhi

For information address:

SAGE Publications, Inc.
2455 Teller Road
Thousand Oaks, California 91320
E-mail: order@sagepub.com

SAGE Publications Ltd.
6 Bonhill Street
London EC2A 4PU
United Kingdom

SAGE Publications India Pvt. Ltd.
M-32 Market
Greater Kailash I
New Delhi 110 048 India

Printed in the United States of America

Library of Congress Cataloging-in-Publication Data

Wilson, Clint C.
    Race, multiculturalism, and the media: From mass to class communication / Clint C. Wilson II, Félix Gutiérrez.
        p. cm.
    Rev. ed. of : Minorities and media: Diversity and the end of mass communication. c1985.
    Includes bibliographical references and index.
    ISBN 0-8039-4628-7 (c: alk. paper). — ISBN 0-8039-4629-5 (pbk.: alk. paper)
    1. Mass media and minorities—United States. 2. Multiculturalism—United States. I. Gutiérrez, Félix. II. Wilson, Clint C.
III. Title.
P94.5M.552U69 1995
305.8'00973—dc20   95-13492

This book is printed on acid-free paper.

95 96 97 98 99 10 9 8 7 6 5 4 3 2 1

Sage Production Editor: Astrid Virding
Sage Typesetter: Joe Cribben

Dedicated to Nancy Hicks Maynard
and the late Robert C. Maynard

Their vision, determination,
and effectiveness inspired us and others
to believe that the First Amendment could belong to
everyone willing and able to fight for it.

CONTENTS

Preface and
Acknowledgments

When the first edition of this book, titled *Minorities and Media: Diversity and the End of Mass Communication,* was published in 1985 it was among the first scholarly works that attempted to chronicle, organize, and analyze the relationship between peoples of color and mainstream "mass media" in the United States. At that time the discussion among media executives, professional practitioners, and communications educators had been under way for more than two decades about how to respond to the issues raised in the 1968 report by the Kerner Commission on civil disorders that took them to task for historic and sustained media maltreatment of non-Whites. For the first time, *Minorities and Media* sought to reveal the commonalities of media treatment of Native, Black, Latino, and Asian Americans instead of singularly focusing on the grievances suffered by any one group or perpetrated by any one medium. The 1994 convening in Atlanta, Georgia, of the first "Unity" conference, bringing media professionals from the four minority journalism associations together for the first time on a national scale, provided a glimpse of the potential power a unified voice can have toward effecting change in media industries. The authors are pleased that their earlier work has stimulated growth of college curricular offerings on pluralizing the media across the United States over the past decade, thereby exposing the new generation of media professionals to the importance of multicultural inclusion in all aspects of public communication.

The number of scholars who have turned their attention to the study of various disenfranchised groups and their relationship to mainstream communications media has grown considerably since publication of *Minorities and Media*. These efforts have broadened the discussion and impacted favorably on the racial composition of media workforces and product content. This book, however, in the tradition of its predecessor, maintains its focus on the four major racial groups as defined herein. The purpose of this edition is to update developments in the areas identified in the first edition and to provide additional analytical and factual information where appropriate. Although the authors acknowledge and welcome the many contributions to the literature of other scholars touching on the topics of this work, no attempt is made in this volume to provide more than an analytical overview of the groups and public media industries it addresses. It is not the purpose of this book, or its predecessor, to be an encyclopedia of all studies in the field.

But, there are significant changes in this book. The title has been changed: *Race, Multiculturalism, and the Media: From Mass to Class Communication*. We believe it more accurately describes the focus of our work and recognizes the fruition of developments we foresaw in *Minorities and Media*. As we noted in the earlier book, the term *minorities* is not only inaccurate in many instances when referring to the cultural groups at issue, but carries the connotation that these groups are less important components in the American social fabric. Thus, use of the term *minorities* is limited in this volume to the extent possible. The authors deem the concept of racial identity as a descriptor to be more useful for this book in context with the subject of mainstream public media. The subtitle of the previous book, *Diversity and the End of Mass Communication*, reflected the authors' view that rapid and sweeping change in the demographic composition of the United States would force change in the way the media do business. Specifically, we predicted that the media's approach would shift from seeking to appeal to a homogenized "mass" audience to a strategy of targeting audience segments along racial and/or other demographic lines. As the reader will discover, the present book recognizes this change to be fully operational at the threshold of the 21st century and the new subtitle, *From Mass to Class Communication*, is self-evident. Public communications media no longer address an amorphous "mass" audience but rather target audiences by demographic classification—thus the emergence of "class" rather than "mass" communication. In addition to the necessary updating of statistical data and documentation of subsequent developments, a chapter has been added to reflect the importance of the public relations profession on media content and corporate communications. Another organizational change is the inclusion of a separate listing of suggested readings reflecting the increase of scholarly activity in this area of study.

Limitations in this work exist in several respects. As noted, it concerns itself only with the four largest racial minority groups in the United States: Native, Black, Latino, and Asian Americans. Other cultural or social groups sometimes categorized as "minorities" (East Indians, people with disabilities, gays and lesbians, women in the workforce, etc.) are not subjects of this work, although some parallels may be seen in their relationships to mainstream media. Similarly, this book does not attempt to address every general audience public communications medium. Therefore, music recording, book publishing, magazine fiction, or other media forms are not within the scope of this work. Despite some advances in recent years, the authors still find that research material on the subject of racial and cultural groups is uneven. For example, there is much less literature on Asian media in the United States than on Black media and less on Native American employment in television than on their images in motion pictures. Thus, it was not possible to tell the complete story of each group in every chapter. Such gaps in research literature, however, continue to suggest areas for future study by students and scholars who are seriously interested in documenting the role of media as they have related to racial groups in the United States.

In this book the terms *Asian* and *Asian American* are used to describe people who trace their origins to the Asian continent, as well as those from the Pacific Islands. The term *Black* is used to describe African Americans and others who trace their origins to the sub-Saharan part of the African continent. *Latinos* is used as an inclusive term for persons of Latin American or Spanish background, including the

Caribbean region. The terms *Native American* and *Indian* are used to describe the native peoples of the continent that Europeans and other immigrants have called America. The terms *White* and *Anglo* are used as applied by the U.S. Bureau of the Census and describe persons of European background who are not Latinos. All terms are capitalized in the text when referring to people of different races and cultures.

The authors wish to reiterate acknowledgments of persons, and their affiliations at the time, who provided assistance during preparation of the first edition of this work. They include graduate research assistants Carey Jue and David Tomsky. Also Luther Luedtke, who provided support when he served as Interim Director of the University of Southern California School of Journalism. Appreciation is also extended to Erwin Kim, a former USC colleague, whose assistance with the historiography of film portions of the text was invaluable. Other colleagues at USC who made important contributions included Lena Chao and Stanley Rosen, of the university's East Asian Studies Center, who assisted in translating portions of the first Asian American newspaper along with graduate student Stanley Chung. Students in our courses at USC brought enthusiasm for the subject of race and the media and were a source of inspiration and encouragement, as was Alice Marshall of Wave Publications.

Important in the development of historical information in the first edition were Michael Emery and Tom Reilly of the journalism faculty at California State University, Northridge. Jorge Reina Schement, University of California, Los Angeles, and Hugo Garcia of the Northeast Newspapers in Los Angeles provided much of the stimulation for sections on audience segmentation.

Also Armando Valdez of Stanford University and Don Carson and Edith Auslander of the University of Arizona provided speaking opportunities and comments that led to some of the concepts developed in that chapter. Carolyn McIntosh, research librarian at the University of Southern California, provided valuable assistance in locating material on topics covered in the book, and staff members of the Margaret Herrick Library, Academy of Motion Picture Arts and Sciences assisted in obtaining photographs.

Gratitude is extended to those who have been gracious with their time and expertise during preparation of this edition of the book.

They include Vernon Stone, Research Director for the Radio and Television News Directors Association; Brenda Alexander of the Howard University Department of Journalism; and numerous colleagues in the Minorities and Communications division of the Association for Education in Journalism and Mass Communications who consistently reinforced the need for completion of this volume. Debra Miller of Florida International University was especially helpful in providing the encouragement and opportunity to develop the information and analysis that became the chapter on public relations. We are also grateful to Elena Gutiérrez of the University of Michigan Department of Sociology for her editing and comments on the first chapter and to Bunty Anquoe and Tim Giago of *Indian Country Today* and Mark Trahant of the *Salt Lake City Tribune* for their insights into coverage of Native Americans. Jon Funabiki of San Francisco State University provided excellent counsel on issues relating to diversity in the media and journalism education, and Aissatou Sidime of Xavier University provided research for the chapter on advertising.

This book also brings to publication the results of research on the end of the mass media supported by Gerald M. Sass of the Gannett Foundation, now The Freedom Forum, in 1985 and 1986. His encouragement and counsel on this project and many other efforts over the past 16 years has been both valued and valuable. This research, which involved an extensive literature review of media trade journals and interviews with advertising and media executives in New York City in the summer of 1985, provided much of the basis for the analysis incorporated in the new title for this edition. We are grateful to Everette Dennis and the staff of The Freedom Forum Media Studies Center (then the Gannett Center for Media Studies) for their help and encouragement of this work during the summer of 1985 and beyond.

Conversations with a number of people helped advance our understanding of the impact of the new technologies on the issues of multiculturalism, media access, and usage discussed in this edition. They include Jorge Reina Schement of Rutgers University; Armando Valdez of Valdez and Associates; Nancy Hicks Maynard of Maynard Partners; Bruce Koon of the *San Jose Mercury News,* and Adam Clayton Powell III of The Freedom Forum Media Studies Center. Thanks also to students and colleagues at Howard University for insight and inspiration and to the staff and editors at Sage Publications for patience, advice, and encouragement during the preparation of this volume.

Most importantly, we must recognize the support, encouragement, and sacrifices made by those closest to us: Mary Julia Wilson and Clint C. Wilson III, and Marìa Elena, Elena Rebeca, Anita Andrea, and Alicia Rosa Gutiérrez. Without their sustaining presence and nurturing expressions the authors could not have completed the task.

— CLINT C. WILSON II
— FÉLIX F. GUTIÉRREZ

PART

1

Introduction

1

Racial Diversity in the Land of Majority Rule

In the spring of 1992, as a massive civil disturbance swept through parts of Los Angeles in the wake of jury verdicts acquitting three of four police officers of all charges of beating a Black motorist, a press conference was called in Beverly Hills. The topic: the riots. The main speaker: Black motorist Rodney King, whose beating by police had been videotaped and widely broadcast.

Without much fanfare and with the cautiousness of someone who had suddenly been thrust into the public spotlight, King simply, but eloquently, called for an end to the violence and asked, hopefully, "Can't we all get along?"

It was an important cry for reason to the residents of the nation's most racially diverse metropolitan areas located in California, the country's most racially diverse state. It was a question that residents of Los Angeles had been struggling with since the city was founded by a multiracial group of settlers sent north from Mexico's Pacific Coast by Spanish authorities in 1780.[1]

It is also a question that has become increasingly important to everyone in the United States as the nation's residents have struggled as they looked for ways to live, and let live, in a nation whose society is increasingly characterized by racial diversity. The riots and

3

the attention on Los Angeles came as the people in the United States were struggling for new ways to come to terms with racial and cultural awareness and identity in a nation that had long been based on common consensus and majority rule.

"No one wants to return to the days when a Euro-centric culture made many blacks, Latinos and Asians feel like outer-space aliens in their own nation; but too much emphasis on what separates us can deepen divisions," the *Los Angeles Times* editorialized several months after the riots.[2]

The newspaper quoted University of California at Berkeley ethnic studies professor Ronald Takaki as calling for people to look beyond their roots to find commonalities bridging their racial and ethnic identities:

> I think people, especially in the post-Rodney King era, are beginning to realize that we just can't study ourselves as separate groups. . . . We've gone beyond the need to recover identity and roots, and now we're realizing that our paths as members of different groups are crisscrossing each other.

These calls to seek and, hopefully, find commonalities and common ground came as the nation continued struggling with unresolved issues of race and culture and at a time when the groups often called "minorities" were becoming more assertive, numerous, and visible in the fabric of the United States. This soul searching had become heightened in the late 1980s and early 1990s as the national discussion on race became more focused, sharper, and divisive. This search also rocked the United States out of the mind-set of race relations earlier cast in the relationships between Blacks and Whites or between colored minorities and a White majority. It was a change that was long overdue.

Who Are the Minorities?

When used in its statistical sense, the term *minorities* refers to groups that are small in number, less than the majority. It had often been applied to people of color in the United States because as individual groups, Blacks, Latinos, Asians, and Native Americans did not comprise a large percentage of the national population. Over time, it became a convenient umbrella category under which any population that is not White could be placed.

It is, however, also a misleading label. It misleads the person using the term and those reading it to think of those who carry the label as small not only in number, but in importance. In a nation based on the democratic principle of majority rule it can make the interests and issues raised by "minorities" appear to be less important than those of the majority. Moreover, it is not always a statistically accurate term. In many cities across the United States the people who are members of groups labeled as racial "minorities" are actually the majority of the city's population when the members of the individual groups are added together. In these cases it is the Whites who are the minority.

The projected growth rates of Asian Americans, Blacks, Native Americans, and Latinos indicate that they will continue to grow at a faster rate than the White population through at least the middle of the 21st century. So even though they may be described in terms that make them appear to be a relatively small part of the current population, census bureau analysts examining factors such as immigration, birthrate, and average family size conclude that the people called "minorities" will continue to grow at a faster rate than the White majority population through the foreseeable future. These demographic changes are part of an evolving racial mix that has been part of the land that is now the United States since the arrival of the first European settlers in the early 1600s.

"The region changed from predominantly Native American to predominantly White Anglo-Saxon Protestant (WASP) in large part due to high mortality on the part of the former and high immigration and fertility on the part of the latter group," wrote population analysts Leon F. Bouvier and Cary B. Davis.

In 1800 close to 20 percent of what, by then was the United States of America, was Black—in large part, the result of high levels of immigration, albeit forced. By 1900, more significant changes had occurred. Blacks were only 10 percent of the population, but among Whites the proportion coming from southern and eastern Europe had grown substantially. . . . What had once been a predominantly WASP society with a Black minority was becoming much more heterogeneous. The proportions of Black and WASP were falling, as immigration reached new highs.[3]

As Bouvier and Davis pointed out, the influx of southern and eastern European immigrants gave rise to a the vision of the United States as a "melting pot" society. The "melting pot" was a popular way of describing the assimilation process of European immigrants to the United States in the late 1800s and early 1900s. Proponents of the model held that immigrants who came to the United States would, within a relatively short period of time, cast aside their European identities, cultures, and languages as they forged or were forced to adopt the loyalties, customs, and language of their new home.

The theory of the melting pot held that it was necessary to forget, or at least submerge, the culture of the homeland in order to be allowed to participate in the benefits of the United States. In essence, assimilation was the price of participation in society.[4] It was thought that within a generation or so the children of the European immigrants would have "melted" into the population of the United States and would no longer be identifiable by the national origin of their homeland. The idea was so dominant that it is reported that some factories held a ceremony in which immigrant workers would enter a stage from one side in their national costumes, pass, and change clothes behind a large symbolic melting pot, and emerge from behind the stage prop pot dressed in the clothes of the American working class.

Today the legacy of the melting pot is found among Americans who know little of their family history, other than that their grandparents or great-grandparents came from Germany, Ireland, Italy, Poland, or some other European country. Even though the grandchildren of those who blended into the melting pot might not be able to speak the language or share the customs of their forebears, there was an increased curiosity about family roots, national heritage, and past customs during the late 1980s and early 1990s, particularly as political changes and ethnic strife occurred in Eastern Europe.[5]

At the same time, there are non-European groups who, because of differences in race, legal status, or geographic proximity to the home country, have never blended, or been allowed to blend, into the melting pot of the United States. Rather than a melting pot, these groups have experienced the United States as a huge pot of stew. As in a stew pot, each group retains its individual identity while maintaining and contributing its distinctive flavor to those of other groups and absorbing some of the flavors of other groups.

All groups have participated in the process of contending with and contributing to the flow of race relations in the United States. This book focuses on the groups who have had the greatest visibility outside of the melting pot: Native Americans, Blacks, Asians, and Latinos.

Demographic Projections

As a nation whose population growth has historically been fueled by immigration, the United States has always had racial, national, and ethnic minorities. But, as noted earlier, the European immigrants who comprised most of the nation's immigrants for much of this nation's history have largely been encouraged to follow the melting pot model of assimilation. Those groups who fell outside of the melting pot have been counted, with varying degrees of accuracy, as separate groups. Racial and cultural designations have always been important in distinguishing between groups in the decennial censuses of the U.S. population. In 1790 the first census counted 757,000 Blacks, 92% of them living as slaves. They comprised 19.3% of the nation's population.[6]

The 1990 census continued to report data for racial minority groups among the 248.7 million residents of the United States. In 1990 the census bureau reported that 199.6 million of those counted were White (80.3% of the population), 29.9 million Black (12.1%), 22.3 million Hispanics or Latinos (9%), 7.2 million Asians and Pacific Islanders (2.9%), 1.9 million Native Americans counted as Indians, Eskimos, and Aleuts (0.8%) and "Other Races" accounted for 9.8 million (3.9%).[7]

It should be noted that Hispanics, who trace their roots to Spain, Latin America, or the Caribbean, can be of any race. The term *Hispanic* was created by the census bureau as an umbrella label for these

TABLE 1.1 Population Percentages in the United States 1970-1990

Group	1970	1980	1990	1990 Total (Millions)
White	—	83.1	80.3	199.6
Black	11.7	11.7	12.1	29.9
Native American	0.4	0.6	0.8	1.9
Asian/Pacific	0.8	1.5	2.9	7.2
Other	—	3.0	3.9	9.8
Hispanic*	4.5	6.4	9.0	22.3

NOTE: * Can be of any race.

people. It can be used interchangeably with the indigenous term *Latino*, the term most often used in this book.

Perhaps more meaningful than the actual figures were the growth rates for the racial minority groups that the census figures revealed for the decade between 1980 and 1990, continuing the sharp growth in their populations that was also present in the decade between 1970 and 1980. The census figures showed that the minority group growth rates continued to outpace the national rate. The census bureau reported the biggest growth was found in the Latino and Asian/Pacific Island groups, although Blacks and Native Americans also posted percentage gains substantially higher than the White majority. As a result, peoples of color continued to increase their share of the national population and continued what has been called "the browning of America.[8]

Overall, the population of the U.S. grew 9.8% from 1980 to 1990, with Whites posting a growth rate of 6% and dropping from 83.1% to 80.3% of the population. In the same period Hispanics grew from 6.4% to 9.0% of the United States' population, a growth rate of 53%. Asians and Pacific Islanders grew from 1.5% to 2.9%, a growth rate of 107.8%; Blacks from 11.7% to 12.1%, a growth rate of 13.2%; and Native Americans from 0.6% to 0.8%, a growth rate of 37.9%; and "Other Races" from 3.0% to 3.9%, a growth rate of 45.1%.[9] When grouped together, the census data showed that Blacks, Asians, Native American, Hispanic, and Other populations grew from 23.2% of the population to 28.7% in 1990 (see Table 1.1).

As steep as this reported growth rate was, it may be less than the reality for people of color. One reason is because the census bureau

Figure 1.1. In the mid-1990s general audience media continued to debate the importance of issues such as affirmative action, multiculturalism, and diversity. This May 1995 edition of *The Atlantic Monthly* features a cover story by Benjamin Schwarz on "The Diversity Myth: America's Leading Export."

admittedly undercounted the nation's population. The most under-counted areas were the inner cities where people of color are often likely to live.[10] The other is that Hispanics, many of whom are either of indigenous backgrounds or of mestizo, mulatto, or other mixed race backgrounds are first asked to indicate race and then to mark their ethnicity. In 1990, 52% of the Hispanics checked the White category, 43% the "Other Race" category, and the remaining 5% Asian, Black, or American Indian. Nearly 98% of the nearly 10 million Americans who chose the "Other Race" category in 1990 also indicated they are Hispanic.[11] But even with the shortcomings of census count, the growth rate of Blacks, Asians, Native Americans, and Latinos has moved steadily upward over the past two decades.

There were many causes cited for the steady growth of racial minorities when compared with overall population trends. One reason is that most racial minority groups have a younger median age than the White population and, thus, are more likely to be within the childbearing, family-rearing ages. Their children are also likely to bear and raise their families in the near future.

Another reason was increased immigration from Asia and Latin America. Although in earlier decades Europe had supplied large numbers of immigrants to the United States, during the 1970s immigration to the United States from Asia and Latin America increased sharply. Some of this was spurred by warfare and political turmoil in certain countries in these regions. Other immigrants were driven by the desire for an improvement in their economic status. But, for whatever reason, the United States continued to be the land of opportunity for these new residents, just as it had been for the earlier European immigrants. The Population Research Bureau reported in 1982 that between 1977 and 1979 immigrants from Latin America and Asia accounted for 42% and 39%, respectively, of the immigrants admitted to the United States, accounting for 81% of the immigrants to the country. Europe accounted for only 13%. In contrast, between 1931 and 1960, Europeans comprised 58% of the immigrants, Latin Americans 15%, and Asians 5%.[12]

These trends continued in the 1980s, the census bureau reported in 1992. Between 1985 and 1990 nearly 5 million immigrants came to the United States, enough to account for one in four foreign-born residents in the country. In 1990 foreign-born residents totaled 19.8

million and accounted for 7.9% of the nation's population, up from
4.7% in 1970. Continuing the trends of the 1970s, the most recent
immigrants were most likely to come from Asia or Latin America, not
Europe. The Immigration and Naturalization Service reported that
in the late 1980s the three most common countries of origin for
immigrants were Mexico, the Philippines, and Korea.[13]

Of the U.S. residents who were born in foreign countries, Mexico
was by far the greatest contributor, accounting for 21.7% of foreign-
born U.S. residents. Other nations in the top 10 are as follows: the
Philippines, 4.6%; Canada, 3.8%; Cuba, 3.7%; Germany, 3.6%; the
United Kingdom, 3.2%; Italy, 2.9%; Korea, 2.9%; Vietnam, 2.7%; and
China, 2.7%.[14]

"The 1980s was the largest decade for people legally immigrating
with 10 million. In the 1990s, we'll have that many or more," INS
spokesman Duke Austin told *USA Today* in 1992. Austin said a new
immigration law in 1990 had increased the number of immigrants.
In 1991 alone, 704,000 persons immigrated to the United States.[15]
The number of immigrants jumped to 846,000 in 1992, the largest
number of recorded immigrants entering the country since the
12-month period ending June 30, 1914.[16] With war, famine, political
repression, and ethnic strife affecting many countries, the United
States planned to admit 122,000 immigrants as refugees in 1993,
most of them coming from East and Southeast Asia.[17]

Another factor spurring the growing racial and cultural diversity
of the United States was the differences in the birthrate of Whites
and non-Whites, with Blacks and Hispanics having more children
than Whites. In the early 1980s, White women averaged 1.76 children, whereas for Latinos the average was 2.6 children and for Blacks,
2.3 children.[18] In the past the census bureau assumed that the
childbearing rates for all racial and ethnic groups would eventually
be the same and that there would be a steady decline in the number
of children each woman would bear. Noting, however, "a dramatic
rise in total fertility levels to almost 2.1 births per woman" and
finding no historical evidence to support the assumption that childbearing rates would become equal, the census bureau abandoned
both positions in a 1992 report.[19]

Analysts of population trends cited other possible causes of the
minority population boom. These included a possible increase in the

number of persons designating themselves as members of minority groups, a change in the racial categories used on census forms, and a stepped up effort accurately to count members of different minority groups by the census bureau. But, whatever the reason, the bottom line was clear. Minorities had grown at a substantially higher rate than the rest of the nation's population and, as a result, comprised a larger percentage of the United States than ever before. Even more important are the projections for the future.

The Impact of Future Growth

Based on the trends noted in the 1990 census it is clear that people of color will continue to grow both in actual numbers and as a percentage of the United States' population for the foreseeable future. The projected growth rate for people of color and its relationship to the White population's trends are a matter of debate among demographers. But, even though they may argue over the slope of the ascending racial minority growth rate curve, they are in agreement about its upward direction.

"Minorities are headed toward the majority," USA Today headlined a front-page story on a 1992 census bureau report projecting population and demographic trends through the middle of the next century. Predicting that the non-Hispanic White percentage of the population will drop to 53% of the population, the census bureau predicted that in 2050 the 383 million residents of the United States will be 21% Hispanic, 15% Black, 10% Asian, and 1% Native American.[20]

Demographers recognize the dangers in predicting the future based on the numbers of the present and the past. The 1992 census bureau report sharply revised some of the assumptions in a report issued just 4 years earlier, which estimated 300 million U.S. residents by 2050 and a slower rate of increase for minority groups.

"The new projections, though very different from our last figures, are conservative in one sense. They assume a continuation of current demographic trends," census bureau demographer Gregory Spencer told the New York Times in 1992.[21] He hoped that the current figures would be more solid because the census bureau had taken into account the racial and ethnic diversity of the nation by analyzing eight distinct groups. Only three racial and ethnic groups had been analyzed for the 1988 report. Among the predictions reported in the *New York Times:*

- The Hispanic population will surpass the Black population as the nation's largest minority group in 2013, when Hispanics will number 42.1 million and Blacks 42 million.
- Illegal immigration will continue at the rate of 200,000 new residents each year until 2050.
- Combined legal and illegal immigration will increase the U.S. population by an average of 880,000 per year through 2050, with immigration reaching as high as 1.4 million in some years.
- Immigration will be more important than birthrate in the population growth of the United States through 2050. By 2050, 21% of the population (82 million people) will be comprised of those who arrived in the United States after 1991 or who were born to parents who arrived after that date.
- Childbearing rates for Blacks and Hispanics will continue to be higher than for Whites.
- The non-Hispanic White population will stop growing in 2029 when it reaches 208 million and will account for a declining share of the population.
- The Black population will nearly double from 1990 to 2050, from 32 million to 62 million.
- The Asian and Pacific Islander population will grow more than five-fold from 1990 to 2050, from 8 million in 1990 to 41 million in 2050.
- The Hispanic population will more than triple from 1990 to 2050, from 24 million in 1990 to 81 million in 2050.

Primary causes for the population shift were based on maintenance of current inflow of people from Asia and Latin America as immigrants to the United States and continued differences in fertility among Whites, Blacks, and Latinos. The projected continuation of these trends promises dramatically to alter the racial and cultural mix of the United States in the 21st century. But the "new" America should not come as any surprise. The signs of the changes, as well as spirited debate and discussion of the implications, moved issues of race and ethnicity into the headlines as people in the United States prepared for the 21st century.

From Melting Pot to Multiculturalism

The racial and cultural trends that would make the new America may have made front-page headlines when they were released by the census bureau in December 1992, but they were not news to demographers and others who had been tracking the nation's changing racial and cultural makeup. A decade earlier the independent Population Reference Bureau reported much the same trends with only slightly different dates and population numbers. In 1982 the authors of the study, Leon F. Bouvier and Cary B. Davis, commented on the implications of such racial changes on the United States.[22]

"There are those who would prefer a 'status quo' society. That is to say a continuation of the present racial and ethnic composition under an Anglo-conformity umbrella," they wrote.

> There are those who see the future demographic changes as marking the onset of a new phase in the ever changing American society—a "multi-cultural" society. In the late 19th century and early 20th century the United States successfully changed identity from WASP to multi-ethnic culture within the White community. In the late 20th and early 21st century, it may once again change towards being the first truly multi-racial society on the planet earth, a multi-cultural society which while still predominantly English speaking would tolerate and even accept other languages and other cultures.[23]

The projected changes have already caused some rethinking among those who became accustomed to the "melting pot" model of assimilation in the United States. The rise of multiculturalism raised sharp national and local debates over issues of race and culture that had long concerned members of racial minority groups and forced others to reassess their vision of race and culture in the United States.

In a 1981 interview, Daniel Levine, Acting Director of the U.S. Bureau of the Census, commented that he no longer saw the United States as a melting pot. Instead, he said, he saw the nation developing as a "confederation of minorities" from different groups, each demanding to be counted by the census and, in his words, "demanding attention addressing their needs or redressing discrimination against them."[24]

In the same interview, Bruce Chapman, Director Designate of the Census Bureau, sounded a more optimistic note. He argued that what have been long identified as "traditional American values" were also part of the value structure of the nation's newest immigrants, particularly Asians and Latinos. He cited the strong family relationships of members of these groups and predicted they would become assets to the nation. "They may want to retain some cultural identification with the old country, but they also want to be unhyphenated Americans," he said.

The debates over the impact of the new America's racial and cultural mix sharpened through the 1980s and into the 1990s, particularly in the field of education. Universities, colleges, and school systems debated over the best ways to educate students and prepare them for a multicultural world. Some argued for the traditional Anglocentric approach as the best way to equip young people to succeed in America, contending that the ways of other cultures are less important in the United States. Others recognized the need for multicultural curricula, as long as the traditions and influence of England and other European nations were recognized as making the greatest contributions to the shaping of the United States. A third approach argued for multicultural curricula, recognizing the contributions of all groups to the United States and affording special attention to the advances of groups that had traditionally been underrepresented in the curricula. A fourth alternative called for educating students in the learning styles and content of people of their own race, such as an Afrocentric approach to education.

In addition to the battles over curricula, in 1992 the 500th anniversary of Christopher Columbus's first voyage to what is now the American continent forced many Americans to reconsider the impact of the subsequent conquest and colonization of the indigenous people and importation of slaves from Africa on the development of what is called the "New World." Similarly, indigenous people throughout the Americas seized the occasion to point out that Columbus's voyages were not necessarily a cause for celebration and to press their cases for recognition and equal rights.

Perhaps most importantly, the debates raised the importance of culture over race. Issues of language, food, lifestyle, and values became more important as people either reclaimed or reinforced cultural elements of their lives that ran counter to the melting pot ideology. And, as intermarriage continued to become more prominent, it became clear that pure racial categories would be more difficult to establish in the future.

Racial and Cultural Minorities: An International Phenomenon

The United States is not the only country with substantial and growing minority populations. Nor is it the only one that has recently experienced racial and ethnic turmoil. During the late 1980s and early 1990s racial, cultural, and religious conflicts among groups tore apart nations on all continents. The conflicts ranged from disputes that had long had international attention, such as disputes between Jews and Arabs in the Middle East and Catholics and Protestants in Northern Ireland, to smoldering conflicts that flared up after political changes, such as battles among Serbs, Slovenes, and Muslims in what had once been Yugoslavia. Conflicts suddenly flared between contending groups, such as Hindus and Muslims in India, and passions were inflamed by new immigration, such as demonstrations for and against immigrant workers in Germany. But, for whatever the reason, the racial and ethnic conflicts were part of a continuing contentiousness among groups that has characterized most of the world's history.

Like the United States, most nations have religious, ethnic, cultural, or racial minority groups within their boundaries. The treatment of members of these groups varies from nation to nation, depending on the political and economic systems of the country, as well as the historical relationship between the dominant and subordinate groups.

For instance, in most colonial situations in which a nation conquers or colonizes the people of another land there are rigid social separations based on class and race. The British, to whom many U.S.

political and social institutions are linked, colonized much of North America and parts of Africa, Oceania, and Asia. The British colonial system maintained strict lines of distinction between the predominantly Anglo colonizers and the people whose territory they came to occupy. "The British colonial code draws the most rigid color line of all," wrote Raymond Kennedy in 1945, when Britain still maintained much of its colonial empire.

> The British have been in contact for a longer time with more dark peoples than any other western nation, yet they hold aloof from their subjects to an unequalled degree. They refuse to associate freely or make friends with other races, and their exclusiveness had engendered a reciprocal feeling toward them on the part of their colonial peoples.[25]

Spain colonized most of Latin America, including what is now the U.S. Southwest from Texas to California. In the Spanish and Portuguese colonies of Latin America the racial situation was less clearly defined. In all countries, the European nation expropriated the lands of the indigenous peoples, making them slaves or peons working the lands in some countries and importing African slaves in others. But, although there were class distinctions between Europeans and native Indians, there was also more intermarriage and elaborate classification systems to label and identify offspring by race. As a result, mixed racial populations of mestizos emerged in Indian countries and mulattos in countries such as Brazil, where Africans were brought to work. The process went so far that one country, Mexico, is considered by many to be a mestizo nation with scattered pockets of native people.

Colonialism in Asia and Southeast Asia was shared by several nations, including Britain, France, the Netherlands, and Spain; each with different policies toward the indigenous residents of the area. Like the Portuguese in Brazil, some colonizing nations also brought in laborers from other areas, Indians from India to Burma and Malaya and Chinese to most of Southeast Asia. As a result, these colonized areas became stratified on three levels: Europeans, immigrant workers, and the natives.[26]

In all of these colonial situations the relationship between minorities and majorities were reversed from what racial minorities have

experienced in the United States. In the colonial situation the numerical minority groups were the European colonizers, who conquered and then governed the native people who outnumbered
them. In this case, the term *minority* could be applied to the Europeans who, though smaller in number, exerted military, political, economic, and social control over the native populations. Thus, although the Europeans may have been a *numerical* minority, they
were not a *power* minority. A legacy of this relationship, and the fight
of indigenous people to regain their rights, could still be seen in the
relationship of Whites over Blacks in South Africa in the early 1990s.

The legacy of colonialism and distinctions based on race are still
found throughout the world. As Charles F. Marden and Gladys
Meyer point out in their book *Minorities in American Society*, nations
as diverse in political and economic structure as South Africa, Israel,
Soviet Russia, and the People's Republic of China have substantial
divisions based on ethnic and racial divisions between dominant
and subordinate groups.[27] The heated conflicts between Blacks and
Whites in South Africa and between Jews and Arabs in Israel and
other parts of the Middle East have been widely reported. Less well
known in the United States is what Marden and Meyer call "the
virtual destruction of small tribal people in Asiatic Russia"[28] and the
annexation of Tibetan people by the People's Republic of China in
the late 1940s.

Except for the Native Americans, who were subjected to colonization by the Spanish and extermination by the English, minority
groups in the United States have followed patterns that are different
from those of other nations. This is because the predominately White
Europeans who were to dominate the country were themselves
immigrants who became the numerical majority. Rather than exert
their control only through a rigid class system, they exterminated or
confined the Native Americans, waged war to take lands held by the
Native Americans and Mexicans, imported Black, Asian, and Latino
labor as it was needed, and encouraged more European immigrants
to come, settle, and develop a new society of White European immigrants in the United States. Between 1820 and 1970, 45 million
immigrants entered the United States, 75% of them from European
nations.[29] It is these immigrants, their children, and grandchildren
who consolidated their identity through the melting pot and became

the new majority in the United States, leaving people of color to be designated as racial minorities.

Does the Term *Minorities* Describe the Present and Future?

In the United States when the terms *majority* and *minority* are used in a racial context they usually refer to White Europeans as the majority and people of color (Native Americans, Asians, Blacks, and Latinos) as the minority. These have long represented both power and numerical relationships in which the White majority both outnumbered and dominated the more racially diverse minority groups. As a result, the word *minorities* became an umbrella term encompassing any group in the United States that was not White.

But the term, though widely used by people of all races, masks the more complex distinctions between dominant and subordinate groups and the diversity within and between the groups bunched under the umbrella. It also distorts the reality of the racial situation in the United States and in the world. For instance, the use of the term has made it appear that racially diverse people such as Asians, Blacks, and Latinos are a minority in the world's population when, in fact, as a group they far outnumber the Whites. Thus, people who may have felt that they were permanent minorities in the United States and elsewhere were, in fact, a much more substantial part of the population elsewhere.

In addition, the term *minority* no longer accurately describes the situation in many urban areas of the nation. By the early 1990s "minorities" were actually the majority of the population in 55 of the nation's largest cities. In 1991, New York City Mayor David Dinkins told a convention of the National Association of Hispanic Journalists that New York is "a city in which no group can claim to be the majority."

But even if the term *minority* did accurately describe the numerical relationship between Whites and non-Whites across the board, the use of the term would still cause unnecessary problems. The umbrella term *minority* may be useful in adding focus and emphasis to the issues that separated people of color from White Americans, such as differences in income, education, and employment. But it also groups people together who have as many differences from each other as they do from the White majority. Although Blacks, Asians, Latinos, and Native Americans may fit conveniently under the label of "minority," there are as many differences within and among these groups as there are between each group and the White majority. In fact, the one characteristic members of these groups universally share is that they are not Anglo Europeans, but then neither are a lot of other groups that are not designated as minorities.

Rather than portraying race relations in the United States in terms of a majority and minorities or dominant and subordinate groups, it is probably more accurate to avoid broad umbrella terms and speak in terms of racial diversity and multiculturalism. For, rather than classifying racial groups as majorities or minorities (and thereby masking the differences within these categories), a focus on racial diversity and multiculturalism signifies a nation with a variety of races and cultures, each one with similarities and dissimilarities within itself and with other groups. Rather than masking the differences between and within different racial groups designated as majority or minorities, the term *racial diversity* describes a nation of different and diverse races. It is a more accurate description of racial conditions in the United States as the nation approaches the 21st century.

Racial Diversity: Problem or Opportunity?

It is this growing diversity that will characterize the nation's population through the foreseeable future. The census and projected growth figures clearly show where the United States is headed in the future. How the media and other institutions react to these demographic changes will, to a large extent, determine whether or not the United States is still considered the land of opportunity. For, even though the figures are clear, it is not so certain that the people of different races will not suffer the same discrimination that has historically faced Blacks, Latinos, Native Americans, and Asians in the United States as they seek education, employment, and housing. For these groups, discrimination continues to be a problem that stands in the way of opportunity.

At the same time, the growing racial diversity can be described as either a problem or an opportunity by the rest of American society. The increasing heterogeneity of the American people forces changes on education, government agencies, and businesses that have become used to conducting their affairs in a certain way. Now, as people come speaking different languages, following different religious practices, and bringing different cultural traditions, these institutions must respond. Some may see the changes as a problem, others as an opportunity to serve new students and consumers. But, whatever the reaction, the trend is unmistakable.

"The message is clear," wrote University of North Carolina sociologist John D. Kasarda in 1984.[30]

> Our major cities are becoming increasingly diverse as their resident populations transform from white, European heritage to black, Hispanic and other minority groups.... These trends are creating not only powerful political bases for minorities (blacks already govern many of the largest cities, including Los Angeles, Chicago, Philadelphia, Detroit, Washington, D.C., Atlanta, and New Orleans) but also unique opportunities for businesses cognizant of rapidly changing urban markets.

Media and Diversity: Maximizing Opportunity?

The growth of racial diversity in the United States has forced the media to reexamine the ways they have traditionally dealt with people of color. As these groups grow at a rate that outstrips the Anglo population both in number and as a percentage of the population, the media executives have to look for new ways to deal with them. And, as Census Bureau Director-Designate Chapman pointed out, continued loyalties to diverse cultural backgrounds and racial groups will make it more difficult for the media to continue to play their traditional role of homogenizing the members of disparate groups into a mass culture or society. Rather than try to address groups as part of the melting pot, media have had to find ways to address them along their cultural and racial identities and, in the process, are reinforcing the diversity rather than changing it.

Too often the growth of a racially diverse population has been portrayed as a *problem* for the media and other institutions, forcing them to change their methods of doing business and making them cater to groups that tenaciously hang on to their cultural roots in a nation in which other immigrants have willingly shed theirs. There are differences in language, culture, religion, and lifestyle that are seen as a threat to Anglo-American values. In one expression of this siege mentality California voters in 1994 passed by a wide majority a "Save Our State" initiative that proponents said would encourage undocumented residents to leave the state.

Some media organizations, despite professing concern over the changing populations, have consciously adopted strategies that appear to be an attempt to avoid minority groups as they moved into the nation's cities. In the 1970s and 1980s, at the same time that the inner cities were becoming increasingly racially diverse, some big city newspapers looked for ways to avoid the potential readers in their neighborhood, but chase those who were living in suburban cities and counties. Using circulation strategies that made it difficult, if not impossible, for residents of ghettos and barrios to subscribe to newspapers, some metropolitan newspapers refused to put news-stands in inner-city areas at the same time they were targeting Anglo readers who had moved to the suburbs by starting or expanding new editions in the outlying areas. The strategies were defended as being based on economics, that the low-income characteristics of Blacks and Latinos made them undesirable newspaper readers. Main-stream advertisers, some publishers argued, wanted affluent read-ers who could afford the products that they advertised. Denying any racist intentions, the newspaper managers said they were merely following the more affluent readers who moved to the suburbs. These strategies, and their impact, were apparent by the late 1970s.

The strategies of newspapers in avoiding the inner city were described by Ben Bagdikian of the University of California at Berkeley in a 1978 article.[31] Bagdikian cited newspapers in different parts of the nation that consciously adopted circulation and news reporting strategies that avoided the growing numbers of minorities and low-income residents in central city areas, while reaching out to readers in the predominately Anglo and more affluent suburbs around those cities.

"We cut out unprofitable circulation, and we arbitrarily cut back some of our low-income circulation," Bagdikian quoted Otis Chandler, then publisher of the *Los Angeles Times,* as saying. Bagdikian also quoted a 1976 memo by an editor of the *Detroit News* ordering staffers to aim the newspaper at people who made more than $18,000 a year and were between the ages of 28 and 40. Such stories, the editor wrote, "should be obvious: they won't have a damn thing to do with Detroit and its internal problems."[32]

"The blackout of news to the central city is usually justified by publishers on the grounds that it is harder to sell papers there, that it is harder to hire and keep delivery people on the job and there is a higher rate of nonpayment of bills," Bagdikian wrote. "That is true, and it has always been true. The difference now is that advertisers don't want that population so now the publishers don't either."[33] Because advertisers wanted affluent readers, newspapers and broadcast media targeted their content to audiences in the more affluent, and predominantly Anglo, suburban areas. Circulation percentages and actual numbers declined in the cities whose names the newspapers proudly wore on their front pages and broadcast stations claimed as their city of license. Broadcasters, although they could not control who watched or listened to their stations and bore no additional costs for having low-income people tuned into their broadcasts, still tried to target news and entertainment programming to more affluent viewers and listeners. The American Broadcasting Company issued a demographic analysis of its audience in the 1970s titled "Some People Are More Valuable Than Others."

"In reporting and emphasis . . . both broadcast and printed news in metropolitan areas have turned their backs on their own cities," Bagdikian wrote.

> This despite a basic communications law that is supposed to exchange a monopoly on the dial for a station commitment to air local issues, and despite the fact that both broadcast stations and papers take their names from the cities they have reportorially abandoned.[34]

Because many of the low-income residents of the central cities were members of racial minority groups, the economic strategies of the publishers and broadcasters had racial overtones as well. Although media managers claimed their emphasis on affluent, suburban audiences was motivated only by their desire to reach the people advertisers wanted to buy their products, the fact remained that many of the low-income people in the inner cities who were unserved by the media were racial minorities.

In 1978 Otis Chandler, in response to a question by a television interviewer, admitted that the *Los Angeles Times* had "a way to go" in adequately covering Los Angeles's minority communities. But he added that it "would not make sense financially for us" to direct the newspaper to low-income readers because "that audience does not have the purchasing power and is not responsive to the kind of advertising we carry."[35]

"So we could make the editorial commitment, the management commitment, to cover these communities," Chandler said. "But then how do we get them to read the *Times*? It's not their kind of newspaper: it's too big, it's too stuffy. If you will, it's too complicated." In a 1979 *Columbia Journalism Review* article by the authors of this book Chandler and other *Times'* executives were quoted as denying that the newspaper approached coverage and circulation from a racial standpoint, although one did admit the strategy meant the newspaper was directed at a predominately Anglo audience. John Mount of the *Times'* marketing research department said, "We don't approach marketing from a racial standpoint. It just happens that the more affluent and educated people tend to be white and live in suburban communities."[36] The newspaper's advertisers were also pinpointed as spurring the strategy.

> Our major retail advertisers have said to us that "We want a certain class of audience, a certain demographic profile of reader, whether that person be black, white, or brown or Chinese or whatever. We don't really care what sex or race they are. But we do care about their income,

Chandler said. He also expressed optimism that more minorities would begin to read the *Times* "as their income goes up and their educational level comes up and they become interested in a paper like the *Times*. Then they become prospects for our advertisers."[37]

The *Los Angeles Times* had killed a short-lived central city zone section in the mid 1970s and in 1978 launched a separate San Diego edition two counties away from its home base. But the situation at the *Los Angeles Times* and other newspapers has changed since the late 1970s. In 1978 the American Society of Newspaper Editors adopted a resolution calling for racial parity in the newsroom by the year 2000 and, although the representation of minorities in the newsroom is still far short of that, affirmative efforts have been made toward integrating minorities into the newsrooms and on the news pages. The employment story is amply told elsewhere in this book. The lesson that the media learned is that the development of a racially diverse population is something that cannot be avoided by the media. Instead of trying to bypass non-White readers and coverage, the news organizations that have made the greatest gains are those that have seen the growing racial diversity as an opportunity, rather than a problem.

The problem approach of many media executives and corporations came about in the early 1970s, just after the first wave of minority media hiring took place as a result of the civil rights movement and federal government pressures in the late 1960s and early 1970s. That first wave of hiring and coverage triggered gains based on tokenism, in which every respectable news organization tried to have at least one Black reporter and, possibly, a Latino, Native American, or Asian American. It was also motivated by a good dose of White guilt for past discrimination against minorities in hiring and coverage.

But by the late 1970s much of that argument had run its course, as media organizations paid at least minimal lip service to the need for integration. By the latter part of the decade the argument for integration had switched to population demographics, focusing on the growing racial diversity in the nation. And, as in previous decades, many well-meaning news organizations saw the growing minority populations as a problem to be solved. The changing racial mix of the nation was seen as something that had to be overcome, a problem that demanded a solution. Thus, the response was often an increase in the tokenism, from one to two Blacks, or a broadening of attention to minorities to include Latinos, Asian Americans, and Native Americans. More attention was also given to coverage of minority issues and special events. These quick-fix solutions to what was seen as a problem sometimes compounded the issue.

For instance, the coverage of minority issues often focused inordinate attention on the more bizarre or unusual elements of minority communities, such as youth gangs, illegal immigration, or interracial violence. Though these are all legitimate topics, the emphasis on such coverage and the near absence of other news stories or dramatic themes involving minorities resulted in a new stereotype of racial minorities as "problem people," groups either beset by problems or causing them for the larger society. Thus, the problem orientation of the media managers was often reinforced by the coverage and dramatic portrayals that people of color were allowed.

There are other difficulties in approaching minorities as a problem. It is inherent in the approach that is dictated when a new situation is seen as a problem, rather than an opportunity. A problem needs to be solved; once it is solved it can be set aside. In the late 1970s and early 1980s, the hiring of minority reporters or staffers became the quick solution to what was seen as a minority problem. Once a minority reporter or actor was hired the minority problem was seen as solved. If the reporter didn't work out or was hired away, the problem reappeared.

Problems also often beg for single solutions; perhaps a throwback to our training in mathematics, in which each math problem has only one solution. Thus, if hiring was seen as a solution to a problem, more hiring of minorities would add more solutions if the problems resurfaced. Editors often looked simplistically at changes in coverage to try to find out what the Black, or Latino, or Native American community "wanted" from the media. Some experimented with Spanish- or Asian-language simulcasts of news programs, some inserted special sections geared for the minority communities on a regular basis, others did extensive special reports on the different minority communities in their circulation or broadcast areas. Not all of these were successful in gaining increased readership, viewership, or acceptance by the minority communities. And, as a result, some media managers became discouraged from trying other approaches.

Finally, a problem is, by definition, an obstacle, an obstruction, a puzzle that stands in the way of someone's progress. It is something that must be overcome, surpassed, or eradicated so that the forward

Figure 1.2. Some general circulation daily newspapers have launched sections targeted to communities of color to improve their news coverage and advertising revenues. The *Los Angeles Times' Nuestro Tiempo* Spanish-language section is published weekly. This cover story features film maker Jesús Treviño and is part of a story on opportunities for Latino film makers in Hollywood.

movement can continue. Thus, when the growing minority populations were seen as a problem by media managers, the approaches, however well intentioned or creative, were geared to overcoming or changing something that was seen as an obstacle. Instead of looking

Publishers on Parade

"Parade reflects Austin's own diversity."

"Austin is a community rich in diversity. It is a city where the traditional American culture mixes with the growing Hispanic population, and the strong individualism of the Southwest complements our rapidly growing high-tech industry. Parade is careful to address and understand the value of the differences among our readers.

"The range of Parade's stories is as eclectic as our readers. Parade covers the important issues such as health, education and literacy, but it chronicles different lifestyles, too, breaking down stereotypes and focusing on the positive. It's a magazine that encourages and touches our readers with a national perspective on many of the issues that face us in Austin.

"Parade has universal appeal; it understands the diversity of our audience, so I'm not surprised at all that it is distributed by more than 340 newspapers across the country. Parade is an important part of our Sunday paper because there's something for everyone in Parade."

Featured in over 340 newspapers
every Sunday.

ROGER S. KINTZEL
PUBLISHER
AUSTIN AMERICAN-STATESMAN

Austin American-Statesman

PARADE

Figure 1.3. General circulation media have tried to keep the mass audience by attempting to address and attract diverse population segments. This cooperative advertisement by *Parade* magazine and the *Austin American-Statesman* touts both publications' interest in drawing an audience in "a city where the traditional American culture mixes with the growing Hispanic population.

for ways to capitalize on the new opportunities presented by the changing population, media managers tried to overcome it because it was seen as a threat to "business as usual."

More recently, media corporations spurred by pressure groups, competition from ethnic media, their own minority employees, or even a growing social consciousness, have come to see the growing minority population as an opportunity, not a problem. Rather than trying just to overcome a hurdle and put the obstacle behind them, they recognize that the United States is growing as a racially diverse nation and that the changing racial demographics are an opportunity for them to gain new audiences and readers. It is this attitude, coupled with the growing racial diversity of the nation, that presages the greatest progress of minorities and the media of communication.

In the 1990s the *Los Angeles Times*, serving the most racially diverse market in the nation, reversed its strategies and turned in a direction opposite from its strategies of the 1970s. The newspaper killed its San Diego edition, citing continuing financial losses since that edition's founding, and launched *City Times*, a new section directed toward inner-city residents of Los Angeles. A few years earlier the newspaper had begun its looking at the long-range opportunities available in racially diverse communities by launching several experimental sections in different languages targeted to Asian and Latino groups. In 1990 the parent Times-Mirror Corporation bought half of *La Opinion*, Los Angeles's Spanish-language newspaper. In 1993 it launched weekly publication of *Nuestro Tiempo*, a Spanish-language tabloid targeting potential Latino readers.

Analysis

As census reports and other data clearly indicate, the current and projected growth of non-White groups in the United States ensure that the nation will be less racially homogeneous in the future than it has been in the past. This growth of racial diversity in a land that has been largely populated by immigrants will continue to create new opportunities in the nation that prides itself as "the land of opportunity." At the same time, as a more racially diverse population challenges the commonly held melting pot theory that once characterized thinking in this country, there will be new stresses and strains.

The communication media of the United States bear a special responsibility in these circumstances, because they share a portion of the responsibility for educating older residents about the new-comers. The media also penetrate the homes of all members of the population through print and broadcast media and assist minority group members by defining the society to newcomers and others outside the mainstream. In the past, media have chosen either to ignore racially diverse populations or to treat them in an unequal manner. The growth of Blacks, Asians, Latinos, and Native Americans throughout the country, however, particularly in urban areas, forces the abandonment of this reaction and adoption of new strategies. As media move beyond tokenism in hiring and content they will grapple with ways to reach audiences, cover news, and provide entertainment programming to a racially diverse society.

It is still too early to project all of the changes that media will undergo as they seek to capitalize on the rainbow of races that will characterize the United States in the future. It is, however, clear that those media that choose to avoid the clearly marked trends will have an increasingly difficult time in capturing a fair share of the audience in areas where non-White groups comprise a substantial and growing portion of the population. The media that do successfully penetrate those audiences will be the media with the greatest chances for success and profitability in the future.

Notes

1. For a sociohistorical analysis of initial race and ethnic relations in California from 1850 to 1900 see Tomás Almaguer, *Racial Fault Lines: The Historical Origins of White Supremacy in California* (Berkeley: University of California Press, 1994).

2. "Really, How Different Are We?," *Los Angeles Times*, Washington Edition, December 3, 1992, p. A10.

3. Leon F. Bouvier and Cary B. Davis, *The Future Racial Composition of the United States* (Washington, DC: Demographic Information Services Center of the Population Reference Bureau, August 1982), pp. 1, 3.

4. For an analysis of this phenomenon see Milton Gordon, *Assimilation in American Life* (New York: Oxford University Press, 1964).

5. For more information see Mary Waters, *Ethnic Options: Choosing Identities in America* (Berkeley: University of California Press, 1990).

6. "U.S. Population: Where We Are, Where We're Going," *Population Bulletin* (Vol. 37, No. 2, June 1982), p. 6.

7. "Racial/Ethnic Changes, 1980-1990," *Black Issues in Higher Education* (May 7, 1992), p. 61.

8. Roberto Rodríguez, " 'The Browning of America'," *Black Issues in Higher Education* (May 7, 1992), pp. 60-62.

9. *Racial/Ethnic Changes*, p. 61.

10. D'Vera Cohn, "Census Bureau Won't Adjust Data for '90 Undercount," *Washington Post*, December 30, 1992, p. A7.

11. Rodríguez, "The Browning of America," pp. 60-62.

12. Bouvier and Davis, *The Future Racial Composition of the United States*, p. 2.

13. Margaret L. Usdansky, "Immigrant Wave Boosts Total to 8%," *USA Today*, December 18-20, 1992, p. 1A.

14. "Foreign-born in the USA," *USA Today*, December 18-20, 1992, p. 9A.

15. Evelyn D. Tan, "Immigrants May Find More of a Promised Land," *USA Today*, November 17, 1992, p. 7A.

16. "Nation Grew in 1992 by 2.9 Million," *Washington Post*, December 31, 1992, p. A4.

17. Tan, "Immigrants May Find," p. 7A.

18. "Non-Anglo Majority Projected for U.S. by 2080," *Public Management* (September 1983), p. 17.

19. Robert Pear, "New Look at the U.S. in 2050: Bigger, Older and Less White," *New York Times*, December 4, 1992, pp. A1, D18.

20. Margaret Usdansky, "Minorities Are Headed Toward the Majority," *USA Today*, December 4-6, 1992, p. 1A.

21. Pear, "New Look at the U.S.," pp. A1, D18.

22. "Non-Anglo Majority," pp. 17-18.

23. Bouvier and Davis, *The Future Racial Composition of the United States*, p. 57.

24. "What Does the 1980 Census Show? Looking Ahead and Looking Back," *Public Opinion*, pp. 15-16.

25. Raymond Kennedy, "The Colonial Crisis and the Future," in *The Science of Man in the World Crisis*, edited by Ralph Linton (New York: Columbia University Press, 1945), pp. 320, as cited in Charles F. Marden and Gladys Meyer, *Minorities in American Society* (New York: D. Van Nostrand, 1978), p. 5. For an analysis of the role of the media in Great Britain and their relationship to racial minorities see Paul Hartmann and Charles Hubbard, *Racism and the Mass Media* (New York: Rowman & Littlefield, 1974).

26. Marden and Meyer, *Minorities in American Society*, pp. 6-7.

27. Marden and Meyer, *Minorities in American Society*, pp. 10-15.

28. Marden and Meyer, *Minorities in American Society*, p. 14.

29. Marden and Meyer, *Minorities in American Society*, pp. 63-64.

30. John D. Kasarda, "Hispanics and City Change," *American Demographics* (November 1984), pp. 25-29.

31. Ben H. Bagdikian, "The Best News Money Can Buy," *Human Behavior* (October 1978), pp. 63-66.

32. Bagdikian, "The Best News," p. 64.

33. Bagdikian, "The Best News," p. 66.

34. Bagdikian, "The Best News," p. 66.

35. Félix Gutiérrez and Clint C. Wilson II, "The Demographic Dilemma," *Columbia Journalism Review,* January/February 1979, p. 53.

36. Gutiérrez and Wilson, "The Demographic Dilemma," p. 53.

37. Gutiérrez and Wilson, "The Demographic Dilemma," p. 53.

2

Communication Media and Society

How much do you know about the people who first lived on what is now called the North American Continent? Think about it. How much do you know about the people who lived in nomadic tribes and in villages across what is now the United States? Do you know what languages they spoke? What they liked to eat? What their customs were? Can you describe how they dressed? Or what their villages looked like? Or how they battled the Europeans who came into their land?

If you're like most people in the United States you probably know something, but not everything, about the answers to these questions. There are some things you know about Native Americans, but probably not as much as you think you should know. At some time or another you've probably seen a movie, or a television documentary, or read a book about Native Americans and their fight to survive on their land.

Now, try to forget about what you have learned from personal experience, textbooks, or school. Try to remember what you know about Native Americans from what you have seen from communication media; from radio, television, newspapers, and magazines. Chances are, you will not remember very much factual information, because, aside from Western movies and an occasional news story, Native Americans are still an invisible minority in the

33

communication media of the United States. The images that have been portrayed often are frozen in the 19th century and do not do justice to the people they try to represent. Movies and television programs have traditionally treated Native Americans as savages who were vanquished by a superior people and civilization. Contemporary Native Americans have been treated by news reports as a problem people, a group either overburdened by its own problems or the source of problems for the larger society.

In a media-dominated society, such as the United States, all of us depend on the media of communication to portray and define those things that we have not personally experienced for ourselves. Thus, we "learn" about others through radio, television, movies, newspapers, and magazines. The portrayals and news coverage of Native Americans and other groups in these media can become reality in our minds, especially if we have no personal experiences to balance them against. This pervasive influence of the media in our society has been amply described and documented by other scholars who have analyzed communication media in modern society.[1]

Functions of Mass Communication in Society

The functions of media in modern society have been described in various terms by different scholars, all of whom agree on the pervasive influence of media on American society. In a 1948 essay often cited by other researchers, pioneer communication scholar Harold Lasswell described the three major functions of communication as:

1. *Surveillance* of the environment, disclosing threats and opportunities affecting the value position of the community and of the component parts within it;
2. *Correlation* of the different parts of society in responding to environment; and
3. *Transmission* of the social heritage from one generation to the next.[2]

Examined in the context of a society containing several racial minority groups and a majority group that, to a large extent, controls the mass communication media of that society, Lasswell's surveillance function assigns to the media the responsibility of looking across the society in order to define and describe the different groups within it. The correlation function of media helps members of the media's audience take stock of the different groups and determine how and where they fit in the society. Finally, the transmission function both defines what the social culture and heritage of the society are and transmits it to other members of the society.

Lasswell noted that although the United States prides itself on being a democratic society built on rational public opinion formed through broad dissemination of information, there is often a gap in information between the leaders and the public. He also noted that communication can be altered when the ruling elements of the society sense a threat.

"In society, the communication process reveals special characteristics when the ruling element is afraid of the internal as well as the external environment," Lasswell wrote.

> In gauging the efficiency of communication in any given context, it is necessary to take into account the values at stake, and the identity of the group whose position is being examined. In democratic societies, rational choices depend on enlightenment, which in turn depends upon communication; and especially upon the equivalence of attention among leaders, experts, and rank and file.[3]

Lasswell's addendum, his last paragraph in the article, reinforces the importance of understanding that communication media may behave differently when a threat is perceived by the leaders of the system, especially when a particular group has been identified. In such cases, the media must portray a consistent message that develops a cohesive opinion of that threat or group among the various components of the society.

Applying Lasswell's functions it is not surprising that most people in the United States know very little about Native Americans. The news media historically treated the native populations as part of the surveillance function, watching the horizon and reporting on them as they defended their lands and culture from the intrusion of the Europeans who came to the American continent in the 18th and 19th centuries. In terms of correlation, they were defined as primitive and pagan peoples who blocked the manifest destiny of the Whites who were destined to populate the North American continent. The native population was often portrayed as worthy only of annihilation, subjugation, or consignment to reservations. Finally, the transmission of the social inheritance of the continent was defined as the culture developed by the European settlers, not the Native American inhabitants, as being the true American culture.

Although most of us may have limited knowledge about the culture and civilizations of the Native Americans, it is not because we were readers of the newspapers and magazines published during the European westward expansion in the last century. For the most part, the images of the people the Europeans called Indians have been shaped by the movies, television programs, and Western novels we have seen or read. These media are not designed to be primarily informative, but to entertain their audiences. That is why in 1959 Charles Wright added a fourth dimension to Lasswell's three functions. Wright's fourth function, *entertainment*, emphasized that communication can also entertain the members of the society.[4] In the case of Native Americans, much of what has been presented as entertainment portrayals has become the reality in the minds of those who have seen Native Americans in movies and on television, but nowhere else.

In addition to these functions, other scholars have noted that communication media also perform important economic functions in the society. Wilbur Schramm and William Porter wrote in 1982 that, though no economist had outlined the economic functions of the media with specificity of Lasswell's other functions, it was possible to enumerate the economic role of the media.

"For one thing, communication must meet the need for an economic map of the environment so that each individual and organization can form its own image of buying and selling opportunities at a given moment," they wrote. "For another, there must be correlation of economic policy, whether by the individual, the organization, or the nation. . . . Finally, instruction in the skills and expectations of economic behavior must be available."[5]

Other scholars have spelled out a more bottom-line approach to describing the economic role of media in American society. Peter Sandman, David Rubin, and David Sachsman once described the economic function of the media as "to make money"[6] in a mass communication textbook. In a later edition they changed the function "to serve the economic system," but listed it as the first function and emphasized its central role in the functioning of media in this society.

"The fundamental economic purpose of the mass media in the United States is to sell people to advertisers," they wrote.

> Economically, the articles in your newspaper and the programs on your radio and TV sets are merely "come-ons" to catch and hold your attention. Advertisers buy that attention from the media, and use it to sell you their products and services. In the process, both the media and the advertisers earn substantial profits.[7]

They could have easily added that the media, including those that do not depend on advertiser support, such as movies, records, videocassettes, some on-line computer services, and some cable television channels, also serve the economic system by functioning within the private sector as corporations that sell a product for a price to an audience, are privately held, issue stock, and generate profits or losses for their owners. Thus, the media must serve the needs of the economic system because, as part of the corporate community, they are private enterprises, rather than tax-supported institutions such as public schools or libraries. Because they are part of the private enterprise system they must behave as other corporations and businesses, seeking revenues and profits by maximizing consumption of their product while lowering the costs of production and distribution.

Combining the work of these and other scholars who have examined the functions of media in society we find that five central functions emerge for media in the United States.[8] These are:

1. *Surveillance,* the sentinel or lookout role of the media watching the society and horizon for threats to the established order and information on people or places of public interest;
2. *Correlation,* interpretation and linking function of the media, which helps the audience understand, interpret, and comprehend the different things that are happening in and out of the society and how they affect each other, as well as stay in touch with others in the society;
3. *Transmission,* the socialization function of the media, which defines the society, its norms, and values, to the audience and through their

portrayals and coverage assists members of the society in adopting, using, and acting on those values;

4. *Entertainment,* the function of the media for diversion and enjoyment, which provides stories, features, music, and films that are designed to make the audiences laugh, cry, relax, or reflect, rather than gain information; and

5. *Economic Service,* the role of the media within the economic system of the society, which in the United States means most media function as corporations serving the needs of their shareholders and other corporations by attracting audiences that will either pay for the media product and/or serve as the target for advertising messages.

Mass Audience, Mass Media, and Race

The media could fulfill all of these functions in American society without treating members of racial minority groups any differently from those in the majority, if it had not been for an economic transformation that was to dictate the direction and form of media development of communication in the industrial society taking shape in the United States in the early 19th century. As originally envisioned by the framers of the U.S. Constitution, media in the United States were supposed to operate in a free marketplace of ideas in which every political group, interest group, or anyone else with the money and motivation would be able to print and disseminate newspapers, books, and pamphlets. It was felt that the new republic's voters, at that time limited to White males, would choose from the wide variety of media available to them and, after weighing the different shades of information and opinion, would make an informed choice at the polling place. Media were seen as both the watchdogs of the government and the critical communication link on which the new democratic society would depend for information. For this reason, the First Amendment to the Constitution prohibits Congress from making laws limiting the freedom of the press, the only portion of the private sector afforded constitutional protection from government.

But in freeing the press from governmental restraints the framers of the Constitution also withdrew from the press the government licenses and subsidies that had been afforded to official government or sanctioned media in Europe and other parts of the Americas. Therefore, the press, although freed from the laws of Congress, was forced to function as a business within the unwritten economic laws of capitalism governing businesses in the United States. While a subsidized partisan press played an important role in the development of early newspapers in the United States, the form of media that would come to dominate the United States through the 1980s emerged in the 1830s.

The newspaper was the *New York Sun*, which appeared in 1833 and sold for only a penny. This first "penny press" took on a new form that was uniquely adapted to the free enterprise system. The newspaper sold for only a penny, but its primary income did not depend on subsidies from a political party, a government in the form of public notices, or the subscriptions of readers. Instead, the newspaper's revenues and profits were to come from advertisers who would pay for the space in the *Sun* to place commercial messages to reach the large readership attracted by the low price. Benjamin Day, founder of the newspaper, envisioned the penny press as a newspaper for the mass audience of city-dwelling workers who would be attracted by the newspaper's lively content, its low price, and the promise of the *New York Sun* that "It Shines for ALL." The newspaper's formula, which was widely imitated, attracted the loyalty of readers. But they were not the only ones to take an interest in the penny press.

"Another person began to take a special interest in the newspaper for the masses," write journalism historians Edwin Emery and Michael Emery.

> This was the advertiser, who was impressed by the amazing circulation of the new medium. Putting an ad in every publication bought by small splinter groups was expensive and ineffective sales promotion. The large circulation of the penny papers now made it feasible to publicize articles for sale that formerly would not have warranted advertising expense.[9]

Given the formula developed by the penny press, media in the United States developed as mass audience media with content designed to attract a wide audience and deliver that audience to advertisers. The space for the advertisement in the newspaper or on the television screen has no economic value by itself. Its worth is derived from the size of the audience that has been attracted to that space by the news or entertainment content of the newspaper and television station. As media strove to accumulate large audiences, they developed content that would attract the widest audience possible and offend the least number.

Rather than a variety of small outlets, each addressing the needs of segments of the society, media in the United States became synonymous with the mass audience. In fact, the terms *mass media* and *mass communication* were used interchangeably to describe the media system of the nation. As a result, media geared for political, national, or racial minorities were consigned to economic second-class standing and members of those groups were either ignored in the mass media attracting the majority society or portrayed in a way that made them palatable to the majority. Mass society in the United States did not necessarily mean a society of the masses, but a society in which the people were amassed into an audience for the messages of the mass media of communication.

The function of the content of the mass media in the 19th century and much of the 20th century has been to reach the lowest common denominator in the society and address the media content to that level; whether it be news, entertainment, or information. Although different media might target different strata within the masses, the basic goal of attracting the largest number of persons at that level has remained the same. The media successful in attracting the mass audience were rewarded by being able to charge higher prices to advertisers or, in the case of records and movies, to purchasers of their product. And it was the advertisers, with their seemingly insatiable appetite for larger audiences for their advertisements, who fueled the media's chase of the mass audience. The critical role of advertising in shaping and directing the development of the mass audience mentality by the media has not always been appreciated by scholars describing the development of communication media in the United States.

"Histories of American periodicals and even of the mass media deal with advertising as if it were a side issue," wrote historian David Potter in 1954.

Students of the radio and of the mass-circulation magazines frequently condemn advertising for its conspicuous role, as if it were a mere interloper in a separate, pre-existing, self-contained aesthetic world of actors, musicians, authors, and script-writers; they hardly recognize that advertising created modern American radio and television, transformed the modern newspaper, evoked the modern slick periodical, and remains the vital essence of each of them at the present time.[10]

Although the range of media has greatly increased in the four decades since Potter wrote and now affords a wider range of content for different segments of American society, the fundamental relationship that he described between advertising and the media has not changed. In the period when the mass audience media dominated all other forms, this relationship dictated that minority groups were treated in the mass media in terms that did not offend or, in fact, reinforced the attitudes of the dominant society toward those groups.

Mass Media and the Collective Consciousness

Advertisers demanded mass audiences to advertise their products; the communication media responded by adopting news and entertainment strategies that would attract the largest numbers of people. Because nearly all of the people in the United States were White—many of them immigrants—Blacks, Latinos, Native Americans, Asians, and other people of color were treated as fringe audiences, not important enough in numbers to dictate the content directed to the mass audience.

The mass audience was by no means homogeneous. In fact, the people in the mass audience were really very different from each other. The challenge facing the mass media was to find common themes and content that would attract people from all of these groups. The media reinforced a collective consciousness in the members of the audience that was necessary to attract large numbers of people in a heterogenous society. It was the task of the mass media to find commonalities among members of the audience; common themes, ideas, interest areas that would attract and not offend the mass audience. With few exceptions this meant that the content of the mass media reinforced, rather than challenged, the established norms and attitudes of the society. To do otherwise would be to risk offending significant numbers in the mass audience and, in the process, lose the large audience demanded by the advertisers.

The society of the United States, characterized by a melting pot mentality in which immigrants from different nations tried to blend together, often treated members of groups who had not assimilated or been allowed to become part of the mainstream as outsiders. Racial minorities that could be identified by color or facial characteristics were often placed outside the melting pot, unable to blend over generations because of physical characteristics. Blacks, Native Americans, Asians, and Latinos were groups whose physical appearance permanently identified them as different from the European Whites who had come from different countries and "melted" into the society of the United States.

They were not only outside of the melting pot, but outside of the focus of the mass media. Their numbers were relatively insignificant in comparison with the White majority and, as a result, they were not considered important components of the mass audience. For the most part, the mass media treated groups not in the mass audience or mainstream either by ignoring them or by stereotyping them. Movies, radio programs, newspapers, and news magazines generally ignored the issues confronting people of color in the United States, as well as their cultures and traditions. When they were treated, it was often in stereotypic roles, such as a Black Mammy, an Indian Maiden, a Latin Lover, or a sinister Asian Warlord. These characterizations of minorities were largely based on the perceptions and preconceptions of those outside of the groups, rather than the realities of the groups themselves. They were pictures as seen through Anglo eyes, rather than a reflection of the realities of the people in these groups.

The images served a useful economic purpose in attracting the mass audience. One characteristic of the mass audience was that it represented people who really were different from each other, who lived in different parts of the country, had different levels of income and education, and came from different cultural backgrounds. It included men and women, young and old, rich and poor. The media needed to communicate across these barriers and develop a common content denominator to which all in the potential audience could relate.

The technique developed by the mass media in dealing with racial minorities and others outside the mainstream involved symbols and stereotypes. The mass media, because they dealt with a wide audience, came to rely on symbols and stereotypes as shorthand ways of communicating through headlines, characters, and pictures. Dramatic portrayals such as those of rich bankers, heroic cowboys, or old spinsters were used so audiences would understand the character the first time it appeared on the screen or in the short story. At the same time, newspapers used symbols such as "right wing," "leftist," and "moderate" in headlines to characterize people or parties in different places on the political spectrum.

These symbols were a useful shorthand for the mass media, because they allowed the entertainment and news media to capsulize much more complex personalities and issues in a shortened character or term. Thus, when the audience at a western movie saw a man come on the screen with a white hat they knew he was supposed to be the hero in the western. Or when the term *leftist* was used in a headline that meant that the group to which the term was applied was on the liberal extreme, bordering on communism. The terms themselves were useful because they became symbols that triggered stereotypes, which Walter Lippmann long ago described as "pictures in our heads." The symbol was the term that called up a whole set of characteristics ascribed to those associated with the term in the minds of the mass audience. It was those characteristics that became the stereotype in the mentality of the audience.

Racial minority groups were among the groups portrayed by symbols and stereotypes in the entertainment and news media. Stereotyped characterizations of Native Americans, Blacks, Asians, and Latinos dominated the portrayals of members of these groups in the entertainment media of movies, radio, fiction, and television through the 1960s. Similarly, news media rarely covered activities in these communities unless, in accordance with the media's surveillance function, they were perceived as posing a threat to the established order or, in accordance with the correlation function, they were covered during colorful cultural festivals. Thus, the mass audience saw only a slice of the minority communities, one that did not jar their preconceptions of these groups. In fact, the media portrayals probably helped legitimize and reinforce such preconceptions.

In the absence of alternative portrayals and broadened news coverage, one-sided portrayals and news articles could easily become the reality in the minds of the audience. Whites might be seen in a wide range of roles in a movie, ranging from villains to heroes. In contrast, Blacks were most often seen as comical mammys, wide-eyed coons, or lazy, shuffling no-goods. There were no alternative portrayals to counter the stereotypes.

Do the Media Have an Effect?

Although it was once thought that the mass media was a "magic bullet" that entered the minds of the audience and could convert it to any opinion or attitude, scholars who have examined the effects of media on society since the 1940s have found that the influence of media is much more limited and complex. They have found that media have their greatest influence when they reinforce rather than attempt to change the opinions of those in their audience. Rather than being pictured as a mere target for a bullet, the mass audience is more accurately described as a complex set of groups and individuals who make selective decisions about which media to use, what to retain from the media, and how to interpret what they see and remember. Media have their greatest effect when they are used in a manner that reinforces and channels attitudes and opinions that are consistent with the psychological makeup of the person and the social structure of the groups with which he or she identifies.

Because of the wide range of social and psychological factors affecting how a person thinks and acts, it is difficult to pinpoint specific effects of media on how people think and act. The reinforcement and channeling effect of media, however, when coupled with the content analyses that have been made on coverage and portrayal of minorities in news and entertainment media, provide an insight into the negative effects of one-sided media images on both Anglos and the members of the minority groups portrayed. Effects do, of course, vary by the age and psychological makeup of the people receiving the messages, and the research in this area is not as well developed as in some other areas of communication research. Nevertheless, the studies that have been done show that negative, one-sided, or stereotyped media portrayals and news coverage do reinforce racist attitudes in those members of the audience who do have them and can channel mass actions against the group that is stereotypically portrayed. The studies also show that bigots watching television programs ridiculing bigotry interpret the program to reinforce their preexisting beliefs. The studies also show that children, both minority and majority, are especially affected by entertainment characters that portray minority groups. Though it is unwise to make general statements about the effect of coverage and portrayals of minorities on the society, it is useful to look at three studies that illustrate cases in which the broad principles of media effects have been found useful in assessing the impact of the media in this area.

News Coverage and Mob Violence: The Zoot Suit Riots of 1943

In the midst of World War II, Los Angeles was the scene of violent attacks by battle-trained American servicemen stationed in Southern California on Mexican, Black, and Filipino youths on the streets of downtown Los Angeles. The attacks targeted minority youth wearing "zoot suits"; long suit coats, pants pegged at the cuff with deep pleats at the waist, and a full head of well-greased hair. The attacks followed and were accompanied by a news media campaign targeting the zoot suited youths as antisocial elements whose dress was out of step with the nation's war effort. Accounts of the zoot suit riots, which occurred in June 1943, often include references to the one-sided coverage of the predominantly Mexican youths in the Los Angeles press.

In 1956 two sociologists, Ralph H. Turner and Samuel Surace, analyzed the press coverage of Mexicans in the Los Angeles press in an effort to determine how the press coverage may have affected the violent attacks on the teenaged youths.[11] Turner and Surace, hypothesizing that the period preceding the riots would be characterized by steady negative coverage of Mexicans in Los Angeles, first studied the coverage of Mexicans in the *Los Angeles Times* from 1933 to 1943. Articles were categorized into one of five categories. First was *Favorable:* stories that emphasized the area's Old California tradition—the romantic, brave, dashing image of Mexicans, religion in the Mexican community or Mexican culture. Second was *Unfavorable:* articles on delinquency and crime or Mexicans as a public burden. Third was *Neutral:* miscellaneous articles including people with Spanish surnames, but not identified as Mexicans in the article. Fourth was *Negative-Favorable:* articles that stated and then refuted accusations against Mexicans, such as, "Not all zoot-suiters are delinquents." Fifth, was *Zooter Theme:* articles identifying the zoot suit dress with crime, sex, violence, or gang activities.

The two sociologists hypothesized that the uniform crowd behavior, such as the organized attacks on Mexican youths by servicemen stationed in the area, would be preceded by media coverage in which the term *Mexican* would be used as an unambiguous negative symbol. They also hypothesized that because of the negative behavior ascribed to those labeled with the symbol, the mob violence against the Mexican youths that would not be tolerated in other circumstances would be sanctioned by the larger society. Turner and Surace felt that both favorable and unfavorable sentiments could be triggered by ambiguous symbols, noting that "even the most prejudiced person is likely to respond to the symbol 'Negro' with images of both the feared invader of white prerogatives and the lovable, loyal Negro lackey and 'mammy.' "[12] But unambiguous symbols representing people outside the boundaries of normal, accepted behavior would trigger "the dictum that 'you must fight fire with fire' and the conviction that a person devoid of human decency is not entitled to be treated with decency and respect."[13] When the symbol loses its positive or neutral elements, the people associated with the symbol can become targets for mob violence that would not normally be allowed in the society, the sociologists wrote. Therefore, in looking at the news coverage the sociologists expected to find a decline in the number of times the term *Mexican* was used in favorable news coverage in the period preceding the mob violence, resulting in the development of an unambiguously negative image for the people labeled with the term.

Their hypothesis was not fully supported by the data gathered before the rioting. In fact, themes classified as favorable by the researchers (primarily those that tended to romanticize the Mexican culture) ranged between 80% and 90% of the stories in which the term *Mexican* was used in the 10-year period before the riots. In taking a closer look at the data, however, they did find support for their hypothesis on the importance of unambiguous negative symbols. Although the percentage of favorable mentions of "Mexican" in the 3-year period preceding the 1943 riots did not decrease, the researchers noted a sharp decline in the number of articles using *Mexican* at all. The term was used in 27 articles sampled between January 1933 and June 1936 and 23 times in articles between July 1936 and December 1939. But it was used in less than half that number, only 10 articles, between January 1940 and June 1943. Thus, given what the researchers considered to be the "favorable" image of the term *Mexican* in the 1930s, the researchers found what they described as "a shift away from all the traditional references to Mexicans during the period prior to the riots."[14]

Their data analysis showed there had been no lessening of coverage of stories concerning Mexicans during the 10-year period, in fact the number of articles rose steadily in the three periods between 1933 and 1943. But there was a decline in the number of articles using the term *Mexican* and an increase in the percentage of articles classified as neutral, negative-favorable, and zoot-suiter. In the first period, favorable articles constituted 80% of the articles coded, but in the last period only 25% of the articles. The percentage of articles coded as neutral increased sharply to 32%, and the authors noted that the category "actually consists chiefly of unfavorable presentations of the object 'Mexican' without overt use of the symbol 'Mexican.' "[15] The percentage of articles in the negative-favorable category also increased, although it was smaller than the others, and, as the authors noted, was based on the overall negative image of Mexicans.

The most startling shift, and the one most supportive of the secondary hypothesis of the researchers, was the sharp increase in the use of the "zoot suit" term and theme as a strictly negative symbol. The zoot-suit theme, which was not used before 1940, accounted for a third of all the articles from 1940 to June 1943. The authors concluded that the introduction of the term and its heavy use in unfavorable circumstances resulted in the development of a strictly negative symbol that triggered no unambiguous or positive stereotypes. It was the association of that symbol with Mexican youth portrayed as having antisocial behavior that helped spur the indiscriminate attacks of servicemen on Mexican youths, including those not wearing zoot suits.

"Unlike the symbol 'Mexican,' the 'zoot-suiter' symbol evokes no ambivalent sentiments but appears in exclusively unfavorable contexts," Turner and Surace wrote.

> While, in fact, Mexicans were attacked *indiscriminately* in spite of apparel (of two hundred youths rounded up by the police on one occasion, very few were wearing zoot suits), the symbol "zoot-suiter" could become a basis for unambivalent community sentiment supporting hostile crowd behavior more easily than could "Mexican."[16]

The researchers found that in the period just before the violent attacks on Mexican teenagers, the newspaper's coverage of the Mexican community in the issues sampled was dominated by the zoot-suiter theme in unfavorable coverage, less use of the term *Mexican* in favorable coverage, and an increased coverage of Mexicans in articles not using the term *Mexican* but portraying the community unfavorably. Of the 15 articles analyzed in the 6 months just prior to the June 1943 attacks, 10 concerned zoot-suiters, 3 were negative-favorable, 2 were neutral, and none were in either the traditional favorable or unfavorable categories. In the 1-month period just before and including the attacks by servicemen on Mexican youths, 74% of the 61 articles on the Mexican community concerned zoot-suiters, 23% were negative-favorable, and 3% were neutral.

Though not ascribing all the blame to the news media for the violent attacks on Mexican youths, the researchers felt that the news coverage may have contributed to the violence and the general public support of the servicemen in two ways. One way was by showing a Mexican name, picture, or using a reference to "East Side hoodlums" without using the term *Mexican* or any other symbol. The second, and more effective according to the authors, was the introduction and use of a new symbol in a strictly unfavorable context.

> It [the new symbol] provided the public sanction and restriction of attention essential to the development of overt crowd hostility. The symbol "zoot-suiter" evoked none of the imagery of the romantic past. It evoked only the picture of a breed of persons outside the normative order, devoid of morals themselves, and consequently not entitled to fair play and due process,

Turner and Surace wrote. They continued,

> The "zooter" symbol had a crisis character which mere unfavorable versions of the familiar "Mexican" symbol never approximated. And the "zooter" symbol was an omnibus, drawing together the most reprehensible elements in the old unfavorable themes, namely, sex crimes, delinquency, gang attacks, draft-dodgers, and the like and was, in consequence, widely applicable.[17]

The Turner and Surace article is valuable because racial symbols triggering commonly accepted images in the minds of the audience have often been used in the news coverage of minorities. Because racial minorities historically have not been well reported in the news media, these symbols are often used at a time when the surveillance and correlation functions of the media are called upon to describe a change in the environment posed by minorities or define how and where minorities fit into the society. A study of national magazine coverage of Mexicans in the United States from 1890 to 1970 revealed a near absence of coverage except when elements of the Mexican population were seen as a threat to society and subject to discriminatory acts by the public or law enforcement officials. In these periods symbols, such as "Zoot-suiters," "Wetbacks," and "Chicanos" in the militant sense, dominated the headlines of national magazines.

More recently, the term *Illegal Alien* has been used to symbolize a person who enters the country illegally and is said to constitute a burden on public resources.[18] A survey of 114 randomly selected articles from California newspapers on undocumented immigration from January 1977 through March 1978 found that nearly half of the articles used the symbols "Alien" or "Illegal Alien" in the headlines.

The largest categories of headlines treated the immigrants as either a law enforcement problem, a drain on public resources, or illegal entrants into the United States; or federal efforts to cope with the issue.[19] Use of the term *Illegal Alien* continued in news headlines and coverage into the mid-1990s, most often referring to immigrants from Mexico. In 1994 Los Angeles police chief Willie Williams drew surprised reactions from a national audience of journalists when he said that the second largest group of undocumented residents in his city came not from a Latin American country, but from Canada.[20]

Bigotry and Bigots Reinforced: The Case of Archie Bunker

When the situation comedy program *All in the Family* hit the airwaves in January 1971 it immediately triggered a debate over its breaking of traditional barriers against racial and ethnic humor in network television. The story line of the program pitted a rascally but hardworking bigot, Archie Bunker, against his liberally minded son-in-law, Mike. Mike, a graduate student, lived in the Bunker household with Archie's daughter and engaged in lively and humorous debates with Archie, who had dropped out of high school and had a blue-collar job. Some lauded the program for tackling racial prejudice and exposing the foolishness of bigotry through the use of comedy. Others argued that the program, by portraying Archie as a lovable bigot, had the effect of sanctioning and even encouraging bigotry.

Norman Lear, the producer of the program, answered the program's critics by arguing that the comedy's story line countered bigotry because Mike effectively rebutted Archie, and that Mike was the one "who is making sense." Archie, Lear wrote in 1971, was seen by the audience as an advocate of "convoluted logic."[21] The program's dependence on racial themes would bring bigotry out in the open and would allow parents to answer children's questions about bigotry, Lear contended. The CBS television network, which aired the program, commissioned a study that showed the program could contribute to a lessening of racial bigotry by humorously exposing its shortcomings. Others defended the program for using a comedy format to belittle those with prejudiced opinions. The Los Angeles chapter of the National Association for the Advancement of Colored People (NAACP) even gave its 1972 Image Award to *All in the Family* for contributing to better race relations.

The program continued on network television for more than a decade and beyond that into syndication on local and cable stations. Its basis of humor moved into other areas as the program and characters evolved. Although several research projects dealt with the impact of the program on its viewers, one of the most important was also one of the first. In 1974, psychologist Neil Vidmar and sociologist/psychologist Milton Rokeach published an article analyzing viewers of *All in the Family* in the United States and Canada and the apparent impact of the program on them. Noting the debate then taking place over the effect of Archie Bunker on bigotry and prejudice, the researchers tested the audience reaction to the program in terms of the previous studies showing the way audiences use selective perception and selective exposure to regulate and filter the media. Under the selective perception hypothesis, Vidmar and Rokeach theorized that viewers with different degrees of prejudice or racism would have different reasons for watching the program, would identify with different characters, and would find different meanings in the outcomes of the programs. Under the selective exposure hypothesis, the researchers proposed that low prejudiced and high prejudiced would not watch *All in the Family* to the same extent. To test the hypotheses they surveyed 237 high school students in a small town in the midwestern United States and a Canadian sample of 168 adults in London, Ontario. The people surveyed were asked to respond to a questionnaire with 11 items designed to probe their reactions to the television program and six questions to measure their ethnocentrism or prejudice.

The initial analysis of the results showed that more than 60% of the respondents liked or admired Archie more than Mike, that 40% of the U.S. respondents felt Archie won at the end of the show, 46% named Mike as the one most made fun of, and 35% saw nothing wrong with Archie's use of racial and ethnic slurs. Results from the Canadian sample followed the same pattern. Vidmar and Rokeach then compared the exposure and interpretations of the program among respondents who were rated as high prejudiced and low prejudiced on the six items designed to measure ethnocentrism and prejudice. Both groups found the program equally enjoyable, but there was a big difference in their reactions to the program. The analysis of data testing the selective perception hypothesis found a number of significant differences showing that people at different levels of prejudice drew different conclusions from watching the same television characters.

"High prejudiced persons in both the U.S. and Canadian samples were significantly more likely than low prejudiced people to admire Archie over Mike and to perceive Archie as winning in the end," the researchers wrote.[22] The high-prejudiced U.S. adolescents were also more likely to report that Archie made better sense than Mike and to report their attitudes similar to Archie Bunker's in 20 years. High-prejudiced Canadian adults also condoned Archie's racial slurs more often and saw the show as poking fun at Archie less often than did low-prejudiced viewers. The researchers summarized that the data "tend to support the selective perception hypothesis—namely, that prejudiced persons identify more with Archie, perceive Archie as making better sense than Mike, perceive Archie as winning."[23] Furthermore, high-prejudiced viewers indicated a number of things they disliked about Mike and low-prejudiced viewers indicated things they disliked about Archie.

Vidmar and Rokeach also found support for the selective exposure hypothesis, but in a different direction than the one proposed by a report commissioned by the CBS television network. Network researchers, assuming that the program would be interpreted as satirizing bigotry, speculated that low-prejudiced persons would be the most avid viewers. But Vidmar and Rokeach researchers found that U.S. teenagers who were the most frequent viewers of *All in the Family* were those in the high-prejudice group. No significant differences were found in the Canadian sample. The data also showed that the most frequent viewers admired Archie more than Mike and condoned Archie's ethnic slurs more than infrequent viewers did. The researchers concluded that the testing of the selective exposure hypothesis showed "*All in the Family* seems to be appealing more to the racially and ethnically prejudiced members of society than to the less prejudiced members."[24]

"Despite the fact that the present study is not an experimental study, the findings surely argue against the contention that *All in the*

Family has positive effects, as has been claimed by its supporters and admirers." Vidmar and Rokeach concluded,

> We found that many persons did not see the program as a satire on bigotry and that these persons were even more likely to be viewers who scored high on measures of prejudices. Even more important is the finding that high prejudiced persons were likely to watch *All in the Family* more often than low prejudiced persons, to identify more often with Archie Bunker and to see him winning in the end. All such findings seem to suggest that the program is more likely reinforcing prejudice and racism than combating it.[25]

Contrary to the claims of the program's producer and network researchers, the findings of Vidmar and Rokeach, as well as subsequent scholars examining the impact of *All in the Family*, were consistent with previous studies on the way the social and psychological makeup of members of the audience influences the manner of choosing which media to use and how to interpret what they see, hear or read. In the classic "Mr. Biggott" studies in the late 1940s, prejudiced individuals were shown cartoons in which the bigoted attitudes of Mr. Biggott were portrayed in an unfavorable light. Instead of seeing the shortcomings of such attitudes, the respondents reinterpreted the meaning of the cartoons to avoid ridiculing Mr. Biggott or to reinforce their own attitudes.[26]

These and other studies have shown that the impact of media is to reinforce attitudes already held by members of their audience, rather than convince people to change them. When the content of the media play on racial prejudice and bigotry, even if these themes are ridiculed, prejudiced persons interpret the message to reinforce their bigoted attitudes, rather than reject or change them.

Television Teaches: Effects of Black Portrayals on Children

Children are particularly vulnerable to media images and portrayals, especially because they are learning about themselves and the society in which they live. The images presented by the media are often the first impressions they have of a group or topic and parents or other adults are not always present to help young children understand what the media are presenting.[27] For these reasons, researchers and education groups have been particularly concerned about the impact of television images on children.

The late 1960s and the 1970s witnessed an increase in the percentage of minority characters, particularly Blacks, in prime-time network television programming. In 1969-1970, half of the television dramatic programs had a Black character and from that season through the early 1980s annual surveys of Blacks in network programming showed that from 6% to 9% of all television characters were Black. The increase in the number of characters, however, did not necessarily mean that Blacks were treated equally with characters of other races. Research cited by communication researchers Charles K. Atkin, Bradley S. Greenberg, and Steven McDermott revealed that Black characters were more often in minor roles and less prestigious jobs than White characters, but were just as industrious, competent, and physically attractive. Blacks were also portrayed as more kind, moral, altruistic, crime victims, and involved in violence and killing than Whites. Blacks also tended to be dominated by Whites in crime dramas, although they dominated Whites in situation comedies. By the late 1970s most of the Black characters were found in situation comedies, where they most often played stereotyped characters who were lower in social status and more beset by problems than Blacks in integrated programs.[28]

To test the impact of such portrayals on White youths Atkin and colleagues surveyed 316 White students in the fourth, sixth, and eighth grades in schools in Michigan and Northern California. The students were asked how often they had watched six network television programs featuring Black casts, if they tried to learn from television, whether television Blacks were like real Blacks, how much they identified with Black characters, to compare portrayals of Blacks and Whites, to compare traits of real Blacks and Whites, asked to estimate the proportion of Blacks in the population, what they learned from television about Blacks, and how much contact they had with Blacks.

In analyzing the responses the researchers found that 30% of the youths watched the six programs weekly or almost weekly. Although only 14% said they watched television to learn about how other people behave, talk, dress, and look, it was clear that the televised portrayals of Blacks had affected the students' "knowledge" of Blacks. Less than a third of the students said they used television to learn about how Blacks dress, behave, and talk. Sixty-six percent said television Blacks "talk" like Blacks in real life, and Black teenagers on television were seen as realistic by 56%, Black men by 45%, and Black women by 44% of the youths surveyed. The researchers also found that the impact of the portrayals on television was mediated by how the youths interpreted those portrayals. Although finding no direct stimulus-response relationship between the way television portrayed Blacks and how real Blacks were perceived by the children, the researchers found that the selective perception of the young viewers could interpret the television programming to reinforce existing racial attitudes.

"The data showing that belief effects depend on the perceptions of the viewer indicate that television's role may be to reinforce prior dispositions rather than cause dramatic changes," Atkin et al. wrote after reviewing the results. "This suggests the important role that parents and schools might play in shaping the process of learning from television, since these sources directly influence attitudes that the viewer brings to the set."[29] The researchers wrote that their findings supported the traditional viewpoint that "what the child brings to TV" is just as important as "what TV does to the child."

Although the portrayals of Blacks may not have a predictable straight-line effect, it has also been shown that Black and White children may learn different things from those portrayals. In an earlier study, Greenberg found Black children were more likely than Whites to watch television programs with Black characters, were more often able to name a show featuring a Black character, and had more positive attitudes toward Blacks on television than did White children.[30] Researcher Alexis Tan concluded in a 1979 study that steady exposure to television entertainment programs that either ignore Blacks or relegate them to low-status roles could lead to low self-esteem among Black viewers.[31] Because of the statistical procedure used to analyze the data, the study did not show a cause-and-effect relationship between television portrayals and low self-esteem among Black adults. Other researchers have also shown that media portrayals may have a greater influence on the development of minority children than on White children.[32]

Media Do Affect Society

The findings of these and other studies are consistent. They show that the media's coverage and portrayal of minorities have an effect on members of both minority and majority groups. But it is a complex effect, one mediated by each person's psychological makeup, social status, age, and how the individual uses the media. It is unlikely that scholars will ever be able to make definitive long-lasting statements regarding the effect of media on minority groups or any other segment of society. This is because communication, unlike chemistry or biology, is a behavioral process. The role and effect of media are not as predictable as the result when two chemicals are mixed at a certain temperature in a laboratory. Communication involves human beings and society, not physical elements undergoing experimentation in a laboratory.

Even when communication researchers replicate experimental conditions as much as possible, they encounter difficulties in generating findings that can be applied to all people in all situations. Furthermore, laboratory findings do not always reflect reality. There are problems with assessing the impact of mass media in society because of the dynamic process. Communication researchers are not dealing with physical properties, but with human attitudes and behavior. The laboratory may be the best setting to observe biological experiments under controlled conditions, but it may be the worst setting for observing social happenings. People do not encounter the media in a sterile laboratory, but in homes, waiting rooms, bars, and so on. What they see, hear, and read in those settings are influenced by the people around them and by their own psychological makeup.

Just because it is difficult, if not impossible, to assess the effects of mass communication on members of society, however, the research findings are clear that certain types of people—including the young, those with predispositions to view members of racially

different groups in a certain way, and members of minority groups
that are not well integrated into the coverage and programming of
the media—are affected to a greater extent than others. As a result,
studies show that young, prejudiced people and members of minority groups are more influenced by minority portrayals in the media
than are others.

Notes

1. For articles on racial issues in the media see *The Media Studies Journal* (Vol. 8,
Number 3, Summer 1994), The Freedom Forum Media Studies Center, Columbia
University. The theme of the issue is "Race—America's Rawest Nerve."

2. Harold Lasswell, "The Structure and Function of Communication in Society,"
reprinted in Wilbur Schramm and Donald F. Roberts, *The Process and Effects of Mass
Communication*, Revised Edition (Urbana: University of Illinois Press, 1971), pp. 84-99.

3. Laswell, "The Structure and Function of Communication," p. 99.

4. Charles Wright, *Mass Communication: A Sociological Perspective* (New York:
Random House, 1959), cited in Wilbur Schramm and William E. Porter, *Men, Women,
Messages and Media* (New York: Harper & Row, 1982), p. 27.

5. Schramm and Porter, *Men, Women, Messages and Media*, p. 27.

6. Peter M. Sandman, David M. Rubin, and David B. Sachsman, *Media: An
Introductory Analysis of American Mass Communication* (Englewood Cliffs, NJ: Prentice
Hall, 1972), p. 14.

7. Peter M. Sandman, David M. Rubin, and David B. Sachsman, *Media: An
Introductory Analysis of American Mass Communication*, Third Edition (Englewood
Cliffs, NJ: Prentice Hall, 1982), p. 9.

8. See Joseph R. Dominick, *The Dynamics of Mass Communication* (Reading, MA:
Addison-Wesley, 1983), pp. 33-49, for a further elaboration of these functions as
applied in contemporary media systems.

9. Edwin Emery and Michael Emery, *The Press and America*, Fifth Edition (Englewood Cliffs, NJ: Prentice Hall, 1984), p. 141.

10. David Potter, *People of Plenty* (Chicago: University of Chicago Press, 1954), pp.
167-168.

11. Ralph H. Turner and Samuel J. Surace, "Zoot-suiters and Mexicans: Symbols
in Crowd Behavior," *The American Journal of Sociology* (Vol. 67, No. 1, July 1956),
pp. 14-20.

12. Turner and Surace, "Zoot-suiters and Mexicans, p. 15.

13. Turner and Surace, "Zoot-suiters and Mexicans, p. 15.

14. Turner and Surace, "Zoot-suiters and Mexicans, p. 18.

15. Turner and Surace, "Zoot-suiters and Mexicans, pp. 18-19.

16. Turner and Surace, "Zoot-suiters and Mexicans, p. 19.

17. Turner and Surace, "Zoot-suiters and Mexicans, p. 20.

18. Félix Gutiérrez, "Making News—Media Coverage of Chicanos," *Agenda* (Vol.
8, No. 6, November/December 1978), pp. 21-22.

19. Gutiérrez, "Making News," p. 23.

20. Willie Williams, Remarks to The Freedom Forum Panel on Coverage of Crime, Unity '94 Convention, Atlanta, July 1994.

21. Norman Lear, "As I Read How Laura Saw Archie . . . " *New York Times*, October 10, 1971.

22. Neil Vidmar and Milton Rokeach, "Archie Bunker's Bigotry: A Study in Selective Perception and Exposure," *Journal of Communication* (Vol. 24, No. 1, Winter 1974), p. 42.

23. Vidmar and Rokeach, "Archie Bunker's Bigotry," p. 43.

24. Vidmar and Rokeach, "Archie Bunker's Bigotry," p. 45.

25. Vidmar and Rokeach, "Archie Bunker's Bigotry," p. 46.

26. Eunice Cooper and Marie Jahoda, "The Evasion of Propaganda: How Prejudiced People Respond to Anti-Prejudice Propaganda," in Wilbur Schramm and Donald F. Roberts, Eds., *The Process and Effects of Mass Communication* (Urbana: University of Illinois Press, 1971), pp. 287-299.

27. For articles on children and the media see *The Media Studies Journal* (Vol. 8, No. 4, Fall 1994), The Freedom Forum Media Studies Center, Columbia University. The theme of the issue is "Children and the Media."

28. Charles K. Atkin, Bradley S. Greenberg, and Steven McDermott, "Television and Race Role Socialization," *Journalism Quarterly* (Vol. 60, No. 3, Autumn 1983), p. 408.

29. Atkin et al., "Television and Race Role Socialization," p. 414.

30. Bradley S. Greenberg, "Children's Reactions to TV Blacks," *Journalism Quarterly* (Vol. 49, No. 1, Spring 1972), pp. 8-9.

31. Alexis S. Tan, *Mass Communication Theories and Research* (Grid Publishing, 1981), p. 261.

32. For a review and analysis of the literature on the effects of television on minority children see Gordon L. Berry and Claudia Mitchell-Kernan, Eds., *Television and the Socialization of the Minority Child* (New York: Academic Press, 1982).

Entertainment
Media Portrayals

From the Live Stage to
Hollywood Before World War II

Any discussion of the portrayals of people of color in American entertainment must include the concept of stereotyping. *The American Heritage Dictionary* defines *stereotyping* as "a conventional, formulaic, and usually oversimplified conception, opinion or belief." In the broadest sense, stereotyping has been employed as a literary and dramatic device since the earliest beginnings of those art forms. It is a means of quickly bringing to the audience's collective consciousness a character's anticipated value system and/or behavioral expectations. Audience members are then able to assess the character against their own value systems and categorize the character as, for example, "the villain" or "the heroine." Stereotypes, therefore, are shortcuts to character development and form a basis for mass entertainment and literary fare.

Stereotyping can be a useful device when used without prejudice. A simplistic example would find a White villain brought to justice by a White hero in an entirely White social environment. The message transmitted to the audience would be that good overcomes evil. Negative stereotyping of non-White cultural groups in a White-dominated environment, however, transmits a far different message when done historically and persistently with prejudice.

Because the concept of prejudice is central to our discussion, let's use the term as James M. Jones has defined it in his book *Prejudice and Racism*. Prejudice, he writes, "is a negative attitude toward a person or group based upon a social comparison process in which the individual's own group is taken as the positive point of reference."[1] In that context our example would transmit not only the notion that good (the dominant cultural group) overcomes evil (the socially subjected culture) but that the latter is evil. Thus, although stereotyping per se may have merits in popular literature and the arts, when combined with prejudice it poses a devastating obstacle to human development and understanding in a multicultural society.

Before examining racial portrayals in American mass entertainment, we should look at the social historic precedents and attitudes in which certain stereotypes were cultivated. This will provide insight into whether the stereotypes were prejudiced and the degree to which social historic factors have been influential in their development and use. We shall consider the social historic experiences in the United States of four non-White groups to determine whether a causal relationship existed between their experiences with Whites and their subsequent treatment in entertainment media.

Native Americans

Native Americans (Indians) were the first peoples of a different ethnicity to confront European settlers on the American continent. The settlers were at once faced with a dilemma of how to coexist with people whom they saw as primitive but who also had some qualities they admired. Writings of early settlers referred to what they considered to be the natives' primitive innocence, their willingness to share food and other essentials of life freely in a communal environment, and their dark, handsome physical appearance. To the White settlers these attributes were "noble." At the same time the settlers also made observations of the natives' proclivity for nudity, open sexual relationships, and incidents of cannibalism. These traits were considered "savage." Thus emerged in colonial-era literature the concept of the "noble savage."

Initially the colonists decided to convert the natives to Christianity in an attempt to assimilate them while the task of creating a European society was under way. Religious conversion was eventually seen, however, as an impossibility, and the colonists rationalized that the natives had to be removed as a barrier to the "civilization" of the continent.

By the mid-1800s the policies for dealing with the "Indian problem" had found their justification in popular literature that first helped to establish the myth of the monolithic "Indian"—without regard for the distinctions of more than 2,000 different cultures, languages, and value systems the concept represented. The literary stereotype was part of the Western frontier writing formula developed after the Civil War. Writers of this genre included Bret Harte and Mark Twain. Readers of this fare were already conditioned to see the natives portrayed in a manner that justified their elimination as a barrier to Western expansion. Twain, Bret Harte, and others wrote of the picturesque scenery and romantic lifestyles of the frontier in contrast with the "savages" who occupied the land. In "Roughing It," Twain described the Gosiute Indians as "scrawny creatures," "treacherous-looking," and "prideless beggars." It remained only for dime-novel author Edward S. Ellis to write during the 1880s and 1890s of the Indian as merely a prelude to a more enlightened White civilization.

Stories of actual and exaggerated atrocities by Indians upon White settlers, who pushed ever westward into the frontier, firmly established a hatred against them that clearly made them both an enemy in war and of the progress of civilization. Literature during the Indian wars is rife with tales of natives burning, looting, raping, and scalping the pioneers who were fulfilling the fervor of "manifest destiny." It was against this backdrop that Frederick Jackson Turner's "Frontier Thesis," presented in 1893, argued that American (White) character had been molded by the experience of the Western frontier. Turner's ideas were accepted to the extent that they pervaded history textbooks into the middle of the 20th century. Elimination or subjugation of the Native American Indian was seen as merely an evolutionary step in the development of industrial America.

Black Americans

In 1619, a year before the arrival of the *Mayflower* on the shores of the American continent, 20 Africans were brought to Jamestown aboard a Dutch pirate ship. The ship's captain offered to exchange his human cargo for a supply of foodstuffs. The young Black men and women, with Spanish names such as Antony, Isabella, and Pedro, were probably originally headed for the West Indies on a Spanish vessel before being intercepted by the Dutch ship.[2] The 20 Africans became the genesis of a Black population that was to have a major impact on the development of the future United States.

Although the facts of slavery in America and its legacy of human indignity have been well chronicled, the roots of its underlying psychosis have been less explored in popular literature. The popular notion regarding the treatment of Blacks and their African ancestors has tended to focus on slavery as a phenomenon of the Southern White attitude based upon geographic and economic considerations. What is often overlooked is that slavery was a part of the Northern experience from colonial times. It is clear that Black racism was a factor in English Calvinist and Puritan religious ideology before those influences were brought to the New World. This affected their attitudes toward Black people in two ways. First, was the Anglo Saxon belief that the color white represented things that were pure, clean, good, and reflected the spiritual light. Black, on the other hand, represented impurity, filth, evil, and spiritual darkness. Both concepts persist to this day. Second, the Puritan concept of predestination relied upon observation to distinguish the "Elect" from the "Damned." Those who seemed relatively prosperous and self-sufficient were deemed superior to those who were enslaved. Against this religiously seated and strongly held attitude the reaction of the English colonists to Blacks in the New World is predictable even among inhabitants of the Northern seaboard. In fact, on New York's famed Wall Street in 1711 slaves were the predominant commodity partly because Puritan law was ambiguous on the subject. One such law of 1641 is revealing:

> There shall never be any bond-slavery, villenage or captivitie amongst us; unlesse it be lawfully captives taken in just warrs, and such

strangers as willingly sell themselves, or are sold to us: and such shall have the libertyes and Christian usuages which the law of God established in Israel concerning such persons doth morally require, provided this exempts none from servitude who shall be judged thereto by Authoritie.[3]

Whites in New England were first to establish what later would be called "Jim Crow" laws in the South as a means of codifying their prejudices against Blacks, although slavery never became a widespread practice in the North for economic reasons. In the South the mythology of the "happy slave," who was content to serve his or her master as the ultimate fulfillment of life, grew as a justification for the exploitation of Blacks. Much of the post-Civil War literature paints a negative image of Blacks designed to reinforce institutional and social racism. Many of the accusations against Black integrity that emerged during Reconstruction are now too familiar: laziness, slow-wittedness, loose standards of morality, fondness for alcoholic beverages, and so forth. Lynchings and other acts of violence against Blacks and those sympathetic to them are ample evidence of the attitudes held by White Americans toward them at the dawning of the 20th century.

Latinos

There is little mention of colonial Mexico in North American literature until the 19th century. Spain ruled Mexico for 300 years (1521-1821) before Mexico won its war for independence. In 1803, however, the Louisiana Purchase removed the vast buffer of territory between the United States and Mexico. The expansionist movement by U.S. settlers into the West and Southwest not only precipitated conflict with Native Americans, as discussed previously, but also lead to war with Mexico in 1846.

Central to the development of relations between Mexico and the United States was the Santa Fe Trail, which was legally opened as a commercial trade route in 1821. The trail ran from Independence, Missouri, to Santa Fe, New Mexico, and became the focal point of friction between White settlers and Mexicans. When some inhabitants of the newly formed Republic of Mexico became disenchanted with their new government, Anglo-American settlers were there in significant numbers to spur the movement for independence by the mid-1830s. In fact, there is much to suggest that American literature of the period was primarily designed to stir up local sentiment for overthrow of the Mexican government in Texas and New Mexico. Thus, Whites engaged in hostilities against Mexicans with Mexican allies during the war for Texas's independence. At the same time, popular literature portrayed in vivid terms the perception of a "cruel" General Antonio Lopez de Santa Anna's massacre of the "gallant" defenders of the Alamo (1836), which included folk heroes David Crockett and James Bowie. Americans were generally persuaded to visualize the Mexican as an inhuman enemy a decade before war with Mexico was officially declared.

Cruelty was not the only negative trait ascribed to Mexicans. Cecil Robinson in his work *Mexico and the Hispanic Southwest in American Literature,*[4] has chronicled the origins of several stereotypes that began to appear in Anglo writings before and during the U.S.-Mexican war. During that war, American naval Lieutenant H. A. Wise wrote that Mexicans were "beyond comparison the laziest and most ignorant set of vagabonds the world produces." George Wilkins Kendall penned:

> Give them but tortillas, frijoles, and chile colorado to supply their animal wants for the day, and seven-tenths of the Mexicans are satisfied; and so they will continue to be until the race becomes extinct or amalgamated with Anglo-Saxon stock.

When Mexicans were not being portrayed in Anglo literature as lazy and indolent, they were assailed for uncleanliness. Texas romance writer Jeremiah Clemens gave his version of the origin of the term *greaser* and why he felt it was appropriate:

> The people look greasy, their clothes are greasy, their dogs are greasy— everywhere grease and filth hold divided dominion, and the singular appropriateness of the name bestowed by the western settlers, soon caused it to be universally adopted by the American army.

In the short story "The Inroad of the Nabajo" by Albert Pike (1934), the women of Santa Fe are described as "scudding hither and thither, with their black hair flying, and their naked feet shaming the ground by their superior filth." It should be noted that several American writers found Mexican women quite charming and wrote at length about their feminine virtues that contrasted sharply with puritanical customs of American women of the era in dress and social demeanor.

A major factor in the attitude of Whites toward Mexico and its people was the negativism toward Mexican ethnicity. Most of the population was either full-blooded native (Indian) or mestizo (mixture of Spanish ancestry and Indian). Anglo-American writers routinely referred with disdain to Mexicans as "these mixed races." But it was the sizeable body of popular literature that grew out of the lore of the Santa Fe Trail that set the tone for American imagery of Mexicans and the southwest. Works such as "The Time of the Gringo" by Elliot Arnold, "Anthony Adverse" by Hervy Allen, and "Adventures in the Santa Fe Trade" by James Josiah Webb established the basic stereotypes by 1900.

Asian Americans

Asian experience in America has a short history prior to 1900, because Chinese immigration didn't begin until the California gold rush in 1848. Japanese people didn't begin to arrive formally until after 1855, when the Japanese government passed laws enabling its citizens to emigrate. We are concerned in this discussion with the Chinese and Japanese because other Asian and Pacific Island peoples were less a social factor in the United States before 1900 and because American attitudes toward the two groups were similar enough as to be virtually indistinguishable. In fact, many Americans never bothered to take note of any differences between Chinese and Japanese people and later came prejudiciously to lump them together as simply the "Yellow Peril."

Because the overwhelming majority of Asian immigration was to California and other states on the West Coast, their social history in

America during the 19th century is focused there. By 1870 there were more than 60,000 Chinese in California who had settled into farming, mining, factory work, and domestic labor after railroad jobs became scarce. Whites, who had come West to seek quick wealth in the gold rush, came to resent the Chinese because they had jobs but many Whites were unemployed. Dennis Kearney, leader of the California Workingman's Party, orchestrated an anti-Chinese movement with the backing of the *San Francisco Chronicle*. Kearney ended every speech with the slogan, "The Chinese Must Go." Kearney and his followers stirred a sentiment of prejudice against Chinese workers, who were highly visible because of their adherence to traditional customs of dress, pigtail hair style, and communal living. Suddenly, after 20 years of serving as a welcome source of cheap labor and having enjoyed a reputation for industry, honesty, thrift, and peaceful disposition, the Chinese were the object of scorn. They were now seen by Whites as debased, clannish, and deceitful. In the 1870s a series of racially motivated incidents of violence occurred in several western towns, resulting in the deaths of numerous Chinese inhabitants.

Finally, in 1882 the first Chinese exclusion law was passed and in 1887 only 10 Chinese immigrated to the United States. Ironically, the Chinese Exclusion Act of 1882 made possible the increase in Japanese immigration. The decline in Chinese immigrant labor proved the fact of White racism because those jobs went unfilled and a serious farm labor shortage developed in California and other western states. Soon there was a demand for Japanese immigrants who had proven farming skills and were willing to work for low wages. Between 1899 and 1904 nearly 60,000 Japanese came to America to meet the labor demand.

History repeated itself when, between 1901 and 1906, the corrupt administration of San Francisco Mayor Eugene Schmitz and his political boss Abraham Ruef used the Japanese as scapegoats when public attention was turned on their own dubious activities. Schmitz's regime was backed by organized labor that claimed the Japanese worked for lower wages and were driving Whites out of the job market. At the same time, Japan was quickly defeating the Russians in the Russo-Japanese War (1904) and going on to eventually seize

Korea. Japan's military successes created apprehension in America that Asians were a threat to Western civilization.

Once again it was the *San Francisco Chronicle* that crusaded in front-page articles against immigration, this time with the Japanese as objects. The *Chronicle* urged and supported a citywide boycott of Japanese merchants in San Francisco. The paper charged the immigrants with maintaining loyalty to the Emperor of Japan. Mass meetings were held denouncing Japanese immigrants, and acts of assault and other violence soon followed against them. The official reaction to what became known as the Yellow Peril was a series of laws restricting Japanese immigrant rights in America. This culminated with passage of the Immigration Act of 1924, banning entry to the United States for all aliens not eligible for citizenship, although the legislation was clearly targeted against the Japanese.

During the height of Yellow Peril hysteria, Chinese and Japanese persons were viewed as devious and vicious. Popular literature warned of the dangers of intermarriage with Asians and charged openly that Asian men purposefully sought White women. These attitudes found their way into entertainment media, as we shall see.

Beginnings of Mass Entertainment: The Live Stage

Now that we have seen the historic social relationships between White Americans and people of color, it is clear White attitudes have been molded negatively toward each of the groups for specific purposes. In each case our definition of *prejudice* (a negative attitude toward the groups based upon a comparison process using White society as the positive point of reference) has been fulfilled. We have also seen these prejudicial attitudes reflected in popular literature and observed how they impacted upon American political, economic, and social life. Our next task is to consider the relationship of these prejudicial attitudes to mass entertainment. To understand that relationship we must take a look at the developmental highlights of mass entertainment in America.

It is no accident that the rise of American mass entertainment coincided with the populist movement, which began in the 1820s and 1830s. The election of Andrew Jackson to the Presidency in 1828 marked the ascension of the "common man" to political and social prominence if not individual economic stature. Cities became population centers and laborers moved there from the farms to become wage earners. The genteel, socially elitist American with his refined cultural tastes was inundated by the onrushing tide of the populist movement.

The pivotal year 1833 marked the beginning of the Penny Press newspaper ushered in by Benjamin Day's *New York Sun* and its symbolic motto, "It Shines for ALL!" Just as Day's unsophisticated newspaper became the reading fare of an audience that clamored for "news" of gossip, sensationalism, and crime, so did live entertainment change to accommodate the tastes of the working class. It was also in 1833 in New York City's Bowery Theatre when an uninhibited audience shouted down the orchestra's symphonic overture and hollered instead for a rendition of "Yankee Doodle"; the audience got its wish. Just as the Penny Press made newspapers affordable for the masses, ticket prices for live entertainment plummeted from several dollars to 25 cents or less.

From the middle of the 19th century to the 1920s, the live stage became the first major mass entertainment medium in America. People in the cities were filling large, ornate theaters, and rural dwellers attended traveling shows housed in tents. Theatrical agents quickly came to understand the imperative of catering to the public's taste. Their reward was a full cash box and lusty cheers; those who failed suffered the wrath of hostile catcalls, hisses, and financial loss. People of color played a figurative, if not literal, role in the development of mass entertainment, because the populist audience demanded their inclusion in theatrical performances. The terms of that inclusion, however, were accommodating to the attitudes and values of the masses. In general, the audience wanted plays with common people (themselves) portrayed as heroes. They wanted foot-tapping music and dance and maintained a strong desire to see anything that fulfilled their perceptions of Black American culture. Perhaps above all, they wanted comedy, and people of color were a convenient foil. "Leave 'em laughing" became an early show business axiom.

One early favorite play had a Native American theme and was titled *The Original, Aboriginal, Erratic, Operatic, Semi-Civilized and Demi-Savage Extravaganza of Pocahontas.* Stereotypical myths of Native Americans, which had been spread by writers such as James Fenimore Cooper and pulp novelists, easily made the transition to the stage. After the Civil War live entertainment took to the outdoor theater arena with "Buffalo Bill" Cody and his "Wild West" show leading the way. Cody played out the American myth of the taming of the West and its Native American Indian population to Eastern audiences while the real Indian wars were being fought across the country. Cody legitimized himself by periodically returning to the West to serve as a scout and Indian fighter. His show played to packed audiences in the United States and Europe for several decades. Other traveling shows, including circuses and variety acts, spread racial stereotypes across America by 1900.

Minstrel shows featuring Anglo-American actors in blackface make-up appeared in the 1830s after an itinerant White actor, Thomas Dartmouth Rice, borrowed a song-and-dance routine from a little Black slave boy he had seen perform on a street corner. Billing himself as "Daddy" Rice he applied burnt cork to his face, dressed in tattered clothing, and performed the borrowed routine as the "jump Jim Crow" dance to the delight of audiences from New York's Bowery Theatre to the London stage.

Edwin P. Christie, a traveling salesman from Buffalo, New York, launched his career as a show business promoter after his travels took him through the South in the 1830s and 1840s. In Louisiana, Christie saw Blacks perform at a public gathering where they were allowed to gather for the amusement of Whites. Impressed with the musical and dance variations he saw, Christie went back to Buffalo, developed his own caricatures of Black personalities for an entertainment variety act, and the minstrel show was born. For decades Blacks could neither perform in nor attend these shows that were based on their musical and dance traditions. Ironically, when Black minstrel troupes did become acceptable to White audiences they, too, were compelled to perform in blackface makeup.

For 80 years the minstrel show was the most popular form of live American entertainment. In its classic form the minstrel show consisted of two acts. Part one employed a minimum of 15 men on stage

in a semicircular seating arrangement with gaudily dressed comedians at the end seats. A nattily attired "interlocutor" stood in the center
and a comedic exchange took place between him and the comedians.
Singers and banjo and tambourine players comprised the rest of the
troupe and songs, dances, rapid-fire jokes, and gags came without
pause. Part two of the show (often called the "olio") was comprised
of recitations, monologues, specialty songs, comedy skits, and bur-
lesque routines. After minstrel shows faded in popularity the olio
concept was expanded into a separate group of acts and became
known as vaudeville. Vaudeville launched the careers of some of
America's most honored performers including George Burns, Bob
Hope, Jack Benny, and Abbott and Costello. It remained only for Al
Jolson to refine minstrel show affectations to indelibly stereotype Black
people in American entertainment. With renditions of *Mammy, Rockabye Your Rockabye Baby to a Dixie Melody, Swanee,* and other songs,
Jolson was being called "Mr. Show Business" as early as 1915 but he
had been a popular fixture since the turn of the century. Jolson was
unquestionably the most popular entertainer in America during the
period. By the time motion pictures began to supplant the live stage
show in popularity, the quintessential stage musical *Show Boat* opened
the Broadway season in 1927 with a favorite White American theme
at its core: the interplay of Blacks and Southern Whites set against
an idyllic romantic background along the Mississippi River.

Racialism in the Movies

Thomas Edison is generally credited with the development of
motion picture technology with his invention of the Kinetoscope in
1889. In 1903 one of his assistants produced the first motion picture
with a storyline, *The Great Train Robbery.* Movies were projected without sound until 1927 when Al Jolson starred in *The Jazz Singer,* the
first "talking" (and, of course, "singing") movie.

Portrayals of people of color appeared very early in motion pictures. As early as 1894 one could view the Sioux Ghost Dance on one
of Edison's contraptions and by 1898 Buffalo Bill's Wild West show
had been committed to film complete with its imagery of the Native

American Indian's collapse before White "civilization." Only a year after *The Great Train Robbery,* Biograph released a one-reel feature (*A Bucket of Cream Ale*) depicting a Black maid employed by a White man. The maid was played by a White actress in blackface makeup. Between 1910 and 1914 several films projected Mexican stereotypes, including a series of works with the term *greaser* in the titles. It was consistent with the treatment of Asian immigrants at the turn of the century that they appeared stereotypically as diabolical personalities in film with the 1916 release of *The Yellow Menace.* Interestingly, in *The Yellow Menace* both Asians and Mexicans combine forces in a subversive plot against the United States.

Although there are many differences between and among the racial and cultural groups under consideration here, a close examination of their treatment in American mass entertainment reveals remarkable similarity. Our review earlier in this chapter of the social historic experiences of these groups shows that Whites held negative prejudicial attitudes against each of them before those attitudes manifested themselves in popular media.

Generally, all characterizations of people of color in early films projected an attitudinal posture of White superiority. That attitude revealed itself on screen through the portrayal of non-Whites as inferior in two major capacities: intellectual and moral. Virtually every characterization of non-Whites was designed to reinforce the attitude of White superiority. Given the low socioeconomic status of working-class Whites during the heyday of the industrial age, movie producers capitalized on audience insecurities by using racial stereotypes to bolster audience self-esteem and reinforce racial attitudes. White insecurities, as reflected in the first 40 years of American popular cinema, were revealed to be a fear of miscegenation and the threat that non-White cultures would have an impact on White social values. Thus, as live stage producers and entertainers profited financially by giving the masses what they wanted, moviemakers quickly developed a symbiotic relationship with their patrons, often at the expense of Americans of color.

Several basic movie themes derived from the attitudinal premises of White intellectual and moral supremacy (Table 3.1), and they were applied at various times to Native, Black, Latino, and Asian Americans alike.

TABLE 3.1 Some Traits Commonly Applied to People of Color in Early Movies

Intellectual Traits	Moral Traits
Preoccupied with simple ideas	Low regard for human life
Inferior strategy in warfare/conflict situations	Criminal behavior
Low or nonexistent occupational status	Sexual promiscuity
Poor speech patterns/dialect	Drug/alcohol abuse
Comedic foil	Dishonesty

With the release of the technical epic *Birth of a Nation* by D. W. Griffith (1915), movies began to institutionalize racial stereotypes. Griffith established a pattern, which would endure for decades, of portraying American Blacks as intellectually and morally inferior to Whites and that carried a strong message against sexual contact between the races. Perhaps the first film to openly proclaim the doctrine of White supremacy over Native American Indians was William S. Hart's *The Aryan*, which was released in 1916. One of the titles projected across the screen of this silent movie also played to the fear of miscegenation and read in part "Our women shall be guarded." As was most commonly the practice in early movies, Whites portrayed all of the non-White characters in both films. (It is interesting to note, however, that genuine Native American Indians were sometimes employed to play minor roles, but the practice was not without problems. Directors found it difficult to teach them how to act "Indian," prompting one observer to write an article on "The Dangers of Employing Redskins as Movie Actors.") An exception was Japanese actor Sessue Hayakawa who was involved in at least two early films in which he portrayed Asian characters. In *Typhoon* (1914) Hayakawa plays a young Japanese diplomat in Paris who, among other things, becomes romantically involved with a French actress. During the course of an argument the woman hurls racial epithets including "whining yellow rat" at the diplomat and he kills her. In *The Cheat* (1915) Hayakawa is cast as a deceitful Asian who schemes to obtain the sexual favors of a naive, but married, White socialite. In both *Typhoon* and *The Cheat* the message is clear: Interracial love leads to tragedy.

Latinos fared no better in the first two decades of American cinema. A series of films denigrating Mexicans appeared, including *Tony the*

Greaser (1911) and *The Greaser's Revenge* (1914). Mexicans in American film were the vilest of characters, who indulged in banditry, pillage, plundering, rape, and murder. The portrayals were so severe that the Mexican government banned such films in 1922 after filing a written protest in 1919 that went unheeded. Hollywood's response was to transport the "greaser" role to other nations or to invent locales with pseudo Latin names. In a perverse manner these films set the stage for the popularity of the mysterious, forbidden "Latin lover" roles that became a movie staple in the 1920s and 1930s. Rudolph Valentino was Hollywood's biggest star in that role.

Hollywood's Heyday: 1930-1945

The fact that stereotypes can, and do, change is evidenced by shifts in racial portrayals during the 15-year period from 1930 to 1945. Although basic attitudes held by Whites toward peoples of color did not undergo significant change, the passage of time altered social relationships between Whites and non-Whites. The result was that Hollywood had to make changes to conform to new realities. Unfortunately, the portrayals did not become more accurate and sensitive to the realities of the non-White experience in America but were merely adjusted to conform to more credible representations. For example, Blacks could not continue to be seen as only criminals and undesirables of various types (the primary theme of the years 1900-1920) because it was clear they had other dimensions of character that were easily observed in "real life." The movie industry response to social reality was simply to shift to new stereotypes that were still consistent with prejudicial notions.

Native American Indian portrayals changed very little between 1930 and 1945, probably because of their unique place in American lore. They symbolized the fulfillment of the American dream—the immigrant's ability to conquer the obstacles presented by a new continent and its existing inhabitants and to harvest its seemingly endless riches as reward. Hollywood adopted the Indian as a living monument to the ideals of manifest destiny and created a stereotype that barely managed to be a facsimile of Native American culture.

Examples include *Drums Along the Mohawk* (1939) and *Northwest Passage* (1940). No distinction was made in the movies between Indian cultures of the Northeast, the Plains, or the Southeast. Feathers, beads, fringed pants, pinto ponies, and halted English dialects were applied indiscriminately to represent the concept of "Indian" to movie audiences. The notion played well across the United States as moviegoers seemingly could not get their fill of "cowboy and Indian" movies and serials. The Native American's role was constantly to help audiences relive his defeat at the hands of the U.S. cavalry and other assorted "good guys." Thus, the major change in Native American movie portrayal from 1930 to World War II was the crystallization of an image. The Indian became an American cliché. Clichés die hard and the movie Indian remained throughout the heyday of Hollywood cinema.

A more pronounced stereotypical shift took place in the movie characterization of Black Americans during the boom period. The venomous, hate-filled disparagement of Blacks epitomized in *The Birth of a Nation* and other films of its era, such as *The Wooing and Wedding of a Coon* (1905), *The Masher* (1907), and *The Nigger* (1915), evolved into less threatening characterizations. The new stereotype played to White perceptions of Black personalities who, in the vernacular of the era, "knew their place" in American society. Blacks now appeared in movies for the purpose of entertaining White audiences within the context of social limitations. They had roles in musicals where they could demonstrate their "rhythmic" talents as singers and dancers. Meanwhile, the supposed inferior mental capacities of Blacks made for hilarious comedy. When in movie character, Blacks were subservient to Whites as maids, mammies, domestics, and sidekicks. The pre-World War II era brought to the screen Stepin Fetchit, Mantan Moreland, and Willie Best. It also produced the "Our Gang" series with the characters of Buckwheat, Farina, and Stymie. When the old days of the antebellum South were recalled by Hollywood, as in *Gone With the Wind*, Blacks played the happy, faithful, and sometimes lazy slaves. Hattie McDaniel received the first Oscar awarded to a Black actor for her portrayal of the dutiful and protective mammy to Scarlett O'Hara in the screen classic. Ms. McDaniel's award as best "supporting" actress was, therefore, doubly symbolic.

Figure 3.1. The portrayal of Native Americans as savages was typical Hollywood fare for decades. This poster for *Drums Along the Mohawk* (1939) promised movie viewers action scenes of Indian Warriors attacking White settlers. (Photo courtesy of the Academy of Motion Picture Arts and Sciences)

Figure 3.2. Mantan Moreland provided comic relief in 15 "Charlie Chan" movies as Chan's chauffeur, Birmingham Brown. As shown in this publicity photograph, Moreland often froze in wide-eyed terror when faced with suspenseful situations, a common Hollywood portrayal of Blacks. (RKO photo, courtesy of the Academy of Motion Picture Arts and Sciences)

Figure 3.3. Hattie McDaniel earned an Oscar for her portrayal of the faithful mammy to Vivien Leigh in *Gone With the Wind* (1939). Hollywood usually depicted Black slaves as being delighted with their servile roles. (MGM photo, courtesy of the Academy of Motion Picture Arts and Sciences)

Perhaps the primary reason for the change in Latino stereotyping during the 1930s was economics. The formal protest and subsequent banning of American moviemaking and distribution in Mexico by the Mexican government in 1922 did not go unnoticed in other Latin American countries. Although Hollywood intended the "greaser" stereotype to be its vision of Mexicans, Central and South American nations took equal offense when filmmakers began to create euphemisms for the roles in an attempt to placate Mexico. Film distribution sales in the affected countries were lucrative, so Hollywood eventually imported Latino actors and actresses to star in sizzling romantic features in an attempt to appeal to the foreign market. It took the film industry a while to learn how to effectively cope with the problem. In the late 1920s and the 1930s, filmmakers promoted Latinos to a more sophisticated level of "greasery." The Latino male was yet to attain personal integrity and social acceptability, but he did, in the words of one movie critic, at least dress well. At the same time it was non-Latino actors such as Noah Beery and Paul Muni who played the Latino roles in *The Dove* (1928) and *Bordertown* (1935), respectively. Alas, the "Latin lover" wasn't even Latino.

One of the traits Hollywood ascribed to Mexicans was a quick temper, and films of this era almost always allowed for a display of irrational Latino temperament. The concept was soon incorporated into female roles, and by the mid-1930s and early 1940s Hollywood had recruited a number of sensuous, tempestuous leading ladies for the purpose. The idea was to appeal to both U.S. and Latin American audiences. Among the new female stars were Delores Del Rio (*The Red Dance*, 1928) and Lupe Vélez (*Hot Pepper*, 1933; *Strictly Dynamite*, 1934; *Mexican Spitfire*, 1940). One concept in the tradition of Hollywood racial portrayals was unchanged, however; interracial movie romances were virtually never successful between Latinos and their White lovers.

By this time relations with Latin America were vital also for political reasons because the United States could ill afford to offend potential allies at a time when war was imminent. This circumstance paved the way for other Latino actors who virtually flooded Hollywood shortly before the outbreak of World War II. The display of Hollywood goodwill and profit motive produced Carmen Miranda, Cesar Romero, and Desi Arnaz, and film titles began to reflect a Latin American flavor (*Down Argentine Way*, 1940; *A Weekend in Havana*, 1941). Concurrently there was a conscious attempt to acquaint American audiences with Latin American history through movies on Benito Juarez and Simòn Bolìvar. Although political and economic pressures combined to accord Latinos the largest degree of change in stereotype among people of color between 1930 and 1945, certain prejudices lingered on screen. In general, Latinos were not seen as people with family values, stable romantic relationships, nor as in pursuit of honorable careers. Moreover, Latino men still had an uncomfortable (for Anglo-American audiences) proclivity for romantic interest in White women.

Figure 3.4. Lupe Vélez, who was born in Mexico, was cast in a series of movies, including *Mexican Spitfire* (1940) as the sexy, tempestuous Latina. (Photo courtesy of the Academy of Motion Picture Arts and Sciences)

With the passage of the anti-Japanese Immigration Act of 1924, their presence in popular films effectively ceased until they were brought to the American conscience once again with the arrival of

World War II. The Yellow Peril, insofar as the Japanese were concerned, was no longer a threat to White American sensibilities during the 1930s. Instead China and its people became the center of American attention in the Far East. China was in the midst of civil war and had been since 1911. Negative racial imagery had been popularly established with the appearance around 1910 of Sax Rohmer's fictional character, Dr. Fu Manchu, in several stories and novels. Fu Manchu soon became a diabolical movie villain and provided Hollywood with an entrée into new stereotypes based upon Chinese warlords. Movies of the genre proved to be highly successful. Among the most profitable of these films that exploited the "mysterious Orient" were *The Bitter Tea of General Yen* (1933), *Oil for the Lamps of China* (1935), and *The General Died at Dawn* (1936). In each of these films the American audience was given the impression that Chinese people are prone to violence, anarchy, corruption, vice, and prostitution, although the central Chinese characters were portrayed in more complex tones. There was no attempt in the movies to explain either why the wars occurred or the role of imperialism in China. Perhaps the only countervailing view was given impetus by Pearl Buck's Pulitzer Prize-winning novel *The Good Earth*, which was published in 1931. The 1938 movie version retained Buck's sensitive account of Chinese peasants as hardworking, loving, family people. There was, however, a strong anti-communist flavor in films about China during the mid-to-late 1930s, with communists depicted most often as the villains.

On the domestic front, the decade of the 1930s belonged to Charlie Chan, who was the Chinese American's cinematic representative, although no Chinese or other Asian actor has portrayed him during the series, which spans six decades with the 1981 release of a Peter Ustinov version. Other White actors who have portrayed the polite, bowing, proverb-spouting detective in the white suit include Warner Oland, Sidney Toler, Roland Winters, J. Carrol Naish, and Ross Martin. Charlie Chan movies were rife with stereotypical affectations. Although Chan seemed the most cerebral of the characters involved in his movie escapades, there were also the "Oriental" traits with which American audiences could identify. Chan was mysterious in his crime-solving techniques; one never knew what thought processes or logic he was employing until the critical moment at the movie's end. White America's memories of the diabolical Asian

Figure 3.5. Charlie Chan, here played by Sidney Toler, in *The Chinese Cat.* Chan epitomized several stereotypes but was, perhaps, the most popular Asian character Hollywood has produced. (Photo courtesy of the Academy of Motion Picture Arts and Sciences)

were readily recalled when Chan offered this advise to one of his many sons: "Keep eyes, ears open. Keep mouth shut." His slow gait, drowsy manner, and halting speech suggested Chan may have spent private moments with an opium pipe. The character's immense popularity with American movie audiences throughout the 1930s and 1940s may have contributed to the pro-Chinese sentiment that existed then.

Hollywood tried to temper its stance toward Latinos as World War II approached, but it revived and escalated its negative portrayals of the Japanese during that period. Because the Chinese peasant enjoyed favored status among Americans in the afterglow of Pearl Buck's *The Good Earth* novel and subsequent movie, Hollywood had little difficulty resurrecting the Yellow Peril theme against Japan as it became a threat to China. The Japanese attack on Pearl Harbor sealed their fate in American cinema but the Japanese Americans who were soon shuttled to "relocation" camps felt the sting of attitudes long since implanted in the mass psyche and nurtured in movie houses. In films produced between 1942 and 1945, Hollywood dusted off the old images of Japanese duplicity, inhumanity, and lust for White women. Unlike the Germans, who were portrayed as a respectable but misguided people under the influence of the Nazi regime, the Japanese were seen in American theaters strafing Red Cross ships, bayonetting children, and delighting in applying torture techniques presumably handed down from centuries of malevolent practice. Examples can be found in *Wake Island* (1942), *Guadalcanal Diary* (1943), and *Objective Burma* (1945).

Analysis

Entertainment stereotypes of non-Whites in American mass media have historical roots in racist attitudes that existed for various social and political reasons against each of the groups prior to their inclusion in media. The stereotypes were based upon negative prejudicial characteristics that, when compared against the values of the majority White society, were deemed to be innately inferior traits. Because the economic success of mass entertainment media in the United States was predicated upon their ability to meet audience demands, mass support for negative and inferior portrayals of people of color indicates that producers satisfied consumer desires. The stereotypes, then, were representative of popular attitudes.

We have also seen that although wide differences exist among the cultural and racial groups under consideration, their portrayals in American mass media have been remarkably similar and are the result of the attitudinal premise of White intellectual and moral supremacy. The fundamental concepts of racial stereotyping were applied consistently in each of the American mass entertainment media forms discussed: popular literature, the live stage, and motion pictures. This was the dubious legacy upon which American entertainment media entered the post-World War II era and the age of commercial television.

▦

Notes

1. James M. Jones, *Prejudice and Racism* (Reading, MA: Addison-Wesley, 1972), p. 3.
2. Lerone Bennett, *Before the Mayflower* (New York: Penguin, 1966), p. 30.
3. W. D. Jordan, *White Over Black: American Attitudes Toward the Negro, 1550-1812* (New York: Penguin, 1969), p. 7.
4. Cecil Robinson, *Mexico and the Hispanic Southwest in American Literature* (Tucson: University of Arizona Press, 1977).

Movies and TV From World War II to the Brink of a New Century

Forces of world history and technology combined to make their impact on the treatment of people of color in American mass media following World War II. During the next two decades there was a war in Korea and U.S. involvement in Vietnam began, signaling a major change in global politics. Domestically, McCarthyism came and went, as did the civil rights movement. The motion picture was in the process of being supplanted as the prime mass entertainment medium by television.

Although motion pictures were entering a transition period and seeking to redefine their niche in American mass entertainment, producers continued to release movies about or including people of color. Stereotypes continued to change in order to reflect the current political viewpoints, racial attitudes, and moods of the White majority audience. Native American Indians were used during the period as metaphors by filmmakers who wanted to make political or philosophical statements about other issues. For example, *Arrowhead* (1953) was seen by critics as an ultra-right-wing allegory of the McCarthy era while *Cheyenne Autumn* (1964) spoke strongly against German extermination camps as well as Indian persecution. Later, both *Soldier Blue* and *Little Big Man* (1970) made statements about American involvement in Vietnam. At the same time, White America (in the midst of the Black-inspired civil rights movement) experienced a guilt complex over the historical and persistent mistreatment of Native American Indians. The result was a series of Hollywood productions designed to purge that guilt including *Hombre* (1967), *Tell Them Willie Boy Is Here* (1969), and *Jeremiah Johnson* (1972). Taking matters further, Hollywood reversed itself on portrayals of two Indian tamers it had immortalized in earlier films. In *Little Big Man* (1970), General George A. Custer is characterized as meeting a just ending at the Little Big Horn massacre as retribution for atrocities perpetrated against the Indians. Similarly, William Cody is portrayed as a mercenary eagerly exploiting Native Americans for the sake of showmanship in *Buffalo Bill and the Indians* (1976). The 1970s can generally be viewed as the decade when movie portrayals became pro-Indian. Although the image of the violent Indian remained into the 1980s, Hollywood tended to mitigate the violence by placing it in the context of survival, self-defense, or retribution. The 1990s brought more sympathetic, although idealized, portrayals of Native Americans to the big screen. Foremost were *Dances With Wolves* and *I Will Fight No More Forever* (1990), *The Last of the Mohicans* (1992), and *Geronimo* (1993).

Black Americans benefited from a shift in White attitudes following World War II when (under the prodding of the National Association for the Advancement of Colored People, other civil rights groups, and the Harry Truman administration) Hollywood began to make films illustrating the folly and unfairness of racial discrimination against them. A catalyst in this movement was the manner in which Black military men had distinguished themselves during World War II in fighting for the cause of American freedom. The evils of prejudice against Blacks were denounced in *Pinky, Lost Boundaries,* and *Home of the Brave* (1949), *No Way Out* (1950), *Blackboard Jungle* (1955), and *The Defiant Ones* (1958). The 1960s belonged to the imagery of the sophisticated Black who was heroic in proportions. Actor Sidney Poitier epitomized the intelligent, cool Black American who harnessed his hidden rage in tolerance to prejudice and ignorance found in Whites of lesser stature in *Guess Who's Coming to Dinner* and *In the Heat of the Night* (1967). Poitier won the Oscar for Best Actor for his portrayal of a handyman who builds a chapel for White European nuns in a rural American community in *Lillies of the Field* (1963).

Figure 4.1. This scene from *Dances With Wolves* (1990) was part of the movement toward more sensitive but idealistic film portrayals of Native Americans that emerged in the 1990s. (Photo courtesy of the Academy of Motion Picture Arts and Sciences)

Harry Belafonte and Sammy Davis, Jr., were two other Black actors who starred in films of the period in roles that showed Blacks in nonthreatening circumstances.

The mid-1960s and early 1970s brought a definitely threatening Black image to the movies as the so-called blaxploitation movies featuring nearly all-Black casts cavorted on screen with the assumption of a militant posture. The civil rights movement led by Dr. Martin Luther King, Jr., was at its zenith. Hollywood again purged its conscience as urban Blacks took revenge against Whites in such movies as *Sweet Sweetback's Baadasssss Song* (1971) and in two urban detective films featuring Richard Roundtree in *Shaft* (1971) and *Shaft's Big Score* (1972). Whites generally showed little box-office interest in blaxploitation movies and the genre soon lost its financial luster. The rest of the 1970s was marked by a trend toward films designed to attract mixed racial audiences. *Cooley High* (1975) and *Carwash* (1976) were examples. In the early 1980s, with the civil rights movement a distant memory, roles for Blacks in motion pictures became extremely scarce, a circumstance they shared with other non-White film craftspeople.

The mid- to late 1980s, however, brought a resurgence of African American presence in cinema due largely to the popularity of two Black comics—Eddie Murphy and Whoopi Goldberg—who had made their marks in television and the stand-up comedy circuit. Murphy proved to have major racial crossover appeal at the box office following a string of movies including *Trading Places* (1983), *Beverly Hills Cop* and its sequel, *Beverly Hills Cop II* (1984 and 1987, respectively), *Coming to America* (1988), and *Harlem Nights* (1989). He continued his success into the 1990s with *Boomerang* and *The Distinguished Gentleman* (1992). Goldberg made her movie debut to critical acclaim in *The Color Purple* (1985) and followed it with *Jumpin' Jack Flash* (1986), *Burglar* and *Fatal Beauty* (1987), and *Clara's Heart* (1988). In the 1990s she starred in *Ghost* (1990), *Sarafina* and *Sister Act* (1992), and *Sister Act II* (1993), among others. Goldberg's roles ranged from purely whimsical and comedic to serious and sensitive portrayals of Black Americans.

Black films with a harsher edge depicting life in urban ghettos also appeared in the 1990s including *Boyz 'N the Hood*, *Jungle Fever*, and *New Jack City* (1991). These works coincided with the emergence of a group of Black film directors who were successful in getting Hollywood to bankroll their efforts. Among them were Spike Lee, John Singleton, and Matty Rich. By the 1990s, Denzel Washington (*Glory*, 1989; *Mo' Better Blues*, 1990; *Malcolm X*, 1992; and *The Pelican Brief*, 1993) had replaced Sidney Poitier as the foremost Black male dramatic actor, closely followed by action/adventure specialist Wesley Snipes who starred in *Jungle Fever* and *New Jack City*, as well as *White Men Can't Jump* and *Passenger 57* (1992), and *Rising Sun* (1993).

The immediate post-World War II period saw a continuation of the relationship established before the war between Latinos and Hollywood that was built on economic considerations. During the war U.S. filmmakers could not distribute their wares to European markets. Latin American countries came to represent 20% of Hollywood's total foreign market business during the era, resulting in the

Figure 4.2. Whoopi Goldberg, shown here in *The Color Purple* (1985), was among the Black performers who moved from night club stand-up comedy ranks to movie stardom in the 1980s. (Photo courtesy of the Academy of Motion Picture Arts and Sciences)

development of joint movie projects. Many movies were filmed in Latin American nations with writing and financing provided by Hollywood. Most of the supporting roles were played by Latino actors, and the alliance lead to an overly positive image of Latino characters as evidenced by such films as *The Fugitive* (1948) and *Way of the Gaucho* (1952). In 1953 a precedent was established with the making of *Salt of the Earth,* in which all of the major roles were portrayed by Latino or Latin American actors.

By the 1960s the Latin American market withered for Hollywood because those countries had developed their own film industries and screen personalities. The number of Hollywood movies utilizing Latino themes dropped drastically, and those that did reverted to old stereotypical forms by reintroducing the "greaser" as an urban gang member. Puerto Ricans were singled out for updated "greaser" treatment in two 1961 films, *West Side Story* and *The Young Savages*. The emphasis was on gang violence in urban America. Hollywood continued the violent "greaser" trend with *Duck You Sucker* (1972), *Bring Me the Head of Alfredo Garcia* (1974), *The Warriors* (1978), and *Boulevard Nights* (1979). A distorted view of the Mexican family was presented in *Children of Sanchez* (1978), but the early 1980s included movies produced and directed by Chicanos (*Seguin*, 1981; and *The Ballad of Gregorio Cortez*, 1982). The 1981 release of *Zoot Suit* followed the success of the play, which began its run in 1978. In *Zoot Suit*, based on an actual incident, the Mexican American is realistically portrayed during a World War II-era race riot in Los Angeles. A series of movies beginning in the 1970s featured the nonthreatening, comedic adventures of "Cheech and Chong" in the Mexican American urban barrio. These films, however, were criticized for their perceived glorification of the drug culture, sexist orientation, and nontraditional lifestyle of the featured characters. In general, Hollywood offerings did little to portray Latinos as part of the social mainstream in the United States during the first half of the 1980s other than in bit parts. A more positive portrayal appeared with the release of *Stand and Deliver* (1988), based on the true story of a Mexican American high school mathematics teacher. Also receiving critical acclaim were *La Bamba* (1987) and *The Milagro Beanfield War* (1988). Generally, however, the late 1980s and early 1990s found Latinos in the storyline background either as street toughs or drug traffickers, as in *Colors* (1988), *Tequila Sunrise* (1989), and *Carlito's Way* (1993).

Japanese portrayals continued to be very negative immediately following World War II as American audiences were offered more war movies. Japanese acts of cruelty and torture were seen in *Tokyo Joe* (1949) and *Three Came Home* (1950). An exception, perhaps inspired by guilt response to the Japanese relocation camps, was *Go for Broke* (1951), which was a positive portrayal of the heroic Japanese American military units that fought in Europe. A major reversal would soon take place, however, between Japanese and Chinese imagery in the movies.

With the coming of the Korean War, the cold war, and McCarthyism, the issue of communism became the focal point of American fears and anxieties. Synonymous with communism were the Soviet Union

Figure 4.3. One of the few Hollywood movies produced in the 1980s and 1990s depicting a positive image of Latinos was *Stand and Deliver* (1988) staring Edward James Olmos. (Photo courtesy of the Academy of Motion Picture Arts and Sciences)

and China. China, whose people had been viewed so warmly by Americans only a decade earlier, was once again seen as home of the Yellow Peril. Japan, on the other hand, was virtually a U.S. satellite and close ally by the late 1950s. Popular movies reflected both attitudes.

The Japanese were initially portrayed with much more sensitivity than at any time since the Immigration Act of 1924. *The Bridge on the River Kwai* and *Battle of the Coral Sea* (1959) are examples of the softer treatment given the Japanese by Hollywood. Even the touchy subject of Japanese-White romance was explored in *Sayonara* (1957) and *My Geisha* (1962). Although such romances did not have happy endings, they were nevertheless not treated as a basic violation of nature.

Meanwhile, China (by now commonly referred to as "Red China" or "Communist China") took on the movie depictions reminiscent

Figure 4.4. Cary-Hiroyuki Tagawa appeared in the *Rising Sun*, a film that drew protests from some Japanese Americans who objected to its stereotypical imagery. (Photo courtesy of the Academy of Motion Picture Arts and Sciences)

of the early 1930s. The Chinese regime was seen as oppressive and exploitive of its own people in *Satan Never Sleeps* (1962) and as a devious threat to the American system in *The Manchurian Candidate* (1962). That same year also marked the release of two films, *55 Days to Peking* and *The Sand Pebbles*, that were set in early 20th century China but that reinforced the image of drug addiction, prostitution, inhumanity, and deceit as staples of Chinese life. From the mid-1970s, following the reopening of diplomatic and trade ties with China, the pendulum swung again in China's favor and Hollywood curtailed its negative portrayals after several fantasy characterizations such as *Dr. No* (1962) and others in the James Bond spy thriller series. A surge of American interest in Oriental martial arts, however, spurred the creation of a series of films featuring almost nonstop violent action scenes showing villains and heroes employing kung fu, karate, and other combative techniques. Chinese American actor Bruce Lee, an acrobatic master of the martial arts, became the catalyst for that motion picture genre that portrayed the Chinese as sadistically violent. Generally, however, his films depicted Chinese characters in both heroic and villainous roles.

In the post-Vietnam era American film producers made the Vietnamese their next target of Asian stereotyping based on the same long-standing attitudes. They were portrayed on screen as crafty, devious, guerilla warfare perpetrators of violence in *The Deer Hunter* (1978), *Apocalypse Now* (1979), and *Platoon* (1986), among others, into the 1980s. From the mid-1980s into the 1990s, White actors Chuck Norris and Jean-Claude Van Damme assumed the mantle of filmdom's leading martial arts masters, often vanquishing Asian foes in the process. Although the Japanese American community voiced concerns about stereotypical characterizations in *Rising Sun* (1993), more sensitive portrayals of Asian peoples surfaced occasionally during the period, including *The Killing Fields* (1984) and *The Last Emperor* (1987). Perhaps the most insightful American film portrayal of Asians in many years was the screen adaptation of Amy Tan's novel, *The Joy Luck Club* (1993). The movie explored Chinese and Chinese American cultural nuances and resulting interpersonal conflicts through the eyes of three generations of Chinese women.

People of Color in the Television Age

Movies of both older and recent vintage did not cease to perpetrate their stereotypical images on either White audiences or people of color after their run in American theaters; many of them have continued to reach the masses via television and video cassette distribution and may do so for years to come. Commercial television began to be a major mass medium in 1948, the year Milton Berle's comedy and variety show spurred the purchase of TV sets in epidemic proportions. People of color were quickly made a part of the new medium, appearing in the traditional roles to which they had been limited in theatrical movies.

🌑 *The Noble Savage Revisited*

Among the first such TV characters was Tonto, the Lone Ranger's "faithful" Indian companion played throughout the series' 8-year run by Jay Silverheels, an actor of Mohawk tribal heritage. *The Lone Ranger* first aired on television in 1949 but had begun as a radio series in 1933. Though the Lone Ranger's mask often made those he encountered in his Western adventures apprehensive, the fact that he maintained a friendship with a Native American Indian made him even more suspect. Tonto's image, however, was positive because he fought for justice in the highest tradition of American folklore. His role as a Native American perpetrated the established stereotypes including the pinto pony, broken English dialect, fringed buckskin attire, and secondary status relative to the White hero.

Unfortunately, the historical portrayal of Native Americans on network television differs little from that experienced in Hollywood. The list of prime-time TV series featuring positive, accurate representations of Native Americans is extremely brief, either as an examination of past or present conditions. Perhaps the only attempt to do so was made in the 1955-1956 TV season when CBS aired *Brave Eagle*. The show sought to portray the Indian viewpoint of the White expansionist movement into his territory during the latter part of the 19th century. The program did feature actual Indian cast members but, ironically, a real Indian (Keena Nomkeena) played the foster son to White actor Keith Larsen who played a Cheyenne tribal chief. There was also an old sage who orally recited tribal history and events—a character also played by a White actor. Nevertheless, the series has not been equaled into the 1990s in its basic objective as a regularly aired network offering, although there have been documentaries and special TV movies that have infrequently appeared with sympathetic themes. *Brave Eagle* was followed by ABC's *Broken Arrow,* which appeared for 5 years (1956-1960). The series, however, featured an all-White cast and the storyline centered around Indian and White cooperation in fighting frontier injustice. During the era when television was dominated by "westerns" (1960s), Indians were mostly relegated to their movie image, serving as either foils or backdrops to the stories of how the West was won. This basic pattern continued into the 1990s. One example was *The Young Riders,* offered by ABC

from 1989 into the early 1990s. In the show Gregg Rainwater played
the role of Little Buck Cross, who was half Kiowa Indian. The storyline
was about the Pony Express era but television sensibilities of the
1980s and 1990s demanded revisionist history of the western frontier
so *The Young Riders* spent most of their time protecting the innocent
and displaying kindness to any Native Americans who happened
to wander into an episode. A different and unique twist came to Native
American TV portrayals with the 1990 arrival of *Northern Exposure*
on CBS. In it Elaine Miles portrayed Eskimo medical receptionist
Marilyn Whirlwind, an unflappable and down-to-earth personality.
The show was a ratings success and continued on prime time into
the 1995 season.

◉ *Black Magic on the Small Screen*

Black Americans have comprised the largest non-White racial
presence in network television. That fact, however, has not resulted
in an altogether satisfactory TV portrayal of the realities of the diversified Black experience in the United States, but more recent history
shows improvement over earlier years. In variety programming,
Blacks appeared frequently as guest performers almost from the
inception of network commercial television. Ed Sullivan featured
them as early as 1948 on his CBS *Toast of the Town* show (later called
The Ed Sullivan Show) as did Steve Allen as host of NBC's *The Tonight
Show* from 1954 to 1957. In 1950 three network shows went on the
air featuring Blacks in their casts as regulars. They were *Beulah, The
Jack Benny Show,* and *The Stu Erwin Show,* and each portrayed Blacks
in subservient, domestic roles. The Beulah character (played first by
Ethel Waters and later by Louise Beavers) was a maid and mammy
figure in a White household who had a scatterbrained girlfriend
(Oriole, played by Butterfly McQueen) and a shiftless boyfriend.
Eddie Anderson portrayed Jack Benny's valet "Rochester" on TV for
15 years and Willie Best, who had played imitative Stepin Fetchit
roles in numerous movies, brought the character to the Erwin show
as the family handyman.

The first show with an all-Black cast made its television debut in
1951, although it had been immensely popular as a radio series since
1929 with its White creators playing the major roles. *Amos 'n' Andy*

was awaited with much anticipation across the nation because the show's creators, Freeman Gosden and Charles Correll, held a widely publicized 4-year search for the Black actors who would bring the show to television. A special televised segment was arranged before a studio audience for Gosden and Correll to introduce the hand-picked cast prior to the first show. In introducing the male actors, the creators occasionally referred to them as "boys," a term long despised by Blacks as a relic of slavery in the United States. The original series lasted 2 years but reruns continued into the mid-1960s, always in controversy over the images it projected about Blacks. Although the show was based on characters with little intellectual capacities or otherwise lacking ethical values and employment, there were Black characters seen as attorneys, business owners, educators, and other professionals. Nevertheless, pressure from civil rights groups forced the program off the air entirely in 1966 when CBS with-drew it from sale. The advent of videocassette technology has made *Amos 'n' Andy* a brisk seller in the home entertainment market into the latter half of the 1990s.

Two other significant programs featuring Blacks prior to the civil rights movement of the 1960s starred male vocalists. In 1952 ABC's 15-minute *Billy Daniels Show* was the first national TV program with a black host. It ran for only 13 weeks—one third of a season by industry standards of the time. A musical-variety show hosted by singer Nat "King" Cole, which aired for 59 consecutive weeks from 1956 to 1957, fared somewhat better. Many prominent entertainers, several sponsors, and NBC executives supported Cole and made con-siderable efforts to keep the show afloat despite poor ratings through-out its 13-month history. Although Cole was an extremely talented vocalist and successful recording star, his show could not win the ratings competition against the popular mainstream programs in its time slot.[1] From the mid-1960s into the mid-1980s Blacks were seen on numerous TV series, usually as comedy-variety show hosts or in situation comedies. Many shows employed what were seen by critics as a single "token" Black character, and from *Amos 'n' Andy* to autumn 1984 there were only four other shows (all situation comedies) with predominately Black casts that lasted more than one season in regular network television: *Sanford and Son* (1972), *Good Times* (1974), *The Jeffersons* (1975), and *What's Happening!* (1976). Of course, the TV

Figure 4.5. The first network TV show to feature an all-Black cast, *Amos 'n' Andy*, debuted in 1951 with (from left) Spencer Williams as "Andy," Tim Moore as "George 'Kingfish' Stevens," and Alvin Childress as "Amos." Protests from civil rights groups forced CBS to drop the series from syndication in 1966.

ratings epoch *Roots* aired as a prime-time miniseries special in 1977 and many believed it served as a catharsis of guilt for Whites over the historical treatment of Blacks in America. An estimated 100 million viewers watched the program over eight consecutive nights, which began several trends in television programming.

Into the mid-1980s the primary roles for Blacks in prime-time network television were still in situation comedies rather than serious dramatic programs. Arguably, however, critics maintained that network television in the 1980s was almost all situation comedies and prime-time "soap opera" serials. Actress Diahann Carroll, who became the first Black woman to star in a network comedy/dramatic series (*Julia*, 1968), made history again in 1984 when she joined the regular cast of ABC's prime-time soap opera *Dynasty*. That same year marked the opening season of NBC's *The Bill Cosby Show*, which became television's number one rated program throughout the mid-1980s, proving that a show with an all-Black cast could be an overwhelming commercial success. The Cosby show's success opened the way for numerous other Black-oriented sitcoms that flooded the airwaves into the mid-1990s. Few of them, however, had the production and scriptwriting qualities that characterized the Cosby program.

The most significant Black comedy/variety show of the early and mid-1990s was Fox network's *In Living Color*, which first aired in 1990. The fast-paced show resembled a hybrid of *Laugh-In* and *Saturday Night Live*, and its success was due primarily to its multitalented writer, producer, director, actor, and comedian, Keenen Ivory Wayans. By the mid-1990s advertisers and their television network cohorts had awakened to the fact that Blacks watched more TV than any other racial group, and in 1994, 25 programs were aired on the four networks either starring or featuring Blacks in major roles. Significantly, however, there were major differences in the viewing patterns of Blacks as compared to the general American audience. A listing of the most popular shows of the 1993 season shows no programs made the Top 10 on both lists.[2]

❋ *Latin Themes Play Again*

Latinos were also brought to the small screen early in television history when the romantic figure of *The Cisco Kid* rode into American homes in 1950. The series aired for 7 years but only in syndication to independent stations. In 1994, some 37 years after the original series ended, its characters were revived with Jimmy Smits in the lead role. *The Cisco Kid* was the first successful syndicated program and was among the first color-filmed series. *The Cisco Kid* had been an entertainment fixture since his creation in the O'Henry short story, "The Caballero's Way." Cisco was originally a bandito-type character in O'Henry's story who preyed on the rich to help the poor, à la Robin Hood. The character was brought to the movies in several productions with various leading men including Duncan Renaldo, who brought the role to TV. Cisco and his sidekick Pancho delighted youngsters, who were the key to their popularity, as they enjoyed a jovial repartee while roaming the Southwest to fight injustice. Renaldo's portrayal was vintage "Latin lover," except he never got romantically involved with the love-stricken ladies given the fact his audience was primarily children. Pancho, played by Leo Carillo, was a rotund, gregarious character who affected the stereotypical speech American audiences had come to expect from movie Mexicans who were not "Latin lovers." Often Pancho would urge his partner, "Hey Cees-ko, let's went!" The next Latino role appeared in 1951 when a White actor, Don Diamond, played El Toro, the Mexican sidekick to the lead in *Kit Carson*.

But the biggest Latino television personality of the early days of television was Desi Arnaz who was Lucille Ball's actual and theatrical husband in the long-running show, *I Love Lucy*. Although Arnaz played a respectable husband who was a band leader, he also played straight man to Lucy's zany schemes. His Latin temperament, which exploded into a torrent of Spanish diatribe when Lucy's ill-fated activities were revealed, was classic stereotyped imagery. The popular series came to television in 1951 and continued in original production until 1961. A swashbuckling adventure show, *Zorro*, debuted in 1957 and although set in early California, it concerned the political struggles of Spanish settlers. Mexicans, however, served only as villains, buffoons, or backdrops to the affairs of the more highly cultured Spanish aristocracy.

In the 1960s, three television programs stood out for their Latino portrayals. In *The Real McCoys* (1957-1963), Tony Martinez played farmhand Pepino Garcia, a role consistent with audience expectations. A non-Latino carried the TV image of the simple-minded Mexican when *The Bill Dana Show* appeared in 1963 for a 2-year run. Dana's opening line with a thick Mexican accent became a virtual national catch-phrase because of his night club act and record sales: "My name, José Jiménez." In the show, Jiménez worked as a hotel bellhop whose ineptness constantly got him into comedic situations. Perhaps the most unusual prime-time TV show centering on Latino characters was *The High Chaparral* (1967-1971). It was one of the numerous "adult westerns" aired during the period and featured an interracial marriage between the daughter of a Mexican cattle baron and a wealthy White rancher. The characters portrayed by Latino actors, however, generally had roles as ranch hands.

In the 1970s there were two network situation comedies based on the Mexican American barrio of East Los Angeles. Most recognized and criticized of the two was *Chico and the Man,* starring Freddie Prinze, which aired for five seasons on NBC beginning in 1974. Chico was a young streetwise character who used his savvy to drum up business for the auto repair garage where he worked. The racial "humor" and image portrayed by Chico was the subject of controversy throughout the show's network existence. In 1976 another "sitcom" was brought to ABC: *Viva Valdez* about an East Los Angeles family. It lasted only 4 months. Two other series featuring Latino actors began in the 1970s and continued until 1983. NBC screened *CHIPS* for the first time in 1977, co-featuring handsome Latino actor Erik Estrada as a California Highway Patrolman with romance on his mind. *Fantasy Island* (1978) starred Ricardo Montalban as the romantic figure host on an idyllic isle. Neither portrayal was very distant from the Latin lover roles that Hollywood had created decades earlier. In 1984, ABC made its second attempt at a sitcom centered on the life of an East Los Angeles barrio family with Paul Rodriguez in *a.k.a. PABLO*. Critics claimed the show was harmful because Rodriguez's jokes were seen as ridiculing Mexican American culture. The program lasted only six episodes and did not return in 1985. A Latino flavor was captured in NBC's *Miami Vice*, which aired from 1984 to 1989 with Edward James Olmos starring as Lt. Martin Castillo, against a backdrop of various drug operatives, many of whom were Latino. A more positive portrayal came in 1986 with Jimmy Smits's role as lawyer Victor Sifuentes on NBC's *L.A. Law*.

The show continued its run into 1994, a year in which Latinos filled only 11 of national television's 800 prime-time roles. But, many pundits expect that the $200 billion Latino consumer market in the United States portends an expanded presence for them in both network and cable TV offerings by the turn of the 21st century.

● *More Yellow Peril*

Asian portrayals came to television in 1949 in an ABC crime show called *Mysteries of Chinatown,* starring White actor Marvin Miller as Dr. Yat Fu. The show was set in San Francisco's Chinatown where Miller's character was in stereotype as owner of an herb and curio shop. The regular supporting cast was all White and, as evidenced by the show's title, was designed to exploit the old stereotype of the "mysterious" Asian. Next to surface was the TV version of *The Adventures of Fu Manchu* (1956), another crime drama with an all-White cast. The program was vintage Yellow Peril imagery with Dr. Fu sending his agents on various missions designed to subvert the cause of Western civilization. The nefarious and wiley Dr. Fu was based in various cities in the Orient as the series dredged up the old Sax Rohmer stereotypes. In fact, the series was facilitated by Rohmer's sale of rights to his creation in 1955 to Republic Pictures. The show was a non-network syndicated production and aired for only one season. Ironically, the following year (1956) it was followed to television by the other venerable Chinese character, Charlie Chan. *The New Adventures of Charlie Chan* was also a syndicated series lasting only one year. Chan was played by J. Carrol Naish but an Asian actor, James Hong, was cast in the role of Chan's "number one son" as Barry Chan. The series was produced in Great Britain and the Chan character operated from London.

In the 1960s, ABC aired an adventure series, *Hong Kong,* which reinforced the Chinese image of intrigue, sexy women, smuggling, and drug peddling. At least two Asian actors were cast as series regulars during its single-year run (1960-1961). The same network brought *The Green Hornet* to prime-time TV for a one-year stay in 1966-1967. The significance of the series was the casting of Bruce Lee as the Green Hornet's sidekick Kato. Lee's weekly demonstration of martial arts skills as he fought crime helped launch the popularity of Oriental self-defense techniques in the United States. Interestingly, *The Green Hornet* was the creation of George Trendle, who also developed *The Lone Ranger.* In both concepts the hero is supported by a trusty ethnic minority sidekick, perhaps for the purpose of adding a fantasy appeal for the mass audience. Sparked by the influence of Bruce Lee was another ABC series, *Kung Fu,* which was a western starring David Carridine and supporting Asian actors including Keye Luke and Philip Ahn. Lee was a consultant to those who developed the *Kung Fu* show and labored under the impression he was to be their choice for the lead role. When Carridine was selected for the part, Lee confided to friends that he had been the victim of racism. *Kung Fu's* producers told Lee they didn't believe a Chinese actor could be seen as a hero in the eyes of the American television audience.[3] The show became a throwback to the "mysterious" Asian stereotype. It aired from 1972 to 1975. With racism standing as a barrier to stardom in the United States, Bruce Lee went to Hong Kong where he achieved superstardom throughout Asia as a film star.

The greatest Asian presence in television began in the 1960s and featured an array of supporting police and criminal characters in the long running CBS series *Hawaii Five-O* (1968-1980). At least three Asian actors appeared as regulars on the show and the lead character, Detective Steve McGarrett, pursued an arch enemy Asian character, Wo Fat, periodically throughout its 12-year tenure. Generally, Asian portrayals in *Hawaii Five-O* were varied and diverse, although definite stereotypes were projected. The show's vulnerability to stereotypical criticism was its portrayal of White superiority and leadership in a predominately Asian environment.

There have been several prime-time shows throughout the history of American television that perpetuated the subservient, humble Asian image. Among them were *Bachelor Father* (1957-1962) with an Asian "houseboy" character played by Sammee Tong and *Bonanza* (1959-1972) with Chinese cook Hop Sing played by Victor Sen Yung. In *The Courtship of Eddie's Father* (1969-1972), Miyoshi Umeki played a housekeeper who was often befuddled by situations that arose in the household. Umeki's character was apparently married to an American because her role was that of "Mrs. Livingston" although

Figure 4.7. Mrs. Kim and her daughter, Margaret, don't exactly see eye to eye on *All American Girl*, which first aired on ABC-TV in 1994. Pictured, from left, are Jodi Long and Margaret Cho. Photo credit: Jerry Fitsgerld.

her mannerisms and philosophy were clearly Japanese as U.S. entertainment media have defined them over the years.

The early 1980s were characterized by a continuation of Asian supporting roles in various sitcoms and dramatic offerings. Two unique programs utilizing Asian themes came to network TV in 1980. A week-long miniseries, *Shogun,* was based on the exploits of a White adventurer in feudal Japan. Although providing American audiences with some insight into Japanese culture, the program placed an emphasis upon the violence of samurai warriors and an aura of the sexual mysticism of Japanese women. NBC brought a variety show called *Pink Lady* to its schedule, featuring a Japanese singing duo of the same name. The two young women were attractive and spoke little English so comic Jeff Altman served as facilitator. As an attempt to bring the demur, humble, and sexy image of the Japanese woman to network television, *Pink Lady* was a failure and was cancelled after less than 2 months on the air. That female image, however, returned to prominence in 1983 when actress Rosalind Chao took a co-starring role in *After M.A.S.H.* In the CBS series, which aired until December, 1984, Ms. Chao's role was as the Korean wife of a White ex-G.I. who had served in the Korean war. A different Asian female portrayal came to television in 1994 with the ABC sitcom *All-American Girl,* featuring Margaret Cho. Cho's character personified a quick-tongued modern Asian woman with a distinctly "American" attitude.

Japanese American actor Pat Morita, who had played the role of Arnold in the long-running (1974-1984) *Happy Days* on ABC, became the star of his own series on the same network. For two seasons in 1987-1988 Morita starred as *Ohara,* a Los Angeles police detective who preferred mystical Asian patience and persuasion over violence in dealing with criminals. Lt. Ohara usually didn't carry a gun but, true to stereotype, would resort to martial arts when necessary.

Analysis

The historical overview reveals stereotyping of non-Whites to be contextual to the social, political, and economic realities of the moment and changes accordingly. At any given historical period the nature of a specific group's portrayal may be much more positive than another's. Basic negative traits, however, have never been totally abandoned, although specific instances of mass guilt purging periodically appear in entertainment media.

Racially prejudicial stereotyping is debilitative in a society, especially one as culturally diverse as that of the United States. Not only does it work against common understanding and the recognition of the brotherhood of humankind, it provides succeeding generations of all racial groups—White and non-White—with distorted self-images. The coupling of biased portrayals with the social and psychological power of mass entertainment threatens the maturation of American society. But the attitudinal change must begin with the people, because producers of popular entertainment are, generally, more motivated by economic incentive than social morality. By the mid-1990s television advertisers and network executives began to offer programs aimed at reaching non-White viewers, specifically Blacks and Latinos, to tap their coveted multi-billion-dollar market potential. The programs were almost exclusively situation comedies, however, and continued to reflect many of the stereotypes of the past. If there is to be significant change it will occur when the people collectively demand it. History shows the audience demanded and got "Yankee Doodle" in place of a symphony. If they demand a symphony of honest and realistic portrayals of people of color from their entertainment media, they will get them. People of color now have enough economic leverage to support such demands.

▓▓▓▓

Notes

1. See J. Fred MacDonald, *Blacks and White TV* (Chicago: Nelson-Hall, 1992), for a comprehensive review of the history of Black Americans as network television performers.

2. "A Television Trend: Audiences in Black and White," *Washington Post*, November 29, 1994, pp. A1, A20.

3. See the account of Bruce Lee's encounter with the producers of *Kung Fu* in Kareem Abdul-Jabbar and Peter Knobler, *Giant Steps: The Autobiography of Kareem Abdul-Jabbar* (New York: Bantam, 1983), pp. 188-189.

PART

3

Nonentertainment Media Portrayals

5

Advertising

The Media's Not-So-Silent Partner

In the late 1960s a lovable cartoon character appeared on television screens and in magazines across the United States. Named the Frito Bandito, this cartoon figure of a mustachioed Mexican bandit with six-gun, broad sombrero, and a sinister smile was a sneaky character who went around houses sneaking Fritos corn chips from unsuspecting mothers. In bullet hole-riddled WANTED posters produced as part of an advertising campaign for the snack food, housewives were advised to buy two bags of the corn chips, because "He loves cronchy Fritos corn chips so much he'll stop at nothing to get yours. What's more he's cunning, clever—and sneaky."[1] Television commercials featured youngsters sneaking corn chips from the family supply, then biting into the crunchy chips as a Mexican-style mustache came across their faces.

The Frito Bandito was a lovable and successful salesman for the Frito-Lay Corporation, maker of the corn chips. He was described by the director of advertising for the company as a "simple character, which is intended to make you laugh, in turn, we hope that this laughter will leave our trademark implanted in your memory."[2] But many Latinos, particularly Chicano activist and civic groups, did not react to the Frito Bandito with laughter. They pointed out that the cartoon character was nothing more than a humorous version of the stereotype Mexican bandit, one who perpetuated and reinforced the stereotype of Mexicans as mustachioed thieves. Protests were organized against the Frito-Lay Corporation and boycotts threatened against television stations airing the commercials. After some local television stations were persuaded in 1970 that the cartoon character was racially offensive and agreed not to air the advertisement, Frito-Lay announced it would cancel what had been a highly successful advertising campaign.

A little more than 10 years later, Frito-Lay launched yet another advertising campaign playing on the Anglo perceptions of Latinos and Latin America. But this time the approach was very different. The product was Tostitos, another corn chip produced by the company, but one that was touted as being authentically Mexican. Rather than featuring an overweight gun-toting mustachioed bandit under a broad sombrero, the campaign was centered on a tall, distinguished Latino, reminiscent of the Latino lovers who populated earlier generations of Hollywood movies. He spoke with a Spanish accent, but this time it was a lilting, cultured accent resonant with careful pronunciations of consonants and vowels that accented the correct pronunciation of the company's product.

In each commercial the stately spokesman for the product told viewers about his fond memories of his growing up as a young boy in his Latin American homeland. Among his fondest memories was coming home from school and play to finding warm corn chips that had just been prepared. He told the viewers how good they tasted and how much he missed them. But, he continued, now corn chips with that same authentic taste and shape were available in the United States and were available to everyone, not just those fortunate enough to come from Latin America. He praised the Tostito corn chips now available in plastic bags at local stores and attested to their authenticity.

This time there were no protests against the commercials from Latino organizations, no threats of boycotts against the product, and no angry letters to the regulatory agencies overseeing broadcasting or advertising. This time Frito-Lay had struck the right chord with Latinos and non-Latinos. The company played on the accepted imagery of Latinos and Latin America, but instead of reinforcing the image of the sneaky Mexican bandit, the company played on the romantic image of the distinguished, cultured Latino, perhaps more a descendent of Spain than Latin America. The campaign, which also ran in media directed to Latinos in the United States, represented a change in the thinking at Frito-Lay from seeing Latinos as the object of humorous stereotypes to portraying Latinos as people with a romantic past that could be brought into your home through the purchase of Tostitos. It was a transition that illustrated an evolution in advertising, an industry that has been identified as being essential to the American character in the United States.

Advertising and Media in the Land of Plenty

In 1950, historian David M. Potter was invited by the Wahlgreen Foundation to prepare six lectures on the American character and the impact of economic abundance on shaping the character of the people living in the United States. In these lectures, which were later published in a revised form in a book titled *People of Plenty,* Potter identified advertising as the "institution of abundance," that unique part of the society "that was brought into being by abundance, without previous existence in any form, and, moreover, an institution which is peculiarly identified with American abundance."[3] He also noted that media scholars up to that time had not recognized the central role that advertising had played in shaping and developing media in the United States.

"Histories of American periodicals and even of the mass media deal with advertising as if it were a side issue." Potter wrote,

> Students of the radio and of the mass-circulation magazines frequently condemn advertising for its conspicuous role . . . they hardly recognize that advertising created modern American radio and television, transformed the modern newspaper, evoked the modern slick periodical, and remains the vital essence of each of them at the present time.[4]

As Potter and subsequent scholars have noted, the development of advertising as a revenue source for print and, later, broadcast media required media managers to develop news and entertainment content that would attract the largest possible number of people. This gave birth to the term *mass media*, which described the ability of the media to attract the large audience to which advertisers could direct their commercial messages. The circulation and rating figures were the bread and butter of the media, because they translated to increased advertising insertions and higher advertising rates. The media attracted the mass audience by developing content with a broad appeal that often was directed to the lowest common denominator of culture in the audience. The advertising, like the editorial and entertainment material it supported in newspapers, magazines, radio, and television, was also geared to appeal to a mass audience that might become potential consumers. This mass appeal by both advertisers and the media they supported was targeted to the audience in the majority, not to racial or other minorities who might happen to pick up a newspaper or listen to a radio program.

Far from being an appendage to the media industry, Potter described advertising as a force dictating the editorial and entertainment content of the media that depended on advertising dollars for their revenues. Mass media charged artificially low subscription fees to boost their circulation, which forced the media to depend on advertisers even more for their revenues. This, in turn, was accompanied by editorial or programming philosophies that place a priority on attracting the largest possible audience. News and entertainment content, wrote Potter, were nothing more than the bait to attract the audience and hold its attention between the commercial messages.

> What this means, in functional terms, it seems to me, is that the newspaper feature, the magazine article, the radio program, do not attain the dignity of being ends in themselves; they are rather means to an end: that end, of course, is to catch the reader's attention so that he will then read the advertisement or hear the commercial, and to hold his interest until these essential messages have been delivered.

Potter continued,

> The program or the article becomes a kind of advertisement in itself—becomes the "pitch," in the telling language of the circus barker. Its function is to induce people to accept the commercial, just as the commercial's function is to induce them to accept the product.[5]

Figure 5.1. Corporations sometimes go to great lengths to appear to be "at home" with communities of color. This advertisement for Miracle Whip salad dressing features a dark-skinned model with braided hair asking her mother "What's up for sup?" The answer is a Soulful Chicken Stir-Fry made with product advertised.

The development of content as bait for the mass audience meant that the mass media included material that would attract the most people and, at the same time, deleted material that had the potential of offending or leaving out any potential members of the audience, Potter wrote. This placed some rigid constraints on media editorial and entertainment content.

"First, a message must not deal with subjects of special or out-of-the-way interest, since such subjects by definition have no appeal for the majority of the audience," he wrote.

> Second, it must not deal with any subject at a high level of maturity, since many people are immature, chronologically or otherwise, and a mature level is one which, by definition, leaves such people out. Third, it must not deal with matters which are controversial or even unpleasant or distressing, since such matters may, by definition, antagonize or offend some members of the audience.[6]

Advertising and People of Color

Given the social and legal restrictions on the participation of racial minorities in the society of the United States during much of this country's history, it is not hard to see how the desire to cater to the perceived views of the mass audience desired by advertisers resulted in entertainment and news content that largely ignored people of color, treated them stereotypically when they were recognized, and largely avoided grappling with such issues as segregation, discriminatory immigration laws, land rights, and other controversial issues that affected certain minority groups more than they did the White majority. Although the entertainment and editorial portrayal of non-Whites is amply analyzed in other chapters of this book, it is important to recognize that those portrayals were, to a large extent, supported by a system of advertising that required the media to cater to the perceived attitudes and prejudices of the White majority and that also reinforced such images in its own commercial messages. For years advertisers in the United States reflected the place of non-Whites in the social fabric of the nation either by ignoring them or, when they were included in advertisements for the mass

Figure 5.2. Rastus, a Black servant, is the longstanding advertising icon for Cream of Wheat and exemplifies the use of racial imagery to sell consumer products.

audience, processing and presenting them in a way that would make them palatable salespersons for the products being advertised. These processed portrayals largely mirrored the stereotypic images of minorities in the entertainment media that, in turn, were designed to reflect the perceived values and norms of the White majority. In this way, non-White portrayals in advertising paralleled and reinforced their entertainment and journalistic images in the media.

The history of advertising in the United States is replete with characterizations that, like the Frito Bandito, responded to and reinforced the preconceived image that many White Americans apparently had of Blacks, Latinos, Asians, and Native Americans. Over the years advertisers have employed Latin spitfires like Chiquita Banana, Black mammies like Aunt Jemima, and noble savages like the Santa Fe Railroad's Super Chief to pitch their products to a predominately White mass audience of consumers. In 1984 the Balch Institute for Ethnic Studies in Philadelphia sponsored an exhibit of more than 300 examples of racial and ethnic images used by corporations in magazines, posters, trade cards, and storyboards. In an interview with the advertising trade magazine *Advertising Age*, institute director Mark Stolarik quoted the catalog for the exhibit, which capsulized the evolution of images of people of color and how they have changed.

"Some of these advertisements were based on stereotypes of various ethnic groups. In the early years, they were usually crude and condescending images that appealed to largely Anglo-American audiences who found it difficult to reconcile their own visions of beauty, order and behavior with that of non-Anglo-Americans," said Stolarik. "Later, these images were softened because of complaints from the ethnic groups involved and the growing sophistication of the advertising industry."[7]

The advertising examples in the exhibit include positive White ethnic stereotypes, such as the wholesome and pure image of Quakers in an early Quaker Oats advertisement and the cleanliness of the Dutch in a turn-of-the century advertisement for Colgate soaps. But they also featured a late 19th century advertisement showing an Irish matron threatening to hit her husband over the head with a rolling pin because he didn't smoke the right brand of tobacco. Like Quaker Oats, some products even incorporated a stereotypical image on the package or product line being advertised.

"Lawsee! Folks sho' whoops with joy over AUNT JEMIMA PANCAKES," shouted a bandanna-wearing Black mammy in a magazine advertisement for Aunt Jemima pancake mix, which featured a plump Aunt Jemima on the box. Over the years, Aunt Jemima has lost some weight, but the stereotyped face of the Black servant continues to be featured on the box. Earlier advertisements for Cream of Wheat featured Rastus, the Black servant on the box, in a series of magazine cartoons with a group of cute but ill-dressed Black children. Some of the advertisements played on stereotypes ridiculing Blacks, such as an advertisement in which a Black school teacher standing behind a makeshift lectern made out of a boldly lettered Cream of Wheat box, asks the class "How do you spell Cream of Wheat?" Others appeared to promote racial integration, such as a magazine advertisement captioned "Putting it down in Black and White," which showed Rastus serving bowls of the breakfast cereal to Black and White youngsters sitting at the same table.

Racial imagery was also integrated into the naming of trains by the Santa Fe railroad, which named one of its passenger lines the Super Chief and featured highly detailed portraits of the noble Indian in promoting its service through the Southwestern United States. In another series of advertisements, the railroad used cartoons of Native American children to show the service and sights passengers could expect when they traveled the Santa Fe line.

These and other portrayals catered to the mass audience mentality by either neutralizing or making humor of the negative perceptions that many Whites may have had of racial minorities. The advertising images, rather than showing people of color as they really were, portrayed them as filtered through Anglo eyes. This presented an out-of-focus image of racial minorities, but one that was palatable, and even persuasive, to the White majority to which it was directed. In the mid-1960s Black civil rights groups targeted the advertising industry for special attention, protesting both the lack of integrated advertisements including Blacks and the stereotyped images that the advertisers continued to use. The effort, accompanied by support from federal officials, resulted in the overnight inclusion of Blacks as models in television advertising in 1967 and a downplaying of the images that many Blacks found objectionable.

"Black America is becoming visible in America's biggest national advertising medium," reported the *New York Times* in 1968. "Not in a big way yet, but it is a beginning and men in high places give assurances that there will be a lot more visibility.[8]

But the advertising industry did not generalize the concerns of Blacks, or the concessions made in response to them, to other groups. At the same time that some Black concerns were being addressed with integrated advertising, other groups were being ignored or singled out for continued stereotyped treatment in such commercials as those featuring the Frito Bandito.

Among the Latino advertising stereotypes cited in a 1969 article[9] by sociologist Tomás Martínez were commercials for Granny Goose chips featuring fat gun-toting Mexicans, an advertisement for Arrid underarm deodorant showing a dusty Mexican bandito spraying his underarms after a hard ride as the announcer intones, "If it works for him it will work for you," and a magazine advertisement featuring a stereotypical Mexican sleeping under his sombrero as he leans against a Philco television set. Especially offensive to Martínez was a Liggett & Meyers commercial for L&M cigarettes that featured Paco, a lazy Latino who never "feenishes" anything, not even the revolution he is supposed to be fighting. In response to a letter complaining about the commercial, the director of public relations for the tobacco firm defended the commercial's use of Latino stereotypes.

" 'Paco' is a warm, sympathetic and lovable character with whom most of us can identify because he has a little of all of us in him, that is, our tendency to procrastinate at times," wrote the Liggett & Meyers executive. "He seeks to escape the violence of war and to enjoy the pleasure of the moment, in this case, the good flavor of an L&M cigarette."[10] Although the company spokesman claimed that the character had been tested without negative reactions from Latinos (a similar claim was made by Frito-Lay regarding the Frito Bandito), Martínez roundly criticized the advertising images and contrasted them to what he saw as the gains Blacks were then making in the advertising field.

"Today, no major advertiser would attempt to display a black man or woman over the media in a prejudiced, stereotyped fashion," Martínez wrote.

Complaints would be forthcoming from black associations and perhaps the FCC. Yet, these same advertisers, who dare not show "step'n fetch it" characters, uninhibitedly depict a Mexican counterpart, with additional traits of stinking and stealing. Perhaps the white hatred for

Figure 5.3. U.S.-based corporations are not reluctant to put advertising in the language of their potential consumers. This advertisement for AT&T appeared in Chinese-language newspapers in the United States.

blacks, which cannot find adequate expression in today's ads, is being transferred upon their brown brothers.[11]

In 1970 a Brown Position Paper prepared by Latino media activists Armando Rendón and Domingo Nick Reyes charged that the media had transferred the negative stereotypes it once reserved for Blacks to Latinos, who had become "the media's new nigger."[12] The protests of Latinos soon made the nation's advertisers more conscious of the portrayals that Latinos found offensive. But, as in the case of the Blacks, the advertising industry failed to apply the lessons learned from one group to other racial minorities.

Although national advertisers withdrew much of the advertising that negatively stereotyped Blacks and Latinos, sometimes replacing them with affluent, successful images that were as far removed from reality as the negative portrayals of the past, the advances made by those groups were not shared with Native Americans and Asians. Native Americans' names and images, no longer depicted either as the noble savage or as cute cartoon characters, have all but disappeared from broadcast commercials and print advertising. The major exceptions are advertising for automobiles and trucks that bear names such as Pontiac, Dakota, and Navajo and sports teams with racial nicknames such as the Kansas City Chiefs, Washington Redskins, Florida State University Seminoles, Atlanta Braves, and Cleveland Indians. Native Americans and others have protested these racial team names and images, as well as the pseudo-Native American pageantry and souvenirs that accompany many of them but with no success in getting them changed.

Asians, particularly Japanese, continue to be dealt more than their share of commercials depicting them in stereotypes that cater to the fears and stereotypes of White America. As was the case with Blacks and Latinos, it took organized protests from Asian American groups to get the message across to the corporations and their advertising agencies. In the mid-1970s, a Southern California supermarket chain agreed to remove a television campaign in which a young Asian karate-chopped his way down the store's aisles cutting prices. Nationally, several firms whose industries have been hard-hit by Japanese imports fought back through commercials, if not in the quality or prices of their products. One automobile company featured an

Asian family carefully looking over a new car and commenting on its attributes in heavily accented English. Only after they bought it did they learn it was made in the United States, not Japan. Another automobile company that markets cars manufactured in Japan under an English-language name showed a parking lot attendant opening the doors of the car, only to find the car speaking to him in Japanese. For several years Sylvania television ran a commercial boasting that its television picture had repeatedly been selected over competing brands as an off-screen voice with a Japanese accent repeatedly asked, "What about Sony?" When the announcer responded that the Sylvania picture had also been selected over Sony's, the off-screen voice ran off shouting what sounded like a string of Japanese expletives. A 1982 *Newsweek* article observed that "attacking Japan has become something of a fashion in corporate ads" because of resentment over Japanese trade policies and sales of Japanese products in the United States, but quoted Motorola's advertising manager as saying, "We've been as careful as we can be" not to be racially offensive.[13]

But many of the television and print advertisements featuring Asians featured images that were racially insensitive, if not offensive. A commercial for a laundry product featured a Chinese family that used an "ancient Chinese laundry secret" to get their customer's clothes clean. Naturally, the Chinese secret turned out to be the packaged product paying for the advertisement. Companies pitching everything from pantyhose to airlines featured Asian women coiffed and costumed as seductive China dolls or exotic Polynesian natives to pitch and promote their products, some of them cast in Asian settings and others attentively caring for the needs of the Anglo men in the advertisement. One airline boasted that those who flew with it would be under the care of the Singapore Girl.

Asian women appearing in commercials were often featured as China dolls with the small, darkened eyes, straight hair with bangs, and a narrow, slit skirt. Another common portrayal featured the exotic, tropical Pacific Islands look, complete with flowers in the hair, a sarong or grass skirt, and shell ornament. Asian women hoping to become models sometimes found that they must conform to these stereotypes or lose assignments. Leslie Kawai, the 1981 Tournament of Roses Queen, was told to cut her hair with bangs by hairstylists when she auditioned for a beer advertisement. When she refused, the beer company decided to hire another model with shorter hair cut in bangs.[14]

The lack of a sizable Asian community, or market, in the United States was earlier cited as the reason that Asians are still stereotyped in advertising and, except for children's advertising, are rarely presented in integrated settings. The growth rate and income of Asians living in the United States in the 1980s and 1990s, however, reinforced the economic potential of Asian Americans to overcome the stereotyping and lack of visibility that Blacks and Latinos challenged with some success. By the mid-1980s there were a few signs that advertising was beginning to integrate Asian Americans into crossover advertisements that, like the Tostitos campaign, were designed to have a broad appeal. In one commercial, television actor Robert Ito was featured telling how he loves to call his relatives in Japan because the calls make them think that he is rich, as well as successful, in the United States. Of course, he adds, it is only because the rates of his long distance carrier were so low that he was able to call Japan so often.

In the 1970s mass audience advertising in the United States became more racially integrated than at any time in the nation's history. Blacks, and to a much lesser extent Latinos and Asians, could be seen in television commercials spread across the broadcast week and in major magazines. In fact, the advertisements on network television often appeared to be more fully integrated than the television programs they supported. Like television, general circulation magazines also experienced an increase in the use of Blacks, although studies of both media showed that most of the percentage increase had come by the early 1970s. By the early 1970s the percentage of prime-time television commercials featuring Blacks had apparently leveled off at about 10%. Blacks were featured in between only 2% and 3% of magazine advertisements as late as 1978. That percentage, however small, was a sharp increase from the 0.06% of news magazine advertisements reported in 1960.[15]

The gains were also socially significant, because they demonstrated that Blacks could be integrated into advertisements without triggering a White backlash among potential customers in the White majority. Both sales figures and research conducted since the late

Figure 5.4. Many corporations promote upscale products to low-income audiences by associating the product with a lifestyle and happiness many of the readers do not enjoy. This liquor advertisement in Spanish invites readers to share their wealth while drinking the product advertised.

1960s have shown that the integration of Black models into television and print advertising does not adversely affect sales or the image of the product. Instead, a study by the American Newspaper Publishers Association showed, the most important influences on sales were the merchandise and the advertisement itself. In fact, while triggering no adverse affect among the majority of Whites, integrated advertisements were found to be useful in swaying Black consumers, who responded favorably to positive Black role models in print advertisements.[16] Studies conducted in the early 1970s also showed that White consumers did not respond negatively to advertising featuring Black models, although their response was more often neutral than positive.[17] One 1972 study examining White backlash, however, did show that an advertisement prominently featuring darker-skinned Blacks was less acceptable to Whites than those featuring lighter-skinned Blacks as background models.[18] Perhaps such findings help explain why research conducted later in the 1970s revealed that, for the most part, Blacks appearing in magazine and television advertisements were often featured as part of an integrated group.[19]

Although research findings have shown that integrated advertisements do not adversely affect sales, the percentage of Blacks and other minorities in general audience advertising did not increase significantly after the numerical gains made through the mid-1970s. Those minorities who did appear in advertisements were often depicted in upscale or integrated settings, an image that the Balch Institute's Stolarik criticized as taking advertising "too far in the other direction and created stereotypes of 'successful' ethnic group members that are as unrealistic as those of the past."[20] Equally unwise, from a business sense, was the low numbers of Blacks appearing in advertisements.

> Advertisers and their ad agencies must evaluate the direct economic consequences of alternative strategies on the firm. If it is believed that the presence of Black models in advertisements decreases the effectiveness of advertising messages, only token numbers of Black models will be used,

wrote marketing professor Lawrence Soley at the conclusion of a 1983 study.

Previous studies have found that advertisements portraying Black models do not elicit negative affective or conative responses from consumers.... Given the consistency of the research findings, more Blacks should be portrayed in advertisements. If Blacks continue to be underrepresented in advertising portrayals, it can be said that this is an indication of prejudice on the part of the advertising industry, not consumers.[21]

Courtship of Spanish Gold and the Black Market

Although Soley stopped short of accusing corporate executives of racial prejudice, he contended that a "counterpressure" to full integration of Blacks into mainstream media portrayals was that "advertising professionals are businessmen first and moralists second."[22] If so, then it was the business mentality of advertising and corporate professionals that led them into increasingly aggressive advertising and marketing campaigns to capture minority consumers, particularly Blacks and Latinos, in the 1970s and 1980s.

Long depicted as low-end consumers with little money to spend, Black and Latino customers became more important to national and regional advertisers of mainstream goods who took a closer look at the size, composition, and projected growth of those groups. Asian Americans, who experienced a sharp percentage growth in the 1970s and were generally more affluent than Blacks and Latinos, were not targeted to the same extent, probably because of their relatively small numbers and differences in national languages among the groups. And, except for regions in which they comprised a sizable portion of the population, Native Americans were largely ignored as potential consumers of mainstream products.

One part of the courtship of Blacks and Latinos grew out of the civil rights movements of the 1960s, in which both Blacks and Latinos effectively used consumer boycotts to push issues ranging from ending segregation to organizing farmworkers. Boycotts had long been threatened and used by minority consumers as economic leverage on social issues. But in the 1960s Black ministers organized the Philadelphia Selective Patronage Program in which Blacks did business with companies that supported their goals of more jobs for Blacks.

Helping people like Yvette means helping so many more.

Yvette Ortiz had no idea where her future would take her. All she knew was she wanted to be a doctor, but she needed help.

At Anheuser-Busch we believe everyone deserves the chance to realize their dreams. That's why for the last eleven years we've been the leading supporter of the National Hispanic Scholarship Fund. Providing over 7,500 scholarships. One of which went to Yvette.

Now, after a few years and lots of hard work, Yvette has reached her dream. And we're all better off for it. Please help us help others. Call 1-415-892-9971 or write:

National Hispanic Scholarship Fund
P.O. Box 728
Novato, CA 94948

THE ANHEUSER BUSCH COMPANIES
GLAD TO BE YOUR NEIGHBOR. PROUD TO BE YOUR FRIEND.

Figure 5.5. Corporations, especially those selling alcohol and tobacco, often associate consumption of their products with good works in communities of color. This advertisement by the Anheuser-Busch Companies promotes its contributions to the National Hispanic Scholarship Fund, which supported a future Latina doctor.

This philosophy of repaying the corporations that invest in the minority communities through consumer purchases was replicated in other cities. It was followed by slick advertising campaigns directed at minority consumers. In 1984 the same line of thinking led to the brewers of Coors beer attempting to end disputes with Blacks and Latinos by signing controversial agreements with the National Association for the Advancement of Colored People (NAACP) and five national Latino groups that committed the brewery to increase its financial support of the activities of those organizations as Blacks and Latinos increased their drinking of Coors beer.

A second, and more influential, element of the courtship has been the hard-selling job of advertising agencies and media specializing in the Black and Spanish-speaking Latinos. Spurred by the thinking of Black advertising executive D. Parke Gibson in his 1968 book *The $30 Billion Negro* and a steady stream of articles on Black and Latino consumers in media trade publications, national advertisers became aware of the fact that minorities were potential consumers for a wide range of products. The advertisers also were persuaded that the inattention they had previously received from mainstream products made Blacks and Latinos respond more favorably and with greater loyalty to those products that courted them through advertisements on billboards and in the publications and broadcast stations used by Latinos and Blacks.

The third, and most far-reaching, element in the courtship was a fundamental change in the thinking of marketing and advertising executives that swayed them away from mass audience media. Witnessing the success they had in advertising on radio stations and magazines targeted to specific audience segments following the advent of television as the dominant mass medium in the 1950s, advertising agencies advised their clients to go after their potential customers identified with market segments, rather than the mass audience. Advertisers found that differences in race, like differences in sex, residence, family status, and age, were easy to target through advertising appeals targeted to media whose content was designed to attract men or women, young or old, suburban or rural, Black or White, Spanish or English speaking. These media, in turn, produced audience surveys to show they were effective in reaching and delivering specific segments of the mass audience. By the mid-1980s, market and audience segmentation had become so important to advertisers that the term *mass media* was becoming an anachronism.

"It is a basic tenet of marketing that you go after markets with rifles, not shotguns. It is foolhardy—and idealistic in the worst way—to try to sell the same thing to everyone in the same way," wrote Caroline R. Jones, executive vice president of Mingo-Jones Advertising, in a 1984 article in the advertising trade magazine *Madison Avenue.*

> Good marketing involves breaking down potential markets into homogeneous segments; targeting the most desirable segments; and developing creative programs, tailored for each segment, that make your messages look different from your competitors'. All of that should be done with the guidance of thorough research on characteristics, beliefs and preferences of the people in the targeted markets.[23]

Like others who have pitched minority audiences to major corporations as ripe targets for slick advertisements, Jones advised advertising professionals reading the magazine to target advertising to Black consumers because *"there's money in it."* Among the factors she cited as making Blacks desirable customers was a reported disposable income of more than $150 million, a "high propensity for brand names and indulgence items," a high degree of "brand loyalty," a young and growing population, growing education and income, concentration in the nation's largest 25 cities, and "its own growing media network."[24]

Much the same approach has been used to sell Latinos to advertising agencies as a target too good to be passed up. A 1965 article on Latino consumers in the advertising trade magazine *Sponsor* was headlined "America's Spanish Treasure," a 1971 *Sales Management* article proclaimed "Brown Is Richer Than Black," and in 1972 *Television/Radio Age* advised readers, "The Spanish Market: Its Size, Income and Loyalties Make It a Rich Marketing Mine."[25] In addition to the characteristics that were cited as making Blacks an attractive market, Latinos have been depicted as being especially vulnerable to advertisements because their use of Spanish supposedly cuts them off from advertising in English-language media. Thus, advertisers are advised to use the language and culture that are familiar with their target audience to give their messages the greatest delivery and impact.

"U.S. Hispanics are most receptive to media content in the Spanish language," wrote Antonio Guernica in a 1982 book titled *Reaching the Hispanic Market Effectively.*[26] Guernica and others have counseled advertisers to package their commercial messages in settings that are reinforced by Latino culture and traditions. These appeals link the product being advertised with the language, heritage, and social system that Latinos are most comfortable with, thus creating the illusion that the product belongs in the Latino home.

"The language, the tradition, the kitchen utensils are different" (in a Latino home) said Shelly Perlman, media buyer for the Hispania division of the J. Walter Thompson advertising agency in a 1983 *Advertising Age* article.

> There are ads one can run in general media that appeal to everyone but that contain unmistakeable clues to Hispanics that they are being sought. It can be done with models, with scene and set design—a whole array of factors.[27]

Corporations seeking the Latino dollar also have been told to picture their products with Latino foods, celebrities, cultural events, community events, and family traditions. The goal has been to adapt the product to make it appear to be a part of the Latino lifestyle in the United States, which often requires being sensitive to the language, food, and musical differences among Latinos in different parts of the nation and from different countries in Latin America.

For both Blacks and Latinos the slick advertising approach often means selling high-priced, prestige products to low-income consumers who have not fully shared in the wealth of the country in which they live. But Blacks and Latinos, who have median family incomes well below national averages, have been nonetheless targeted as consumers for premium brand names in all product lines and particularly in liquor, beer, and cigarettes. In response, Black and Latino community groups and health organizations in the 1990s protested the targeting of alcohol and tobacco products to their communities and, in some cases, forced outdoor advertising companies to restrict the number of such billboards in these communities.

Through the 1990s, corporations making and marketing products ranging from beer to diapers tried to show Blacks and Latinos that consumption of their goods is part of the good life in America. It may not be a life that they knew when they grew up in the ghetto, barrio, or in another country. It may not even be a life that they or their children will ever achieve, but it is a lifestyle and happiness they can share by purchasing the same products used by the rich and famous. Prestige appeals are used in advertising to all audiences, not just minorities. But they have a special impact on those who are so far down on the socioeconomic scale that they are especially hungry for anything that will add status or happiness to their lives and help them show others that they are "making it." The advertisements promote conspicuous consumption, rather than hard work and savings, as the key to the good life.

> The Black consumer is not unlike other consumers when it comes to the basic necessities of life—food, clothing and shelter. There is a difference, nevertheless, in the priority the Black consumer adopts in the pursuit of happiness; in other words, in how he structures the *quality* of his life. Some differences are by choice. And some differences are because of *lack* of choice,

wrote Caroline Jones in *Madison Avenue*.

> The Black consumer must often react to what he has *not* been able to enjoy or choose, or what he must choose from among products that have not overtly invited him to use them . . . in general the Black consumer all too often has learned to live with his feelings of being ignored altogether or excluded psychologically.[28]

"In the light of life's uncertainties, Blacks also seek instant gratification more than do Whites, who can enjoy 'the good life' earlier and longer," she added, citing a successful advertising campaign for Polaroid cameras that courted Blacks with the line "Polaroid Gives It To You Now."[29] This means that advertisers can strike responsive chords at different levels with minority groups than with the White majority.

Latinos, particularly recent immigrants or those who have moved up from the economic level of their parents, may also share these feelings. To both groups, advertising is corporate America's welcome mat, the happy face that lets them know that they are important enough to be recognized. By recognizing elements of the Black or Latino experience that may have been ignored by White Americans, the advertisers also play on national or racial pride to boost sales of their products. In the 1970s, Anheuser-Busch commissioned a series of glossy advertisements commemorating the Great Kings of Africa, and Schlitz produced a Chicano history calendar. These and similar advertising campaigns provided long overdue recognition of Black and Latino heritage, but they also prominently displayed the corporate symbols of their sponsors and were designed to boost the sale of beer more than to recognize overlooked historical figures and events.

Because the goal of advertising is to promote sales and consumption of the products advertised, advertising agencies serve no moral code other than to promote the products as ethically as possible to stimulate consumption. Print and broadcast media that penetrate the segments of the mass audience that the advertisers wish to cultivate have been the beneficiaries of the increased advertising emphasis on Blacks and Latinos. Most surveys show that Blacks and Latinos depend more on radio and television than print media, a fact that is probably more related to their lower median level of education and the wide availability of Black and Spanish-language broadcasting than any innate racial differences among members of these groups and Whites. Accordingly, most of the millions of dollars that national advertisers spend to reach these minority audiences is spent on broadcast media.

The media targeted to non-Whites are eager to promote themselves as the most effective way to reach consumers of color. In 1974 one of New York's Black newspapers, the *Amsterdam News*, vigorously attacked the credibility of a New York *Daily News* audience survey that showed it reached more Black readers than the *Amsterdam News*. In a 1979 *Advertising Age* advertisement, *La Opinión*, Los Angeles's Spanish-language daily newspaper, promised advertisers it could show them how to "Wrap Up the Spanish-language Market." Advertising is the lifeblood of the print and broadcast media in the United States, and media that target people of color have been quick to promote themselves as the most effective vehicles for penetrating and persuading the people in their communities to purchase the products advertised on their airwaves and in their pages.

How Loud Is the Not-So-Silent Partner's Voice?

The relationship between racial minorities and advertising has undergone dramatic changes since the early 1960s. Blacks have been the most visible in the changes that have occurred in both mainstream and segmented advertising, although Spanish-speaking Latinos also have become more important as a market segment. In spite of experiencing the greatest percentage growth of any racial group in the years between 1970 and 1990, Asian Americans were only beginning to be recognized as a major economic force by the mid-1990s, primarily in media targeted to Asian American audiences. Given the projected growth figures for Asians in the United States, it appears inevitable that the group will be increasingly important as a market segment in the future, particularly if Asian Americans continue to demonstrate income and education levels that are above national norms and if they respond to racially sensitive advertising in media directed to Asian Americans. In order for this to happen, however, advertisers will need to launch campaigns that successfully negotiate the different languages and cultures of the different Asian American nationalities in the United States.

Native Americans, divided between the cities and rural areas, have become largely invisible in mainstream advertising, except for the automotive and sports team nicknames previously noted. The noble Super Chief has gone the way of the passenger train he once advertised, as have the caricatures that once stereotyped Native Americans in advertising. The small percentage that Native Americans comprise of the population in urban areas and their geographic dispersion in rural areas make them less attractive for mainstream advertisers looking at potential growth markets. As far as advertising is concerned, it appears that, except for local advertising and goodwill advertising by some major corporations, Native Americans will

Figure 5.6. Advertisers often associate their products with arts and culture that have been ignored by the general audience media. This Budweiser beer advertisement praises the "Latin American craftsmen (who) have found the natural warmth and richness of sculpted wood."

Figure 5.7. Native Americans have not been targeted as a consumer market by many major corporations, but companies producing products of particular interest to them do advertise in Native American newspapers. This advertisement is for computer clip art featuring Native American images.

continue to be treated as the Most Invisible Minority through the 1990s.

National advertisers in mass audience media appear to be reluctant to learn from the experiences with one group in dealing with others. Thus, Blacks, Latinos, Asians, and Native Americans have all had to fight individual battles against stereotyping and racially offensive advertisements. Blacks, the most visible racial minority in network television and general interest magazine advertising, still comprise only a very small percentage of the characters in those media. Asians and Latinos are still infrequently used in mainstream advertisements. Gains have been noted in the use of Black celebrities, such as Bill Cosby, Michael Jackson, and Gladys Knight, in advertising with a "crossover" appeal to both Blacks and non-Blacks. Given the use of different languages and the smaller sizes of the groups, it would appear that integration of Latinos and Asians into mainstream advertising will most likely follow the crossover model, such as the Tostitos commercial or Olympic skating champion Kristi Yamaguchi. Such advertisements afford the advertiser the advantage of reaching the majority of potential consumers, including English-speaking Latinos and Asians.

Minority-formatted publications and broadcasters depend on advertising to support their media. They have benefited from the increased emphasis on market segmentation by promoting the consumption patterns of the audiences they reach and their own effectiveness in delivering persuasive commercial messages to their readers, listeners, and viewers. But advertising is also a two-edged sword that expects to take more money out of a market segment than it invests in advertising to that segment. Black and Spanish-language media will benefit from the advertising dollars of national corporations only as long as dollars are the most cost-effective way for advertisers to persuade Blacks and Latinos to use their products. This places the minority-formatted media in an exploitative relationship with their audience, who because of language, educational, and economic differences sometimes are exposed to a narrower range of media than Whites. Advertisers support the media that deliver the audience with the best consumer profile at the lowest cost, not necessarily the media that best meet the information and entertainment needs of their audience.

Figure 5.8. Univision is the largest Spanish-language television network in the United States. This advertisement reports that "America's Hispanic market is 26 million people, strong, and growing. And 'sí' they spend over $240 million on goods and services each year."

The slick, upscale lifestyle used by national advertisers is more a goal than a reality for most Blacks and Latinos. It is achieved through education, hard work, and equal opportunity. Yet advertisers promote consumption of their products as the short-cut to the good life, a quick fix for low-income consumers. The message to their low-income audience is clear: You may not be able to live in the best neighborhoods, wear the best clothes, or have the best job; but you can drink the same liquor, smoke the same cigarettes, and drive the same car as those who do. At the same time, advertising appeals that play on the cultural or historical heritage of Blacks and Latinos make the products appear to be "at home" with minority consumers. Recognizing the importance of national holidays and the forgotten minority history, they have joined with Blacks and Latinos in commemorating dates, events, and persons. But they also piggy-back their commercial messages on the recognition of events, leaders, or heroes. Persons or events that in their time represented protest against slavery, oppression, or discrimination, are now used to sell products.

Advertising, like mining, is an extractive industry. It enters the ghetto and barrio with a smiling face to convince all within its reach that they should purchase the products advertised and purchase them often. It has no goal other than to stimulate consumption of the product; the subsidization of the media is merely a by-product. But owners of minority-formatted media, having gained through the increased advertising investments of major corporations, now have greater opportunities to use those increased dollars to improve news and entertainment content and, thus, better meet their social responsibility to their audience. Unlike advertisers, who may support socially responsible activities for the purpose of promoting their own images, minority publishers and broadcasters have a long, though sometimes spotty, record of advocating the rights of the people they serve. Their growing dependence on major corporations and national advertising agencies should do nothing to blunt that edge as long as the audiences they serve continue to confront a system of inequality that keeps them below national norms in education, housing, income, health, and other social indicators.

Notes

1. "Using Ethnic Images—An Advertising Retrospective," *Advertising Age* (June 14, 1984), p. 9.

2. Tomás Martínez, "How Advertisers Promote Racism," *Civil Rights Digest* (Fall 1969), pp. 8-9.

3. David M. Potter, *People of Plenty* (Chicago: University of Chicago Press, 1954), p. 166.

4. Potter, *People of Plenty*, p. 168.

5. Potter, *People of Plenty*, pp. 181-182.

6. Potter, *People of Plenty*, pp. 184-185.

7. "Using Ethnic Images," p. 9.

8. Cited in Philip H. Dougherty, "Frequency of Blacks in TV Ads," *New York Times*, May 27, 1982, p. D19.

9. Martínez, "How Advertisers Promote," p. 10.

10. Martínez, "How Advertisers Promote," p. 11.

11. Martínez, "How Advertisers Promote," pp. 9-10.

12. Domingo Nick Reyes and Armando Rendón, *Chicanos and the Mass Media* (Washington, DC: The National Mexican American Anti-Defamation Committee, 1971).

13. Joseph Treen, "*Madison Ave. vs. Japan, Inc.*," *Newsweek* (April 12, 1982), p. 69.

14. Ada Kan, *Asian Models in the Media*, Unpublished term paper, Journalism 466: Minority and the Media, University of Southern California, December 14, 1983, p. 5.

15. Studies on increase of Blacks in magazine and television commercials cited in James D. Culley and Rex Bennett, "Selling Blacks, Selling Women," *Journal of Communication* (Autumn 1976, Vol. 26, No. 4), pp. 160-174; Lawrence Soley, "The Effect of Black Models on Magazine Ad Readership," *Journalism Quarterly* (Winter 1983, Vol. 60, No. 4), p. 686; and Leonard N. Reid and Bruce G. Vanden Bergh, "Blacks in Introductory Ads," *Journalism Quarterly* (Autumn 1980, Vol. 57, No. 3), pp. 485-486.

16. Cited in D. Parke Gibson, *$70 Billion in the Black* (New York: Macmillan, 1979), pp. 83-84.

17. Laboratory studies on White reactions to Blacks in advertising cited in Soley, "The Effect of Black Models," pp. 585-587.

18. Carl E. Block, "White Backlash to Negro Ads: Fact or Fantasy?" *Journalism Quarterly* (Autumn 1980, Vol. 49, No. 2), pp. 258-262.

19. James D. Culley and Rex Bennett, "Selling Blacks, Selling Women."

20. "Using Ethnic Images," p. 9.

21. Soley, *The Effect of Black Models*, p. 690.

22. Soley, *The Effect of Black Models*, p. 690.

23. Caroline R. Jones, "Advertising in Black and White," *Madison Avenue* (May 1984), p. 53.

24. Jones, "Advertising in Black and White," p. 54.

25. Félix Frank Gutiérrez, *Spanish-language Radio and Chicano Internal Colonialism*, Doctoral Dissertation, Stanford University, 1976, pp. 312-314.

26. Antonio Guernica, *Reaching the Hispanic Market Effectively* (New York: McGraw-Hill, 1982), p. 5.

27. Theodore J. Gage, "How to Reach an Enthusiastic Market," *Advertising Age*, (February 14, 1983), p. M-11.

28. Jones, "Advertising in Black and White," p. 56.

29. Jones, "Advertising in Black and White," p. 56.

Public Relations

An Opportunity to Influence the Media

In 1992 the Public Relations Society of America chose "At the Crossroads" as the theme for its annual conference. As public relations professionals and educators met in Kansas City in October of that year, it was noted that the conference theme could well be the theme of their discussions on multiculturalism in public relations as well. This is because 1992 and much of the 1990s have been years of discussion, dialogue, and debate on issues of race, diversity, and multiculturalism. Both public relations educators and professionals found themselves "at the crossroads" as they met to discuss and map out their own diversity plan.

Setting the stage for some of the discussion was a research paper on career influences, job satisfaction, and discrimination described by people of color in public relations by Eugenia Zerbinos of the University of Maryland and Gail Alice Clanton of the American Trucking Association.[1] The study, which had been judged the "Top Faculty Paper" by the Association for Education in Journalism and Mass Communications Minorities and Communications Division in 1991, presented one of the most comprehensive analyses to date of diversity issues in public relations.

In their paper Zerbinos and Clanton quickly summarized the demographic statistics and growth projections for people of color that

139

make the subject of diversity a hot topic for more than academic discussion. Having set the stage with population projections, they then turned the spotlight to issues of diversity in public relations.

Diversity and Room for Growth

In 1990 the census bureau counted 167,000 persons working as public relations specialists. Of these, 7% were Black and 4.3% Hispanic, 1.7% Asian/Pacific Islanders and 0.3% Native Americans/Eskimos/Aleuts—14% of the public relations workforce.[2] This is about the same percentage as in broadcast newsrooms. In 1991 the U.S. Bureau of Labor Statistics reported 173,000 persons working in public relations, 8.3% of them Black and 3.1% Hispanic.[3]

But a greater number of non-Whites in the population or in public relations does not automatically translate to more power or influence. The most immediate result is that people of color face more of the reality they already know. The most immediate corporate response has been in market segmentation and penetration strategies designed to tap the purchasing power of these groups.

A growth in the dollars spent by African American, Latino, Asian and Pacific Islander, and Native American consumers has made them more and more attractive as targets for advertising and the media advertisers' support. What's more, these groups are growing at rates faster than the overall population growth in the United States. If current trends continue these markets will comprise about 30% of the American population in another 11 years.

These figures make people of color attractive as consumers and advertising targets and that is where most of the attention by advertising executives and public relations agencies was placed during much of the 1980s and 1990s. But the diversity message need not stop there. Instead, it can be extended to include the positive values that a diversified workforce brings to an organization's ability to understand and communicate to audiences of different races, cultures, languages, and nationalities. This is a point that has already been made by Marilyn Kern-Foxworth of Texas A&M University, the most prolific scholar analyzing multicultural trends in public relations.

Public relations and marketing executives should realize what an asset they have in their own employees or fellow officers who are African American, Native American, Latin American or Asian American. Members of these communities are also valuable assets when companies attempt to communicate and market to other countries . . . by bridging cultural and communication gaps,

wrote Kern-Foxworth.[4]

Even with the census bureau's admitted undercounting of people of color in mind, it should be clear that public relations has a long way to go to narrow the gap between the estimated 7.5% that minorities make up of the public relations workforce and the 20% to 25% that we make up in the population. Until positive steps are taken in that direction, the public relations profession will continue to encounter difficulties in capitalizing on the multicultural and multinational opportunities described by Kern-Foxworth and others.

Why Public Relations?

But the case for the diversity agenda in public relations education is even more than social justice and demography. It is more than urging others to "Do the right thing." Or, as Newspaper Association of America President Cathie Black says, to "Do the thing right." And it should go beyond copying the efforts of the print, broadcast, and advertising side of the profession to be racially inclusive. It is an initiative that could be driven by the very essence of this country's professed democratic ideal: freedom of speech.

Print journalists and journalism educators are quick to package their work in the wrappings of the First Amendment and rightfully proclaim their right to a free press. Similarly, advertisers present arguments for the right of commercial free speech and broadcasters warn against the threats to free press and free speech that they feel are posed by government regulation. The case for the sometimes competing First Amendment rights of print media, broadcasters, advertisers, and new media technologies are most often fashioned and focused by public relations professionals.

But where is the public relations profession in this turf battle for the First Amendment high ground? On many campuses its place in the mass communication curriculum is affected by the "last hired, first fired" mentality that people of color also have faced for many years. Public relations sometimes is seen as a adjunct to other media training, not a profession that can or should exist on its own. Its place on campus is often argued within and among educators, both in and out of schools of journalism and mass communication. Administrators love the public relations enrollment, but many question the value of the curriculum.

But when it comes to the importance of a diversity agenda, public relations should take a back seat to no one. If public relations practitioners and educators would wrap themselves in the First Amendment rights of freedom of expression, the free marketplace of ideas, and the right both to send and to receive information they would find their case parallels the need for diversity raised by other media professions.

In many ways, the practice of public relations is like the practice of law. Public relations professionals believe in the free marketplace of ideas, just as lawyers believe in the legal system. Just as attorneys believe that everyone deserves his or her day in court, public relations practitioners feel, or should feel, that every viewpoint deserves to have its best case made in the court of public opinion. Just as attorneys learn to craft legal arguments before the court, public relations professionals are skilled in shaping the public presentation of the viewpoints of those whom they represent to the media and the public. The message is important, but most important is the right of message to be expressed and received. Less important is the messenger.

Public Relations Influence on the News Media

The level of influence that public relations has on the news media is a lesson the authors learned in the 1960s when, finding themselves with a journalism education but no real opportunity to enter the nearly all-White newsrooms of Southern California general circulation newspapers, they worked with the Black Student Union (BSU) and United Mexican American Students (UMAS), community organizations and antipoverty agencies to present the issues of Chicanos and Blacks to the news media. Much of this work involved gaining coverage for pickets, protests, demonstrations, marches, and all the other activism many of us now associate with the 1960s. But it also focused on gaining coverage and understanding for the need for youth job training, community credit unions, neighborhood beatification efforts, and drug diversion programs.

In these efforts we learned two important lessons we had not been taught in earning our journalism degrees. For one, we learned that public relations workers are critical to the selection and presentation of the day's news. Second, we learned that journalists too often file inaccurate stories about non-Whites because they are influenced by biases and misunderstandings of who these racial and cultural groups are, what they believe, and what they want.

In the 1960s, this meant that news professionals often portrayed stories from the Black and Brown communities in terms of conflict, activism, and militancy. Too often they covered a demonstration by focusing on the demonstrators, not the issues behind the demonstration. In the 1990s, journalists often focus on people of color in stories of "problem people" either beset by problems or causing them for the larger society and "zoo stories" focusing on these communities during colorful observances of Chinese New Year, Kwanzaa, Mexican Independence Day, or Native American pow-wows. Once again, the journalists see these communities through a lens that filters out certain elements of the story and allows others to pass through to the audience.

Racial diversity in public relations can help lead journalism students and news professionals. Public relations expertise and experience is needed for forceful, effective, and accurate presentation of the reality of the multicultural groups that now make up our nation to the news and information media. Public relations professionals are also needed to help journalists overcome their misunderstandings of racially and culturally diverse communities if they are accurately to report them.

The need for multiculturalism in public relations is no less strong in the 1990s than it was in the 1960s. With the increased racial diversity in this country—coupled with the proliferation of targeted, segmented, and micro media—the need for people of color to learn and practice public relations is even greater. Similarly, students of all races and backgrounds need to learn to appreciate and understand cross-cultural communication if they are to be effective in their profession. These skills will be even more important over the next generation as more of us from racially diverse backgrounds—and our issues—are in a position to speak and be heard.

Diversity in Public Relations

No doubt the opportunities will be there. Diversity of the population is continuing to translate to diversity of messages and messengers and to create multiple opportunities for public relations practitioners and educators. Ketchum Public Relation's Senior Vice President and Director of Media Services, Jonathan Schenker, cited increased diversity in demographics as one of 10 key media trends in 1992 and beyond, noting that demographics will have a huge influence and that people of color will be featured as matter-of-fact, not as exceptions to the rule.

"Consider these audiences when creating press kits, and hiring spokespeople," Schenker wrote. "Multiple spokespeople might be necessary for some national campaigns." Schenker predicted continued diversity and demassification on the media side as well, predicting a continuation of the trend of narrowcasting and media targeting to special audiences. He notes, "Expect more of these [targeted] publications and an equal, if not higher, number of them to fail."[5]

People of color working in public relations share both professional and personal commitment to their work, as well as concerns about its commitment to diversity. Of the 140 public relations professionals of color responding to Zerbinos and Clanton's survey, nearly two thirds (63.6%) were women, the average of the ages was 37, about half were married, nearly a quarter had undergraduate degrees in journalism, and 11% had graduate degrees in journalism or communication. Of those responding to the survey, 70% had titles indicating managerial or supervisory responsibilities, but only 64% supervised a staff.

Practitioners reported that they were most satisfied with the networking opportunities and their present job function. They were least satisfied with the interaction with other non-White practitioners and with their participation in public relations. Nearly half (48%) said they considered leaving the field. Those in corporations were less satisfied than those in public relations firms and were also less satisfied with networking opportunities. Those in firms were most satisfied with networking opportunities.

Many cited perceived discrimination based on race in terms of either promotions, access to a project, access to a public relations position, or salary increases. A moderate relationship was perceived between leaving the field and perceived discrimination. High satisfaction level indicates public relations professionals of color have developed coping mechanisms to endure what they perceive as a hostile environment.[6]

Kern-Foxworth's earlier survey of 196 non-White public relations professionals found the typical respondent to be a Black female, age 38, who has worked for 9 years in public relations and has attained a middle-level position with earnings of $38,337 per year.

More than half had degrees in journalism, public relations, or communications. Having a journalism degree was more important in determining role than having degrees in other areas. Those with journalism degrees were more likely to be responsible for writing, editing, and producing material to present management's position, but were less likely to guide management through step-by-step planning and programming.

> The analysis supports the assumption that larger organizations do not allow minorities the opportunity to advance in their careers. The more people employed in the organization for which minorities work, the lower their salaries and the less chance they have to become expert prescribers.

Kern-Foxworth found a gap between the role that minorities assign to themselves (middle-level management) and that they actually fulfill (communication technician, not problem-solver). "This mis-conception indicates that what they perceive perhaps is not the reality of the situation."[7]

No doubt their skills are increasingly needed in developing man-agement strategies and media messages. Kern-Foxworth asserts that one of the reasons that the R. J. Reynolds $10 million, African American targeted venture in Uptown cigarettes went up in smoke is because the company did not use a Black agency to research and assess community and opinion leader reactions in the targeted community.[8]

> Companies have realized that they must reach all of the racial and ethnic groups in their markets and in their communities. That increasing aware-ness has led to greater opportunities in the form of growing numbers of minority-owned advertising and public relations firms and in the form of aggressive recruiting of Black, Hispanic, Asian American and Native American professionals by other firms,

Gloster and Cherrie wrote in 1987.[9]

But is there an interest in increased diversity on the management side? Maybe not. A 1989 survey of 50 key corporate and agency public relations executives by the Atlanta Association Council for Public Relations yielded responses from only 18, of whom 5 responded they were willing to discuss the issue further.[10]

Zerbinos and Clanton's 1990 survey offered many, and varied, reasons for the scarcity of non-White public relations professionals. Among them: lack of awareness of the opportunities, racism, lack of role models, lack of encouragement, limited growth offered by the field, their lack of essential skills, negative reputation of the field, and belief that other fields are more accessible. The most influential factors in career choice were an early interest in communication and the opportunity to work with people. Least influential were high school counselors.[11]

Those in the field have mixed, though somewhat positive, feelings about the their professional field. Gilliam's qualitative study of 10 Black women who are public relations managers mentioned the importance of targeting Black women as heads of households, the need for successful Black women to share their experiences, and the fact that more Black participants than the White ones felt that Whites were uncomfortable working with Blacks. The study cited an Atlanta survey showing that, although women outnumbered men two to one in public relations, their earnings were lower and Black women earned less than White women.[12]

Diversity Practices in Public Relations Education

Public relations educators had both an excellent opportunity for advancement and a clear agenda of needs to be addressed in the 1990s. Some of these are:

1. Too few non-White students are oriented toward journalism once they reach college. They know little about journalism, and other professions are better known to them. Educators should identify and reinforce the high achievers with the motivation and drive to be successful.
2. Professors should use racially and culturally inclusive textbooks and classroom materials in their teaching. There has been little research on inclusiveness of textbooks, which have a great influence in portraying the field, its practice, and practitioners to aspirants and students of the field.
3. People of color are not newcomers to the profession, nor are their newspaper histories separate from their public relations history. The first Black, Native and Asian American newspapers in this country were all founded as public relations or public advocacy vehicles: *El Misisipí* to rail against Napoleon's takeover of Spain, *Freedom's Journal* was founded "to plead our own cause," the *Cherokee Phoenix* to advocate a tribal identity and disseminate tribal news to the Cherokees and the native viewpoint to a wider audience, and the *Golden Hills News* to Christianize the Chinese and to advocate respect for them among the forty-niners in the gold rush.

A Public Relations Education Diversity Agenda

By reinforcing to their students the economic advantages of working in a corporate environment and stressing the opportunities for community service as part of public relations, professors can help students understand the unique opportunities in public relations. Community involvement is encouraged, not discouraged, on the public relations side of the communications profession.

The other media professional associations, such as the American Society of Newspaper Editors, offer models of multicultural programs that public relations faculty and professionals can replicate, emulate, and improve upon. Similarly, non-White professional associations can also help to establish links for internships, mentors, part-time faculty, and campus speakers. The Los Angeles-based Hispanic Public Relations Association's 80 to 100 members annually raise $10,000 in scholarships and look for contacts on campus.

Mentoring programs with professionals, internships, early tracking, and a national competition to select, train, place, and follow up will help to attract and keep the best students in public relations. Contacts with historically Black colleges, schools that are members of the Hispanic Association of Colleges and Universities (HACU), and campuses with large minority student enrollment will also help identify and nurture public relations faculty and students. Such contacts should be seen as a two-way street. Public relations agencies and educators who have only focused on general audiences can learn from the students and faculty at predominately non-White campuses as they work with them.

In a world of demassified society and media, those who are aware of and able to function in more than one culture and to work in more than one medium will be the most advantaged. Public relations students and professionals must know how to communicate with people of all cultures and to use all the media at their disposal. It is therefore crucial that everyone gain an understanding of the crossover skills necessary to communicate effectively with diverse audiences through diverse media.

Notes

1. Eugenia Zerbinos and Gail Alice Clanton, *Minority Public Relations Practitioners: Career Influences, Job Satisfaction and Discrimination*, Top Faculty Paper, Minori-

ties and Communications Division, Association for Education in Journalism and Mass Communication, Montreal, Canada, August 1992.

2. U.S. Bureau of the Census, *1990 Census of the Population Special Report 1-1,* "Detailed Occupation and Other Characteristics From the EEO File for the United States," p. 3.

3. U.S. Bureau of Labor Statistics, *Monthly Labor Review* (January 1992), "Employment and Earnings," p. 186.

4. Marilyn Kern-Foxworth, "Black, Brown, Red and Yellow Markets Equal Green Power," *Public Relations Quarterly* (Spring 1991), p. 30.

5. "How New Media Trends Affect PR Activities," J. R. O'Dwyer Co., Inc., PR Services, April 1992.

6. Zerbinos and Clanton, *Minority Public Relations Practitioners.*

7. Marilyn Kern-Foxworth, "Status and Roles of Minority PR Practitioners," *Public Relations Review,* Fall 1989, pp. 42-44.

8. Marilyn Kern-Foxworth, "Advertising and Public Relations: An Educator's Perspective," *Black Issues in Higher Education,* June 6, 1991.

9. D. Gloster and J. Cherrie, "Communication Careers: Advertising or Public Relations May Mean Opportunity," *Equal Opportunity* (Spring 1987), pp. 36-39 as cited in Kern-Foxworth, "Status and Roles," p. 40.

10. Interassociation Council for Public Relations in Atlanta, "Report of the Interassociation Council for Public Relations Survey," Atlanta, GA, 1990, as cited in Zerbinos and Clanton, *Minority Public Relations Practitioners,* pp. 7-8.

11. Zerbinos and Clanton, *Minority Public Relations Practitioners,* pp. 9-15.

12. Juliet Nicole Gilliam, "Black Women in Public Relations: Climbing to the Top," Master's Thesis, Graduate School of the University of Maryland, 1992.

7

The Press

Adding Color to the News

News—which Americans receive every day via newspapers, radio, television, magazines, and personal computer information services—is a vital commodity. Researchers call news reporting in these media the "surveillance" function of mass communication, the task of surveying the trends and events occurring in society and reporting those that seem to be most important and consequential to the society's well-being. Without such information people would be seriously hindered in their ability to participate in the political affairs of the republic or to make business, professional, and personal decisions. Obviously, tens of thousands of events and activities take place daily in the United States and throughout the world, but only a minuscule fraction of them are reported through the major national or local news media.

The most important characteristic of news is "consequence" (importance).[1] In other words, those who make decisions about news media content first consider the importance of the event to the audience. This process is, of course, subjective, but the decision makers (theoretically, at least) stake their professional livelihood on their ability to provide the information most desired and needed by society.

Another, closely related, social role of news media is the "correlation" function, or the task of analyzing the selected news, offering

150

analysis and opinion to the society concerning its potential impact, and/or suggesting what should be done about it. Often, social policies are formulated by opinion leaders with the assistance of news media as a forum.

Researchers have labeled the persons who are involved in the news selection process "gatekeepers" of information because they are in the position of either letting information pass through the system or stopping its progress. Performance of the gatekeeping function results in what some scholars have called "agenda-setting" for the society. The process of filtering out huge volumes of information while allowing only a few items to reach the audience is an act that by itself adds credence and importance (consequence) to the surviving events and issues. The extent to which gatekeepers bear responsibility for the flow of news information and set the agenda in the United States is a topic of discussion among social scientists. It is clear, however, that gatekeepers are vitally influential in the process. The perspective of American values, attitudes, and ambitions brought to society have largely been those of gatekeepers and others with access to media.

Historically, and continuing to the present, non-Whites have not been gatekeepers in mainstream American mass media. Their near exclusion from the process is the subject of the next chapter, but the effect of that exclusion is our present concern. Coverage of people of color in American news media has been and remains a reflection of the attitudes held by gatekeepers and those who influence them. The frequency and nature of the coverage of non-Whites in news media, therefore, reveal the attitudes of the majority population throughout American history as much as do portrayals in entertainment media. News coverage may be more significant, however, because of its role and function in society: entertainment is "make-believe," but the news is "real." Because news content, in theory, reflects what is really important to society, the coverage of people of color in mainstream news media provides insight into their social status. By their professional judgments, the gatekeepers of news reveal how consequential they regard non-Whites in American society by determining the ways in which they are interpreted to the general audience.

North American newspaper press history began in 1690 with the publication of the ill-fated *Public Occurrences,* which was banned after its first issue because editor Benjamin Harris failed to get approval from Boston colonial authorities. Significant here is the mention of Native American Indians in at least two articles within the small four-page newspaper. Throughout the colonial period, references appeared in the press concerning both Indians and Blacks. Indians were of interest because of both the French and Indian War and the uneasy relationship between them and the White settlers. Blacks were the subject of advertisements for slave auctions and notices for runaway slaves. For most of the first 100 years after the founding of the republic, press coverage continued to focus on the "Indian problem," and the issue of abolition of slavery began to receive notice, along with Black runaways.

Newspapers, however, did not reach the vast majority of the population until the forces of technology, public education, and the political rise of the "common man" made the Penny Press in the 1830s the first truly "mass" medium in the United States. Since then, news about people of color in White news media has been characterized by developmental phases commonly experienced by each of the groups under consideration. Five stages can be identified historically: (a) exclusionary, (b) threatening issue, (c) confrontation, (d) stereotypical selection, and (e) multiracial coverage phases. The first four phases were so uniformly practiced by news media as to become virtually established as covert policy. In the 1990s the final phase may be viewed as embryonic and possibly destined to become news media policy in the future.

Exclusionary Phase

The fact that each non-White group had an initial social presence and contributed to the historical development of American life without any systematic inclusion in the reporting of public affairs reveals their status as inconsequential entities insofar as the gatekeepers of information were concerned. The inference to be drawn was that people of color were not an important consideration to the well-being of society. This is made clear in such a sacrosanct document as the Declaration of Independence, in which the phrase "all men are created equal" was understood to exclude Indians and Blacks. The point was so obvious that there was no need to insert the word *White* between *all* and *men*. Furthermore, the U.S. Constitution specified (Article 1, Section 2) that for purposes of determining the number of members in the House of Representatives, a state could not count the Indian population, and each slave counted as only three fifths of a person. Free Blacks were generally prevented from participating in political affairs by requirements of extensive property holdings as a qualification to vote.

Although the policy of virtual exclusion of people of color in news coverage may seem benign, it had a significant impact on the historical development of race relations in the United States. Its most immediate effect, as noted above, was to signal the status and role Whites accorded non-Whites in society. Lack of coverage of peoples of color in White news media had the effect of asserting their lack of status, a powerful social psychological message delivered to Whites and non-Whites alike. Ultimately, exclusion from news media coverage signified exclusion from American society, because the function of news is to reflect social reality. For that reason, racial exclusion in news set the course followed by the other phases of non-Whites' treatment in news. It was a course of alienation between Whites and non-Whites.

Threatening-Issue Phase

When non-White cultural groups first begin to appear as subjects of news media reports it is because they were at the time perceived as a threat to the existing social order. Threat is grounded in fear. As may be expected, Native Americans were the first to attract the attention of the news media because of the uneasy relationship between them and White settlers. The ambivalence manifested in the "noble savage" attitude of Whites toward Indians was the result of fear of Indian resistance to colonial expansion. Although the European settlers were intruders on the natives' soil, the colonial and early national press began to characterize their Native American hosts in the role of adversary with heavy use of the term *savages.* Newspapers, therefore, made it easy to justify the displacement of Indians by focusing coverage on acts of Indian violence to reinforce the savagery theme. "Civilized" Whites were made to seem heroic for any actions, however extreme, resulting in the overthrow of "savages." By the time the Penny Press era reached its zenith, the Indian wars of the West were in full spate.

Similarly, Blacks were the object of fears that set the press awash in a flood of articles speculating on the aftermath of emancipation. In the far West, Chinese laborers became the focus of fears they would displace Whites from the labor market, and the *San Francisco Chronicle* led the press attack against them during the 1870s. In the 1950s the same fear manifested itself in the California press, as headlines blared against the Mexican immigrant workers they labeled "wetbacks." The 1980s and 1990s saw the press indiscriminately use the terms *illegals* and *aliens* to depict Latinos, who argue that when used as nouns, the labels are dehumanizing and inaccurate. A report by San Francisco State University's Center for Integration and Improvement of Journalism explained that "Individuals can commit illegal acts . . . but how can a human being be deemed an 'illegal' person?" The report further noted that the term *alien* conjures up images of creatures who are invaders from another planet.[2] A 1990 article in New York City's *Downtown Express* newspaper characterized the expansion of the Lower East Side Chinatown with a headline reading "There Goes the Neighborhood."[3] In 1991 the *Daily Breeze* in Torrance, California, headlined a front-page story about changing demographics in its circulation area as an "Asian Invasion"[4] and rekindled White fears of a Yellow Peril.

As the 21st century approaches, there remains increasing fear among media critics that oversimplifying news coverage of people of color contributes to racial polarization by making them scapegoats for the nation's problems and fueling White fears and hatred of other racial groups and lifestyles. A research study titled "The News As If All People Mattered" reported that the media often reduce complex conflicts into simply one side versus another. The study concludes that

The media further stimulate polarization by such actions as treating subgroups within communities of interest differently, repeating inflammatory comments without challenge or balancing statements, omission of relevant news, disregard for certain communities, quoting and referencing sources predominantly from one subgroup.[5]

Confrontation Phase

When a non-White group stimulates fear and apprehension in the general population, the response is inevitably a social confrontation. News media, having already brought the threat to society's attention and exacerbated racial polarization, then proceed to cover the response. The response is often violent in nature, such as the Indian wars of the westward expansion, the Mexican War, or the lynchings of Blacks in the South, Mexicans in the Southwest, and Asians in the West. At other times the response culminates in legislative action, such as segregation laws, peace treaties, immigration laws, or the creation of agencies such as the Bureau of Indian Affairs. On still other occasions, race riots dominate the news with a historical consistency that has involved virtually every non-White racial group.

American news media generally approach confrontation coverage of race-related issues from the perspective of "us versus them." It is a natural progression from the exclusionary phase: News people think of non-Whites as outside the American system, thus their actions must be reported as adversarial because they are seen as threats to the social order. Until the late 1960s, news headlines and text were filled with racial epithets in reporting on these social confrontations, thereby encouraging conflict instead of conciliation. When the Kerner Commission on civil disorders issued its report in 1968, it condemned this historical trend in news coverage by a press that "has too long basked in a White world, looking out of it, if at all, with White men's eyes and a White perspective."[6] More than during any other phase, it is during confrontation that news media have the opportunity to exhibit leadership in race relations; unfortunately, their historical track record has been poor and continues so into the 1990s.

An example was the coverage of civil unrest in Los Angeles following initial verdicts in the 1992 Simi Valley trial of policemen accused in the beating of Black motorist Rodney King that had been videotaped by a witness. A report issued by the National Association of Black Journalists[7] noted that although major news organizations had sufficient representation of Black reporters on their staffs, coverage of the ensuing "riots" was severely flawed. Among the findings were that many Black reporters assigned to the event from mainstream media throughout the United States had their stories filtered through White editors, resulting in stories skewed toward the preconceived biases and attitudes of White middle-class America. The most glaring result was the fixation on the riots as being racially motivated in the context of Black versus White "establishment" when, in fact, they were class motivated. Involvement in the unrest transcended race as Latino, Black, and Asian peoples joined in the looting and burning in a display of frustration targeted more toward despair over their socioeconomic plight than race-based hatred for each other. Much of the media reportage ignored the geographic range of the Los Angeles upheaval that showed a pattern across ethnic communities and revealed the true common denominator to be poverty. The informational disservice was the superficial and oversimplified coverage that distorted isolated events to make them appear in conformity with existing mainstream attitudes.

Stereotypical Selection Phase

After society has met the perceived threat of a non-White racial group via confrontation, social order must be restored and transition must be made into a postconflict period. Although conflicts between Whites and other racial groups have been numerous throughout American history, none of the conflict resolutions have resulted in the disappearance of non-Whites from the American social landscape. News media reportage, therefore, moves into another phase designed to neutralize White apprehension of people of color while accommodating their presence. Information items that conform to existing White attitudes toward other groups are then selected for inclusion in news media and given repeated emphasis until they reach thematic proportions.

Examples include news stories that ostensibly appear to be favorable to non-Whites, as in the cases of "success stories," where a person has risen from the despair of (choose one) the reservation, the ghetto, the barrio, Chinatown, or Little Tokyo. These stories accomplish the two objectives of stereotypical selective reporting: (a) The general audience is reassured that non-Whites are still "in their place" (i.e., the reservation, ghetto, etc.) and (b) those who escape their designated place are not a threat to society because they manifest the same values and ambitions as the dominant culture and overcome the deficits of their home communities. In the early 1980s, one of the nation's largest metropolitan newspapers headlined a story concerning a Black woman's appointment to the presidency of a major university with reference to her being the "granddaughter of [a] former slave." The headline fulfilled the objectives of stereotypical selection by invoking the image of Black slavery even though the issue had no relevance to the instant "news" event. Similarly, the same newspaper headlined a story on the election of its city's first Asian American councilman with a reference to his being the "grandson of a Chinese laundryman." At a moment of signal personal achievement, the newspaper came forth to put the persons of color "in their place" and thereby legitimize their accomplishments in the eyes of the Anglo audience. At the same time, such stories tangentially give credit to the social system that tolerates or praises upward mobility of non-Whites without facilitating it.

Other types of thematic stories also appear during the stereotypical selection phase of news coverage and, unfortunately, they are far more numerous. In the years since the 1968 issuance of the Kerner Commission report, the news media have responded to the call for better reporting of non-White groups with imbalanced coverage. People of color are more likely to pass the gatekeeper if they are involved in "hard news" events, such as those involving police action, or in the "colorful" soft news of holiday coverage, such as Chinese New Year, Cinco de Mayo, and Native American festivals. Other reporting in recent years has emphasized non-Whites on "welfare" who live in crime-infested neighborhoods; lack educational opportunity, job skills, and basic language skills; and, in the circumstance of Latinos and Southeast Asians, are probably not documented as U.S. citizens.

The news media have served to reinforce existing stereotypes. The old stereotypes of non-Whites as violent people who are too lazy to work and who indulge in drugs and sexual promiscuity are prominent. In fact, the preponderance of such reporting has lead some observers to say the news media have offered an image of non-Whites as "problem people," which means they are projected as people who either have problems or cause problems for society. The legacy of news exclusion thus leads to the general audience seeing people of color as a social burden—the "us versus them" syndrome carried to another dimension.

Multiracial Coverage Phase

Multiracial news coverage is the antithesis of exclusion. If it is to become the goal and policy of American news media, the last vestiges of prejudice and racism must be removed from the gatekeeper ranks. At present this phase is still largely a vision, but it is within the grasp of a society determined to include all Americans in the quest for social and economic equality. This does not mean that all news about non-Whites will be good news, but that non-Whites will be reflected in all types of news. News will be reported from the perspective that "us" represents all citizens. A major step in the process, of course, is the increased employment of non-Whites in news media professions. Equally important is an increased sensitivity among news media personnel to be attentive to untold stories from non-White communities and to the cultivation of news sources there.

The result should be a functional information surveillance system that promotes social understanding and alleviates unwarranted fears based on prejudices. In the meantime, major changes must be made in the training of journalists and in applied news philosophy if news reporting concerning non-White racial groups is to improve.

Obstacles to Multiracial News

The issue of more equitable employment of people of color in news media professions represents an obvious opportunity to effect more accurate reporting of their role in society and merits detailed discussion, which is provided in the following chapter. For the moment, however, it is important to look at other factors currently working against the achievement of culturally integrated news reporting in the United States. Progress toward this phase depends on the ability to overcome two major obstacles that have become matters of entrenched journalistic policy. Overcoming the first requires a renewed commitment to the ideals espoused by media owners and editors from the inception of professional news reporting standards; overcoming the second necessitates a change in the basic "news values" journalists apply to their work.

If news media reporting does expand to encompass wider representation, it will have to rededicate itself first to the principle that meeting the substantive communication needs of society is its first priority. The news media obligation to provide information and interpretation of issues and events to society is essential to the development and maintenance of an enlightened citizenry. A major barrier to more racially comprehensive news coverage has been preoccupation with profit incentive, as media "marketing" of the news has led to, among other questionable practices, an increased emphasis on information targeted to high-economic-profile audiences. Among some major metropolitan daily newspapers, increased circulation among affluent readers has become the primary objective, and broadcast media seek higher audience ratings to attract major advertisers. Because people of color are vastly underrepresented in the upper-middle- to upper-class income economic categories, they have been shortchanged in news media coverage.[8] This approach to news reporting has affected both the frequency and nature of their coverage. Although news media, operating under the free enterprise system, have every right to pursue profits, they should not do so at the expense of their social responsibility to serve the informational needs of society. The surveillance function of mass communication requires that news media inform society about the perspectives, aspirations, and contributions of all its components.

As noted earlier, the Kerner Commission provided insight into the nature of a major news media problem: the values applied to news judgment. The commission noted that news was determined from "a White perspective." In other words, priorities of importance were based solely upon an event's significance to the White majority. This notion was instilled in future journalists at the very earliest stages of their training. News was virtually defined as being events of consequence to the majority population audience, which meant Whites. This concept was easily made practicable because the social system ensured that news sources (persons of authority and social standing in the fields of politics, business, education, law enforcement, the military, etc.) were White. Journalism educators taught their students that the essence of good news reporting was the attribution of facts gathered from authoritative sources. Those news sources, unfortunately, represented in disproportionate numbers White ideals and values held in common with the journalists and gatekeepers who reported on their activities. The perspective of non-Whites, therefore, was not "newsworthy." Even in reporting events about non-Whites, the news sources sought by reporters to interpret them were invariably White ones. This practice was a primary reason for the alienation and distrust of news media by citizens of color.

Because America's non-White communities generally have not been reported on in the mainstream context by news media, their stories have not been told adequately. Numerous sources of information have yet to be tapped, and a lot of work remains before a semblance of balance is attained that will provide an accurate assessment of the non-White experience in the United States. In the 1970s and early 1980s, news media began to make inroads via special newspaper series and broadcast documentaries on specific issues of concern to people of color. In the 1990s, however, the task of integrating them into the news requires ongoing inclusion of their views regarding all major issues confronting society. To accomplish that objective, journalism educators and news professionals will have to redefine news values to include the perspectives of a wider spectrum of American citizens. Examples of attempts to forge a change in the 1990s include content audits of news topics and news sources by newspapers; guideline stylebooks for journalists on proper usage of terms and labels; the Multicultural Management Program at the

University of Missouri School of Journalism; total community coverage programs of the Robert Maynard Institute for Journalism Education in Oakland, California; and the development of multicultural newsroom training workshops at the American Press Institute in Reston, Virginia. One result may be a change in the composition and priorities of issues on the national agenda.

Newsroom Policy and Race

We have observed that the misrepresentation of people of color in news media is partly the result of long-standing policies concerning news values and economic incentive. The Kerner Commission report was the watershed for national recognition of news media dereliction of responsibility, but change has come very slowly. Professional news organizations began to address the issues of non-White training, employment, decision making, and coverage publicly in 1968. The years since, however, were generally characterized by an increase in stereotypical selection-phase reporting, notable exceptions notwithstanding. This suggests the difficulty of changing policy in news organizations. The nature of newsroom policy was set forth by sociologist Warren Breed in his work, "Social Control in the Newsroom."[9] Among the major findings in Breed's study of daily newspapers was that every paper has policies that are covert and that often contravene ethical standards of professional journalism, including policies concerning issues of politics, business, and class consideration.

Because the policies are covert and, therefore, not written and codified for persons new to the staff, they must be learned by other means. Among the ways new reporters learn policy are by observing the content of the newspaper or news broadcasts, noting which material has been edited from their own work, conversing with staff members concerning the preferences and affiliations of superiors, and noting the priorities assigned to news story ideas discussed in planning conferences.

A common complaint of non-White reporters working in mainstream newsrooms is the pressure of unwritten policy applied to their stories and "news angle" ideas. This is the manifestation of news being defined in terms of the dominant cultural perspective. Both non-White and White reporters face sanctions when policy is violated. Sanctions include reprimand, loss of esteem among colleagues, and lessening of opportunity for upward mobility in the organization. A revealing look at how newsroom policy affects news coverage of people of color from the vantage point of a staff newcomer is presented below.

Content Observation. A contemporary reporter intent upon analyzing the news editorial product issued by his or her organization would find reportage of non-Whites ranging from the threatening issue to confrontation to stereotypical selection phases, depending on the historical moment and ethnicity of the group involved. The absence of a fully integrated approach to either individual reports or general coverage would be a strong indicator of organizational policy. Conversely, stories about non-Whites focusing on special occasions—such as Cinco de Mayo, Chinese New Year, or Dr. Martin Luther King, Jr.'s, birthday—to the exclusion of more substantive reporting is likewise indicative of policy. Observation of multiracial views being included in reporting environmental issues, alternative energy sources, foreign policy, or the defense budget would signal the newcomer that such efforts on his or her part would be welcome. Past performance, therefore, becomes a policy statement as strong as any written or orally expressed edict—perhaps stronger. In certain contexts it is easier to challenge formal policies, because they are often accompanied by a procedure for making changes to them. It is difficult for the newcomer to counter the explanation that conditions exist "because that's the way we do things around here." It is more likely, however, that the force of content observation will not elicit inquiry from a newcomer anxious to accommodate him- or herself to the work environment. The compelling instinct is to conform in order to survive.

Editing by Superiors. A more direct means of conveying policy is the editing process. Newsroom editors are gatekeepers and enjoy professional superiority over staff reporters. The journalist who produces newspaper or broadcast material that is inconsistent with policy will be edited, either by alteration or by deletion of offending work. As such editing relates to news about non-Whites, the professional explanation—if any is given—is that the item lacks "newsworthiness" or that lack of space or time prevents its inclusion. Because it is the reporter's job to get work into print or on the air, the inability to achieve those objectives reflects upon professional competence. Editing is not necessarily a sanction against the newcomer, but it often denotes a policy infringement, and one or two applications are usually enough to complete indoctrination.

Informal Conversation. When staff members gather around the water cooler or have lunch together, the conversation often provides insight into policy. Mention of political and/or civil affiliations and preferences maintained by executive superiors suggests to the astute newcomer issues and topics to emphasize or avoid. Attitudes held by peers toward other racial groups is evidenced by their informal conversation and comments about race-related news stories. Policy facilitates a newsroom atmosphere and when consensus is apparent, whatever the issue may be, newcomers quickly get the message.

The informal conversation of newsroom colleagues, however, need not be supportive of the views and attitudes of superiors. For the newcomer's purposes, even negative conversation regarding the attitudes of superiors is sufficient to convey policy. Staff members aren't obliged to agree with policy, only to adhere to it.

News Planning Conferences. Journalists who become privy to news story planning meetings can observe the hidden force of policy in action. The priority ranking of news events, activities, and ideas for future reporting assignments reflects the thinking of executives and editorial gatekeepers. The reception and "play" given to race-related news as opposed to other comparable items reveals policy clearly. This is where the relative consideration of values is weighed, where the perception of social consequence is manifest. Even the decision to do a special series on one racial group or another only highlights the ongoing neglect of established policy to provide the general audience with a complete surveillance of the social landscape. The news perspective is askew, but the newcomer accepts it as "standard operating procedure."

Sanctions for Policy Violations. Although organizational policy works subtly but effectively as a barrier to multicultural news coverage, the sanctions for policy violations are equally subtle. There are four major sanctions that are self-motivated and psychologically self-imposed but nonetheless real. An important reason for newsroom conformity to policy is the reporter's desire to hold the esteem of peers. Few journalists, apart from those who attain national prestige, gain consistent recognition for performance. In the absence of letters or phone calls from the public, perhaps the greatest job satisfaction is the acknowledgment from fellow staff members of a job well done. Newcomers to a staff arrive with the desire to demonstrate quickly their right to "belong" by earning the respect of colleagues. Any violation of policy would cast the newcomer as incompetent or, worse, as a rebel.

As is true of most American professionals, journalists seek the rewards of career advancement. The fear of not getting the challenging assignments that lead to promotions and recognition by superiors is a strong motivation to learn and conform to policy. Because policy virtually defines the parameters of news value, breaches severely handicap a staff member competing with several peers for promotion.

A third major sanction is the desire of journalists to please superiors who have afforded them opportunity for employment. With that desire is a feeling of obligation to submit to policies and procedures (published or otherwise) established by management.

Finally, there is the ever-present possibility of job loss if policy is violated. Although it is rare for a reporter to be fired over misinterpretation of policy, journalists who violate policy may become subject to scrutiny. It is not difficult for an editor or management superior to find other reasons to terminate policy transgressors or to make them feel "uncomfortable" on the job. One example of the latter is the continued assignment of routine work that offers no prospect for personal satisfaction or peer recognition except to denote one's status "in the dog house."

It must be understood that newsroom policies and sanctions work against change in news coverage of non-Whites without regard for the racial heritage of reporters. Non-white journalists lament the newsroom atmosphere that forces them to see their profession from a White perspective. They complain that colleagues and superiors, not overtly racist but insensitive or ignorant, evaluate their perform-ance on culturally biased news criteria. To focus too heavily on race-related issues jeopardizes peer esteem, and work on such issues rarely results in the kind of recognition that leads to promotion. Given the nature of the various factors supporting traditional news-room policy, the slow progress made toward more equitable and accurate news reporting concerning racial groups in American me-dia becomes understandable but not excusable.

Analysis

Communications media make up a vital social component that enables a social system to exist and function. The role of news trans-mission is to reflect the realities of the societal well-being by alerting society to dangers within and without and by providing an agenda of issues for consideration. Individuals involved in that process are termed "gatekeepers" of information. Because non-Whites began their American experience as social outsiders, they have, by long-standing tradition, been excluded from roles in mainstream news gathering and reporting institutions. Information concerning non-Whites that does get processed through the news media is filtered, almost entirely, through members of the dominant Anglo culture.

Historically, news media reporting of non-Whites can be viewed in characteristic phases that, depending upon specific time and circumstances, have been experienced by Native Americans, Blacks, Latinos, and Asians alike. Initially, non-Whites are excluded from news reports because they are not deemed part of the social system. Their continuing presence, however, soon leads to their being reported as threats to society. Social response to the perceived threat leads to conflict and results in confrontation news reporting. Once the con-frontation crisis subsides, news media begin reporting stereotypically selected items to reassure their audience that the non-White group is no longer a threat. Multicultural news reporting looms as a promise on the horizon as increased opportunity for people of color to participate in the information gatekeeping process becomes reality.

Obstacles remain, however, in the path leading to multicultural news reporting. First is the placement of profit motivation before the responsibility to inform society accurately about the contributions, ambitions, frustrations, and issues important to all of its racial segments; a necessity for its most prosperous survival. The tendency for some media to cater to economically advantaged audiences at the expense of lower socioeconomic levels (where a disproportionate number of non-Whites are found) impedes multicultural news coverage. Other media, under the guise of providing news, merely exploit prurient interests to attract the largest audience for profit. In both instances the result is inadequate and inaccurate reporting of essential information inclusive of all viewpoints.

A second obstacle to racially inclusive news media reporting is the distorted sense of news values held by many news professionals. Traditional reporting procedures have defined news from a White perspective. Although news media have been nationally cognizant of the need to change their approach since the Kerner Commission report of the late 1960s, progress toward integrated reporting has been extremely slow. Necessary reorientation of the reporting process has been inhibited because traditional prejudicial news values had become ingrained as matters of newsroom policy.

Newsroom policy, evidenced by the work of sociologist Warren Breed, is often a hidden phenomenon that is effective in maintaining philosophical control of the news-gathering and -reporting process. Because professional journalistic mores preclude formal written policy curtailing freedom of expression among staff members, a covert system has evolved to teach and enforce policy. Newcomers learn policy by observing the organization's news content produced by peers, by noting which types of their own material are deleted in the editing process, by listening to informal conversation among peers concerning policy, or by participating in news content planning conferences.

Sanctions, which maintain enforcement of newsroom policy, are also subtle but effective. They include the desire of reporters to earn and maintain the esteem of peers, to advance up the organizational ladder, to fulfill obligations to employers, and to protect their jobs. These sanctions affect White and non-White reporters alike.

American society will not achieve the goal of multicultural news coverage that accurately reflects an image of itself until the concept of news is redefined to include non-White perspectives. The consequences of failure to do so will result in a nation that falls short of its own vision and purpose for existence. Much of the responsibility for change must come from news media organizations where dedicated, conscientious efforts must be made to examine whether outmoded and counterproductive policies are preventing progress toward multicultural reporting.

Notes

1. For a discussion of the definition of news and news values see any of several basic newswriting texts, including Curtis MacDougall, *Interpretative Reporting* (New York: Macmillan, 1982) and William Metz, *Newswriting* (Englewood Cliffs, NJ: Prentice Hall, 1985).

2. Center for Integration and Improvement of Journalism, "News Watch: A Critical Look at Coverage of People of Color," Report from the Center for Integration and Improvement of Journalism, San Francisco State University (1994), p. 44.

3. Cited in "Project Zinger: The Good, the Bad and the Ugly," Report from the Center for Integration and Improvement of Journalism, San Francisco State University, and Asian American Journalists Association (August 1991), p. 4.

4. "Asian Invasion: South Bay's Chinese, Japanese, Korean Populations Swell," *Daily Breeze* [Torrance, CA], March 24, 1991, p. 1.

5. M. J. Bridge, "The News as if All People Mattered," cited by Debra Gersh, "Promulgating Polarization," *Editor & Publisher* (October 10, 1992), p. 30.

6. Kerner Commission, *Report of the National Advisory Commission on Civil Disorders* (New York: Bantam, 1968), p. 389.

7. "The L.A. Unrest and Beyond," Special Report, National Association of Black Journalists, Reston, VA, August 1992.

8. See Félix Gutiérrez and Clint C. Wilson II, "The Demographic Dilemma," *Columbia Journalism Review* (January/February 1979), pp. 53-55, for a report on how socioeconomic factors affected news coverage strategies in the *Los Angeles Times*.

9. Warren Breed, "Social Control in the Newsroom," *Social Forces*, May 1955. Also, reprinted in Wilbur Schramm, *Mass Communications*, Second Edition (Urbana: University of Illinois Press, 1960).

PART

Strategies
for Coping

History

Journalism's Colorful Firsts

When most people think about the beginnings of media in the United States, they often look at Europe as the foundation of both the technology and system of media. Journalism history is often told in terms that emphasize the English-speaking traditions of media but ignore the historical past of other people. Although it may be useful to look to Europe to find some of the roots of media in the United States, a scholar looking there and nowhere else will get only a partial view of the media's rich history. Communication is a basic human activity and people of all races and cultures have taken part in it.

Communication Before the Europeans

Journalism historians Edwin Emery and Michael Emery describe some of the earliest forms of communication.

Around 3500 B.C. the Sumerians of the Middle East devised a system of preserving records by inscribing signs and symbols in wet clay tablets using cylinder seals and then baking them in the sun. They also devised a cuneiform system of writing, using bones to mark signs in wet clay.

171

They wrote,

> Pictographs or ideographs—drawings of animals, commonly recognized objects, and humans—were popular in the Mediterranean area, China, India, what is now Mexico, and Egypt, where they became known as hieroglyphs. There is evidence that a system of movable type was devised in Asia Minor prior to 1700 B.C., the date of a flat clay disk found in Crete. The disk contained forty-five different signs that had been carved on individual pieces of type and then pressed into the clay.[1]

The Phoenicians created an alphabet in 1500 B.C. and used colored fluids to outline its symbols to produce the pictographs. About 1,000 years later the Egyptians began using reeds from the Nile River to make papyrus, on which scribes using brushes or quills would mark with hieroglyphics. The different sheets of papyrus were then joined to form scrolls, which were stored in centers of learning. Around A.D. 100 parchment made from animal skins was used for special manuscripts or scrolls. But it was the Chinese who made the greatest two inventions leading to modern communication, paper and printing. Emery and Emery describe their contributions.

"At about this same time (A.D. 100) the Chinese invented a smooth, white paper from wood pulp and fibres and also discovered a way to transfer an ideograph from stone to paper after inking the surface," they wrote.

> Wang Chieh published what is considered the world's oldest preserved book from wood blocks in A.D. 868. Large blocks could be carved so that one sheet of paper, printed on both sides, could be folded into thirty-two pages of booksize. Feng Tao printed the Confucian classics between 932 and 953 and in about 1045 the artisan Pi Sheng was inspired to devise a set of movable clay carvings—a sort of earthen ware "type"—that could be reused.[2]

The technology of wood-block printing was not introduced in Europe until Marco Polo returned from China in 1295. But the Asian technology sped ahead, Emery and Emery write. Movable metal type of copper or bronze came into use in Korea in 1241.

Record keeping and communication were also important in what was to become Latin America before the arrival of the Spanish in

1492. The native Incas, Aztecs, and Mayans all had elaborate systems of recording, transferring, and storing records, including scribes who wrote on bark tablets and artisans who recorded information and pictures in stone carvings. The Incas, governing a territory that rose precipitously from the ocean to the mountains, used an elaborate network of runners to transmit messages of importance throughout their empire. The Aztecs, who developed both a university and libraries, used an early form of mass communication by hanging colored banners on the main public square of their capital city of Tenochtitlán, which is now known as Mexico City.

Although Hollywood movies have popularized the image of North American natives communicating through tom toms, war drums, and smoke signals, the intertribal communication systems were actually more complex and systematic than the movie image. A complex network of trails and footpaths spanned the continent and was traversed by specially trained couriers authorized to carry messages between tribes. James E. and Sharon M. Murphy described communication between tribes before the arrival of the Europeans.

"A complex system of native communications covered most of North America before white contact," they wrote.

> It was a unique network of trails and footpaths that crisscrossed the continent, passing through dense forests, over rivers and streams, across mountains and meadows. Traversing these trails were Indian runners, known as tribal messengers, who were officially recognized by governing systems such as those of the Iroquois in the East, the Cherokees in the South and Southeast, the Yuroks in the Northwest, and the Eskimos in present-day Alaska. Other tribes, having less complex tribal governing structures, named and trained young men, and sometimes young women, to act as messenger communicators carrying news from tribe to tribe. Their extraordinary strength and endurance, their fleetness of foot, and their intimate knowledge of the land amazed early European immigrants.[3]

Africans south of the Sahara Desert, divided into three chief groups and many tribes, also developed systems for recording and communicating information. Like the natives of North America they also used "talking drums" to communicate from village to village and transferred information between tribes and other parts of the world along land and water trade routes. Rock painting was a key activity for the ancient residents of the Kalahari Desert near the Southern tip of Africa, as well as in the Sahara Desert in the north. Literature, often in the form of folk tales performed with music, passed along folk tales and important events from generation to generation. In some tribes special persons known as *griots* memorized the history of the tribe and passed it along to younger members, as well as those who would carry on the telling of history after they died.

Early Printing in America

Like the history of communication and printing in the world, the history of printed media in the Americas starts with a group other than the English-speaking colonists. The first printing press to come to the Americas was brought from Spain to what is now Mexico in 1535, more than 100 years before the English colonists brought their first printing press to Harvard University in 1638. The earliest printing in the Americas, which was licensed by the Spanish royalty to printer Juan Cromberger of Seville, was built on the native languages and alphabets of the indigenous peoples. The Spanish saw the main use of the press in printing government notices and proclamations, as well as catechisms to be used in converting the Aztecs and neighboring tribes to Catholicism. Therefore, the first booklets produced on the printing press were bilingual, using a European language such as Spanish or Latin in one column next to the same text in a native language, such as Nahuatl or Tarascan, in the next column. Armed with this bilingual format, the Spanish continued on their mission of conquering and converting the native tribes.

But the press was used for more than printing government documents and religious texts. In 1541 a terrible storm and earthquake struck Guatemala City, south of Mexico City. After the storm a notary public by the name of Juan Rodríguez wrote what has been identified as the first printed news reporting on the American continent. Rodríguez's story of the storm and its destruction of the city was taken to Mexico City, where it was printed in an eight-page booklet by the operator of Cromberger's printing house, Juan Pablos, his pressman, Gil Barbero, and a Black slave whose name was not recorded. The front page of the booklet, giving readers a foretaste of the news reporting that would follow it, began with an attention-getting headline.

"Report of the Terrifying Earthquake Which Has Reoccurred In the Indies in a City Called Guatemala," the news report blared in large type. "It is an event of great astonishment and great example so that we all repent from our sins and so that we will be ready when God calls us."[4] The actual report began on an inside page that began with a dateline and gave Rodríguez's first-person account of what had happened.

The news report, which was distributed in Mexico City, was the forerunner of what was to become a popular form of news reporting in New Spain, as the Spanish colonies were then called. Based on a European model, they were called *hojas volantes* (literally, flying pages or bulletins) and *relaciones* (reports) and were issued when major news occurred, when the government had a major announcement, or when ships bearing news of world events docked at Veracruz. As more presses arrived in New Spain more printers took up the practice of printing and selling these irregularly issued news booklets. Mexican historian Julio Jiménez Rueda wrote that it was through the *hojas volantes* that "people knew of the death and coronation of kings, wars in Europe, earthquakes and calamities."[5]

By 1600, nearly 40 years before a printing press had even arrived in the English colonies, the presses of New Spain had produced at least 174 books. An additional 60 books have been identified without dates or verification.[6] The booklet format was also used in the first regularly issued printed news reports in America, the four volumes of the *Mercurio Volante* published by Carlos de Siguenza y Gongora in Mexico City in 1693. Among the news covered in one of the issues of the *Mercurio Volante* was an account of the unsuccessful attempts of the Spanish to conquer and colonize the native inhabitants of what is now New Mexico.

Although the Latino roots of communication media were long overlooked or ignored by media historians, it has not always been that way. In 1810 Isaiah Thomas began the first history every written of American journalism, the *History of Printing in America*, with a 10-page chapter on printing in Spanish America, but that chapter was deleted when his book was reprinted in 1874. Journalism historian

Frank Luther Mott mentioned the 1541 Mexico City news report in a footnote reference to his 1941 journalism history text, but claimed that "no regularly published newspaper on the continent antedated the earliest Boston papers."[7] In 1984, however, the fifth edition of Emery and Emery's *The Press and America* included a new two-page section on the Spanish influence in American journalism, including a reproduction of the 1541 news report. In addition, in 1977 and 1979 *Journalism History* devoted the cover and several articles to the contribution of Latinos and the Latino press in the evolution of news media on the American continent. These Latin American roots have influenced the development of the press in the United States, as well. Newspapers were published for the Spanish-speaking residents of Texas and New Mexico in the years before those territories were acquired by the United States in the 1840s.

As important as the contributions of Blacks, Latinos, Asians, and Native Americans have been in creating and developing their communication systems and media in other civilizations and countries, the focus of this book is to examine these groups as they have interacted with communication media in the United States, with an emphasis on commonalities and differences among the groups. All groups have had active media addressing the needs and interests of their communities in this country for more than a century. But there is far more description and analysis of the Black, Native American, and, to a lesser extent, Latino press than there is of the historical roots of media directed toward Asians. For this reason, and to avoid possible generalizations that are not supported by evidence, this chapter will describe the commonalities in the history of media directed toward Latinos, Blacks, Native Americans, and Asians.

The first newspapers for Latinos, Blacks, Native Americans, and Asian Americans all began in the 19th century. They were preceded by media targeted to other groups, most notably the Polish- and German-speaking residents of the English colonies and the new nation. They developed in the same era as the first mass circulation press pioneered by Benjamin Day, the *New York Sun* in 1833. But, despite the closeness of their chronological beginnings, there is another, more meaningful, commonality drawing together these different newspapers started at different times in different cities for four different racial groups. They were all started as a response to a crisis. The four newspapers (in chronological order) are the first Latino newspaper, *El Misisipí*, founded in New Orleans in 1808; the first Black newspaper, *Freedom's Journal*, founded in New York City in 1827; and the first Native American newspaper, *Cherokee Phoenix*, founded in New Echota, Georgia, in 1828; and what apparently is the first Asian American newspaper, *Kim-Shan Jit San-Luk, The Golden Hills' News*, founded in San Francisco in 1851 or 1854.

The First Latino Newspaper: *El Misisipí* (1808)

El Misisipí was founded in the midst of the Napoleonic Wars in Europe, when France had conquered much of the European continent, including parts of Spain. New Orleans, a major seaport built where the Mississippi River flows into the Gulf of Mexico, was the port of passage for commerce and travelers coming in and out of the United States from Europe, as well as the Spanish colonies in the Caribbean Sea, Central America, and South America. The newspaper was a four-page publication printed primarily in Spanish, but with English translations of many of the articles and almost all of the advertising. It was started by an Anglo firm, William H. Johnson and Company, and was printed on the press of the Louisiana *Gazette*. Although the newspaper is cited in a number of journalism history sources, not much is known about its founders, and only two copies remain from its 2-year printing run.

A translation of the one copy remaining in the United States, however, reveals the crisis under which the newspaper's readers were living. With Napoleon campaigning in Europe and attempting to establish a puppet regime in Spain, *El Misisipí* is filled with reports from other newspapers and sea captains of events in Europe, including a story on the uprising of citizens in Madrid against Napoleon's forces. The newspaper also speculates on the possibility of England ending its hostilities with Russia and entering the war on the side of Spain against France. All the news is from outside of New Orleans and almost all of it concerns the war in Europe, including a long commentary on the events. Because there was no wire or electronic

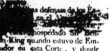

Figure 8.1. *El Misisipi* (1808), the first Latino newspaper in the United States, used both Spanish and English, including a bilingual advertisement for Don Juan Rodriguez, Attorney-at-Law, in the lower right-hand corner, as this 1808 edition shows. (Wisconsin State Historical Society)

dissemination of news, most of the stories the newspaper published were several months old and, at times, differed with each other. In a separate column the editor would comment on the different reports and their possible implications for Spain. The newspaper was also distinctly pro-Spanish, denigrating officials of the puppet regime established by Napoleon and speculating on the possibility of England entering the war against France on the side of Spain.

El Misisipí relied heavily on news reports taken from other newspapers, a common practice at that time, and reports of sea captains and sailors arriving from foreign ports. Among the articles in the only surviving issue of the newspaper in the United States, published October 12, 1808, are articles from the *Boston Chronicle* and a newspaper identified as the *Diario de New York* (New York *Daily*). Because the Boston newspaper's name was not translated to the Spanish word *Cronica* and used the Spanish word *Diario* in the New York reference, there is some speculation that the *Diario de New York* may have also been a Spanish-language newspaper. However, no listings of a newspaper called the *Diario de New York* or the New York *Daily* are found in the accepted newspaper references for New York at that time, although there was a newspaper named the New York *Daily Advertiser* published in 1808.

The front page of the October 12, 1808, edition carries the report of the Madrid uprising in all of its three columns, adding only a brief notice of its publication schedule (Wednesdays and Saturdays), subscription rates (8 dollars a year, half payable in advance), and language policy ("in both languages or in the one wanted"), and a bilingual advertisement for Don Juan Rodríguez, Abogado (lawyer), with a Spanish version on top of an English translation of the same message. Rodríguez took the advertising space "to inform his friends and the public in general that from this date he will reside at his plantation, better than a league below the city," but added that he would "still continue to keep his office in town, in the house of Doctor Deveze, No. 16 Main Street, where he will execute any business in the line of his profession from ten o'clock a.m. till four p.m."

Inside the paper, the second page offered the report "of a correspondent" on the problem of separating facts from the official news, private reports, and rumors emanating out of war-torn Europe. *El Misisipí* summarized what its editors felt were the latest factual information, naming the Bayonne *Gazette* as the source and calling that periodical "an official organ of the usurpers of the thrones of France and Spain." The newspaper then engaged in some of its own interpretation of the news:

> Madrid has long been in the possession of the French and the patriots of Spain are not to be duped by the mockeries of Bonaparte, however solemnized by a recreant minister of religion.

Citing victories against the French in Spain and Portugal, *El Misisipí* continued:

> We think therefore that nothing has yet appeared to discourage the friends of freedom. To hold their own ground is much for the patriots at the commencement of the struggle. Their armies will increase and improve in a far greater degree than those of the enemy.[8]

The fourth page was devoted entirely to advertising, almost all in a bilingual format in which the Spanish copy ran in a space above the English text. Everything from ships, to hardwood, to supplies for sailors was advertised in the bilingual format. The advertising reveals something of the commerce and trade taking place in the sea and river port of New Orleans, which had been acquired by the United States from France only 5 years earlier and had briefly been part of the Spanish empire. One company, A. & J. M'Ilvain, Grocers, No. 43, on the Levee, offered sugar, coffee, tea, and a "general assortment of groceries" along with "2500 lbs. James River Chewing Tobacco, 1000 bushels Indian Corn, 2000 feet Walnut plank." The firm advised ship's captains preparing to sail: "SEA STORES Put up at the shortest notice." Another advertisement advised readers that "Five or six gentlemen may be accomodated with Genteel Boarding in a private family, at the rate of 20 Dollars per month."

The largest advertisements, taking up nearly all of the second and third columns, were for Mrs. Zacharie, who offered "a handsome assortment of DRY GOODS" and *La Rionda*, apparently a dealer offering for sale two brigantines, the *Sophia* and the *Minerve*, each "with all her tackle," two houses on St. Phillip Street, and a long list of goods such as 800 tons of Campeachy Logwood, 40 bales of sarsaparilla, and 22 trunks of "Callicoes."

Even though it was the first Latino newspaper in the United States, *El Misisipí* exhibited many of the characteristics that were to be found in the other Latino publications that were to follow it. For one, it was apparently directed toward a Spanish-speaking audience that had come to the United States because of warfare and political turmoil in their homeland, a consistent theme in immigration from Latin America and the Caribbean. Second, it was bilingual, recognizing the importance of both the English and Spanish languages to the Latino community. Third, its news content was heavily influenced by events happening elsewhere, just as much of the content of Latino media over the years has been dependent on news from Latin America. And, fourth, like many of the Latino publications that were to follow, it apparently was operated as a business venture, devoting one fourth of its space to advertising in both Spanish and English.

The First Black Newspaper: *Freedom's Journal* (1827)

A different kind of crisis triggered the founding of *Freedom's Journal* on March 16, 1827, by the Reverend Samuel E. Cornish and John Brown Russwurm. The crisis was slavery, which kept Blacks as property in much of the United States. White Abolitionists favored the ending of slavery and had campaigned against it in the press, printing accounts of slavery written by freed Black slaves. After an attack on the abolitionists and Black leaders in the New York *Enquirer*, Cornish and Russwurm (who was the second Black person to graduate from a college in the United States) decided it was time for Blacks to start their own weekly newspaper. In the first edition of the four-page newspaper the editors eloquently stated their reasons:

We wish to plead our own cause. Too long have others spoken for us. Too long has the public been deceived by misrepresentation in things which concern us dearly, though in the estimation of some mere trifles; for although there are many in society who exercise toward us benevolent feelings, still (with some sorrow we confess it) there are others who enlarge upon that which tends to discredit any person of color.[9]

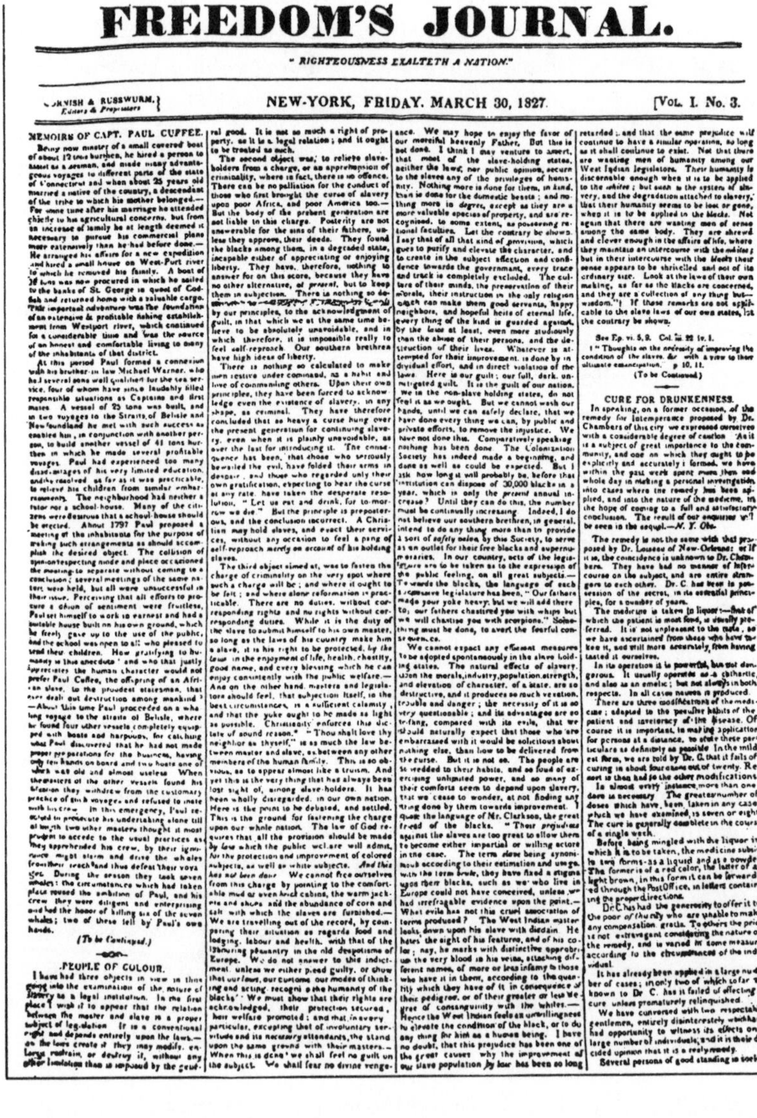

FREEDOM'S JOURNAL.

"RIGHTEOUSNESS EXALTETH A NATION."

CORNISH & RUSSWURM, *Editors & Proprietors* — NEW-YORK, FRIDAY, MARCH 30, 1827. — [VOL. I. No. 3.

MEMOIRS OF CAPT. PAUL CUFFEE.

Being now master of a small covered boat of about 12 tons burthen, he hired a person to assist as a seaman, and made many advantageous voyages to different parts of the state of Connecticut and when about 25 years old married a native of the country, a descendant of the tribe to which his mother belonged.—For some time after his marriage he attended chiefly to his agricultural concerns, but from an increase of family he at length deemed it necessary to pursue his commercial plans more extensively than he had before done.—He arranged his affairs for a new expedition and hired a small house on West-Port river to which he removed his family. A boat of 18 tons was now procured in which he sailed to the banks of St. George in quest of Codfish and returned home with a valuable cargo. This important adventure was the foundation of an extensive & profitable fishing establishment from Westport river, which continued for a considerable time and was the source of an honest and comfortable living to many of the inhabitants of that district.

At this period Paul formed a connexion with his brother-in-law Michael Warner, who had several sons well qualified for the sea service, four of whom have since laudably filled responsible situations as Captains and first mates. A vessel of 25 tons was built, and in two voyages to the Straits of Belisle and Newfoundland he met with such success as enabled him, in conjunction with another person, to build another vessel of 41 tons burthen in which he made several profitable voyages. Paul had experienced too many disadvantages of his very limited education, and he resolved as far as it was practicable, to relieve his children from similar embarrassments. The neighborhood had neither a tutor nor a school-house. Many of the citizens were desirous that a school-house should be erected. About 1797 Paul proposed a meeting of the inhabitants for the purpose of making such arrangements as should accomplish the desired object. The collision of opinion respecting mode and place occasioned the meeting to separate without coming to a conclusion; several meetings of the same nature were held, but all were unsuccessful in their issue. Perceiving that all efforts to procure a union of sentiment were fruitless, Paul set himself to work in earnest and had a suitable house built on his own ground, which he freely gave up to the use of the public, and the school was open to all who pleased to send their children. How gratifying to humanity is this anecdote! and who that justly appreciates the human character would not prefer Paul Cuffee, the offspring of an African slave, to the proudest statesman, that ever dealt out destruction among mankind?—About this time Paul proceeded on a whaling voyage to the straits of Belisle, where he found four other vessels completely equipped with boats and harpoons, for catching whales. Paul discovered that he had not made proper preparations for the business, having only ten hands on board and two boats one of which was old and almost useless. When the masters of the other vessels found his situation they withdrew from the customary practice of such voyages and refused to mate with his crew. In this emergency, Paul resolved to prosecute his undertaking alone till at length two other masters thought it most prudent to accede to the usual practices as they apprehended his crew, by their ignorance might alarm and drive the whales from their reach and thus defeat their voyages. During the season they took seven whales: the circumstances which had taken place roused the ambition of Paul, and his crew they were diligent and enterprising and had the honor of killing six of the seven whales; two of these fell by Paul's own hands.

(To be Continued.)

PEOPLE OF COLOUR.

I have had three objects in view in thus going into the examination of the nature of slavery as a legal institution. In the first place I wish it to appear that the relation between the master and slave is a proper subject of legislation. It is a conventional right and depends entirely upon the laws.—As the laws create it they may modify, enlarge, restrain, or destroy it, without any other limitation than is imposed by the general good. It is not so much a right of property, as it is a legal relation; and it ought to be treated as such.

The second object was, to relieve slaveholders from a charge, or an apprehension of criminality, where in fact, there is no offence. There can be no palliation for the conduct of those who first brought the curse of slavery upon poor Africa, and poor America too.—But the body of the present generation are not liable to this charge. Posterity are not answerable for the sins of their fathers, unless they approve, their deeds. They found the blacks among them, in a degraded state, incapable either of appreciating or enjoying liberty. They have, therefore, nothing to answer for on this score, because they have no other alternative, *at present*, but to keep them in subjection. There is nothing so de- [illegible] by our principles, to the acknowledgment of guilt, in that which we at the same time believe to be absolutely unavoidable, and in which therefore, it is impossible really to feel self-reproach. Our southern brethren have high ideas of liberty.

There is nothing so calculated to make men restive under command, as a habit and love of commanding others. Upon their own principles, they have been forced to acknowledge even the existence of slavery, in any shape, as criminal. They have therefore concluded that so heavy a curse hung over the present generation for continuing slavery, even when it is plainly unavoidable, as over the last for introducing it. The consequence has been, that those who seriously bewailed the evil, have folded their arms in despair, and those who regarded only their own gratification, expecting to bear the curse at any rate, have taken the desperate resolution, "Let us eat and drink, for to-morrow we die." But the principle is preposterous, and the conclusion incorrect. A Christian may hold slaves, and exact their services, without any occasion to feel a pang of self-reproach *merely on account of his holding* slaves.

The third object aimed at, was to fasten the charge of criminality on the very spot where such a charge will be; and where it ought to be felt; and where alone reformation is practicable. There are no duties, without corresponding rights and no rights without corresponding duties. While it is the duty of the slave to submit himself to his own master, so long as the laws of his country make him a slave, it is his right to be protected, *by the laws* in the enjoyment of life, health, chastity, good name, and every blessing which he can enjoy consistently with the public welfare.—And on the other hand, masters and legislators should feel, that subjection itself, in the best circumstances, is a sufficient calamity, and that the yoke ought to be made as light as possible. Christianity enforces this dictate of sound reason.* "Thou shalt love thy neighbor as thyself," is as much the law between master and slave, as between any other members of the human family. This is so obvious, as to appear almost like a truism. And yet this is the very thing that has always been lost sight of, among slave-holders. It has been wholly disregarded, in our own nation. Here is the point to be debated, and settled. This is the ground for fastening the charge upon our whole nation. The law of God requires that all the provision should be made *by law* which the public welfare will admit, for the protection and improvement of colored subjects, as well as white subjects. *And this has not been done.* We cannot free ourselves from this charge by pointing to the comfortable mud or even *brick* cabins, the warm jackets and shoes and the abundance of corn and salt with which the slaves are furnished.—We are travelling out of the record, by comparing their situation as regards food and lodging, labour and health, with that of the labouring peasantry in the old despotisms of Europe. We do not answer to this indictment, unless we either plead guilty, or show that our *laws*, our customs our modes of thinking and acting recognise the humanity of the blacks.* We must show that their rights are acknowledged, their protection secured, their welfare promoted; and that *in every* particular, excepting that of involuntary servitude and its *necessary* attendants, they stand upon the same ground with their masters.—When this is done we shall feel no guilt on the subject. We shall fear no divine vengeance. We may hope to enjoy the favor of our merciful heavenly Father. But this is not done. I think I may venture to assert, that most of the slave-holding states, neither the laws, nor public opinion, secure to the slaves any of the privileges of humanity. Nothing more is done for them, in *kind*, than is done for the domestic beasts; and nothing more in *degree*, except as they are a more valuable species of property, and are recognised, to some extent, as possessing rational faculties. Let the contrary be shown. I say that of all that kind of provision, which goes to purify and elevate the character, and to create in the subject affection and confidence towards the government, every trace and track is completely excluded. The culture of their minds, the preservation of their morals, their instruction in the only religion which can make them good servants, happy neighbors, and hopeful heirs of eternal life, every thing of the kind is guarded against, by the *laws* at least, even more studiously than the abuse of their persons, and the destruction of their lives. Whatever is attempted for their improvement, is done by individual effort, and in direct violation of the laws. Here is our guilt; our full, dark, unmitigated guilt. It is the guilt of our nation. We in the non-slave holding states, do not feel it as we ought. But we cannot wash our hands, until we can safely declare, that we have done every thing we can, by public and private efforts, to remove the injustice. We have not done this. Comparatively speaking nothing has been done. The Colonization Society has indeed made a beginning, and done as well as could be expected. But I ask how long it will probably be, before that institution can dispose of 30,000 blacks in a year, which is only the *present* annual increase? Until they can do this, the number must be continually increasing. Indeed, I do not believe our southern brethren, in general, intend to do any thing more than to provide a sort of *safety valve*, by this Society, to serve as an outlet for their free blacks and supernumeraries. In our country, acts of the legislature are to be taken as to the expression of the public feeling, on all great subjects.—Towards the blacks, the language of each successive legislature has been, "Our fathers made your yoke heavy, but we will add thereto; our fathers chastised you with whips but we will chastise you with scorpions." Something must be done, to avert the fearful consequences.

We cannot expect any efficient measures to be adopted spontaneously in the slave holding states. The natural effects of slavery, upon the morals, industry, population, strength, and elevation of character, of a state, are so destructive, and it produces so much vexation, trouble and danger; the necessity of it is so very questionable; and its advantages are so trifling, compared with its evils, that we should naturally expect that those who are embarrassed with it would be solicitous about nothing else, than how to be delivered from the curse. But it is not so. The people are so wedded to their habits, and so fond of exercising unlimited power, and so many of their comforts seem to depend upon slavery, that we cease to wonder, at not finding any thing done by them towards improvement. I quote the language of Mr. Clarkson, the great friend of the blacks. "Their *prejudices* against the slaves are too great to allow them to become either impartial or willing actors in the case. The term *slave* being synonimous according to their estimation and usage, with the term *brute*, they have fixed a stigma upon their blacks, such as we who live in Europe could not have conceived, unless we had irrefragable evidence upon the point.—What evils has not this cruel association of terms produced? The West Indian master looks down upon his slave with disdain. He hates the sight of his features, and of his color; nay, he marks with distinctive opprobrium the very blood in his veins, attaching different names, of more or less infamy to those who have it in them, according to the quantity which they have of it in consequence of their pedigree, or of their greater or less degree of consanguinity with the whites.—Hence the West Indian feels an unwillingness to elevate the condition of the black, or to do any thing for him as a human being. I have no doubt, that this prejudice has been one of the great causes why the improvement of our slave population *by law* has been so long retarded; and that the same prejudice will continue to have a similar operation, so long as it shall continue to exist. Not that there are wanting men of humanity among our West Indian legislators. Their humanity is discernable enough when it is to be applied to the *whites*; but such is the system of slavery, and the degradation attached to slavery, that their humanity seems to be lost or gone, when it is to be applied to the *blacks*. Not again that there are wanting men of sense among the same body. They are shrewd and clever enough in the affairs of life, where they maintain an intercourse with the *whites*; but in their intercourse with the *blacks* their sense appears to be shrivelled and not of its ordinary size. Look at the laws of their own making, as far as the blacks are concerned, and they are a collection of any thing but—wisdom."† If these remarks are not applicable to the slave laws of our own states, let the contrary be shown.

* See Ep. vi. 5, 9. Col. iii. 22 iv. 1.

† "Thoughts on the necessity of improving the condition of the slaves, &c. with a view to their ultimate emancipation." p. 10, 11.

(To be Continued.)

CURE FOR DRUNKENNESS.

In speaking, on a former occasion, of the remedy for Intemperance proposed by Dr. Chambers of this city we expressed ourselves with a considerable degree of caution. As it is a subject of great importance to the community, and one on which they ought to be explicitly and accurately informed, we have within the past week spent more than one whole day in making a personal investigation into cases where the remedy has been applied, and into the nature of the medicine, in the hope of coming to a full and satisfactory conclusion. The result of our enquiries will be seen in the sequel.—*N. Y. Obs.*

The remedy is not the same with that proposed by Dr. Loiseau of New-Orleans: or if it is, the coincidence is unknown to Dr. Chambers. They have had no manner of intercourse on the subject, and are entire strangers to each other. Dr. C. has been in possession of the secret, in its essential principles, for a number of years.

The medicine is taken in liquor:—that of which the patient is most fond, is usually preferred. It is not unpleasant to the taste, as we have ascertained from those who have taken it, and still more accurately, from having tasted it ourselves.

In its operation it is powerful, but not dangerous. It usually operates as a cathartic, and also as an emetic; but not always in both respects. In all cases nausea is produced.

There are three modifications of the medicine; adapted to the peculiar habits of the patient and inveteracy of the disease. Of course it is important, in making application for persons at a distance, to state these particulars as definitely as possible. In the mildest form, we are told by Dr. C. that it fails of curing in about four cases out of twenty. Resort is then had to the other modifications.

In almost every instance, more than one dose is necessary. The greatest number of doses which have been taken in any case which we have examined, is seven or eight. The cure is generally complete in the course of a single week.

Before being mingled with the liquor in which it is to be taken, the medicine subsists in two forms—as a liquid and as a powder. The former is of a red color, the latter of a light brown, in this form it can be forwarded through the Post Office, in letters containing the proper directions.

Dr. C. has had the generosity to offer it to the poor of this city who are unable to make any compensation gratis. To others the price is not extravagant considering the nature of the remedy, and is varied in some measure according to the circumstances of the individual.

It has already been applied in a large number of cases; in only two of which so far as known to Dr. C. has it failed of effecting a cure unless prematurely relinquished.

We have conversed with two respectable gentlemen, entirely disinterested, which have had opportunity to witness its effects on a large number of individuals, and it is their decided opinion that it is a real remedy.

Several persons of good standing in society

Figure 8.2. *Freedom's Journal* (1827), the first Black newspaper in the United States, carried news of general interest to Blacks, as well as strident opposition to slavery and calls to protect the rights of free Blacks in the northern states. (Journalism History)

Freedom's Journal is often described as an aggressive newspaper
that agitated forcefully against slavery and for the rights of free Blacks
in the North. But the newspaper was not only an Abolitionist or
Black civil rights periodical. It also built a sense of Black consciousness and community identity among Blacks throughout the United
States. It was able to do this because the newspaper reflected the broad
interests of Blacks, some of which continue to the present time. In
addition to news and hard-hitting editorials, the newspaper offered
information, features, culture, and entertainment to its Black readers.
Its first issue reflected the broad interests of its editors and readers,
carrying news from Haiti and Sierra Leone; the first part of a serial
on Captain Paul Cuffee, a Black Boston shipper; a poem entitled
"The African Chief"; and advertising for the B. F. Hughes' School of
Colored Children of Both Sexes. Throughout its years, *Freedom's
Journal* ran regular columns titled "Foreign News," "Domestic News,"
and "Summary." These columns, which were based on news taken
from other newspapers, were highly sensational. The "Summary"
column was especially noted for its exploitation of the staples of
sensational reporting: blood and sex.[10]

The newspaper was virulent in its opposition to slavery and in its
advocacy of the rights of freed Blacks, however. Its editors also did
not hesitate to attack the mainstream media to reinforce the importance of the alternative viewpoint that *Freedom's Journal* presented
on these issues. Walter C. Daniel wrote of *Freedom's Journal* in his
guide to the Black press:

> The editor of the New York *Enquirer* was attacked in a subsequent issue
> as one "whose object is to keep alive the prejudice of the whites against
> the coloured coummunities of New York City." Other articles dis-
> agreed with the platform of the American Colonization Society which
> advocated returning Afro-Americans to Africa and reported on lynch-
> ing. Russwurm believed in universal education as a critical need for
> Blacks who would be respected by White Americans.[11]

Russwurm left the newspaper in 1828 to become an editor and
official in Liberia, a part of Africa that the Abolitionist movement
had established to return freed slaves to Africa. The newspaper
continued to be published by Cornish under the title *Rights of All*
until it apparently folded in 1829. Lionel C. Barrow, Jr., noted the

important role of *Freedom's Journal* in establishing an important precedent as an alternative to the mainstream press in a 1977 article that
closed with the following passage:

> *Freedom's Journal* gave Blacks a voice of their own and an opportunity
> not only to answer the attacks printed in the White press but to read
> articles on Black accomplishments, marriages, deaths that the White
> press of the day ignored. Slavery is no longer here, but its vestiges are
> and today's reporters and publishers—Black and White—could do
> well to study the *Journal*, adopt its objectives and emulate its content.
> Blacks still need to "plead our own causes," and will need to do so for
> sometime to come.[12]

Like many of the Black and other newspapers for non-White readers
that were to follow it, *Freedom's Journal* filled an important void. It
did more than take issue with the coverage and editorial positions
that were found in the White press and present an alternative to
them. It also reported events of interest to Blacks with dignity and
pride, demonstrating that its Black readers, though victims of racism, had a broader range of activities and interests than what was
presented in the mainstream press of the era. Over the years the
Black press has continued to fulfill this dual role to its readers. On
one side, they have raised the concerns and protests of Blacks when
confronted with slavery, segregation, and discrimination. On the
other, they have reported on the organizational, social, religious,
and other activities and interests within the Black communities that
have too often been ignored by the White media.

The First Native American Newspaper: *Cherokee Phoenix* (1828)

Like the first Latino and Black newspapers, the first Native American newspaper was born of a crisis, in this case the federal government's efforts to displace the Cherokee Nation from the millions of
acres of land it held in North Carolina, Georgia, and Tennessee. It
was because of this crisis that the first Native American newspaper,
the *Cherokee Phoenix*, was born to unify and express the opinion of
the Cherokee people.[13]

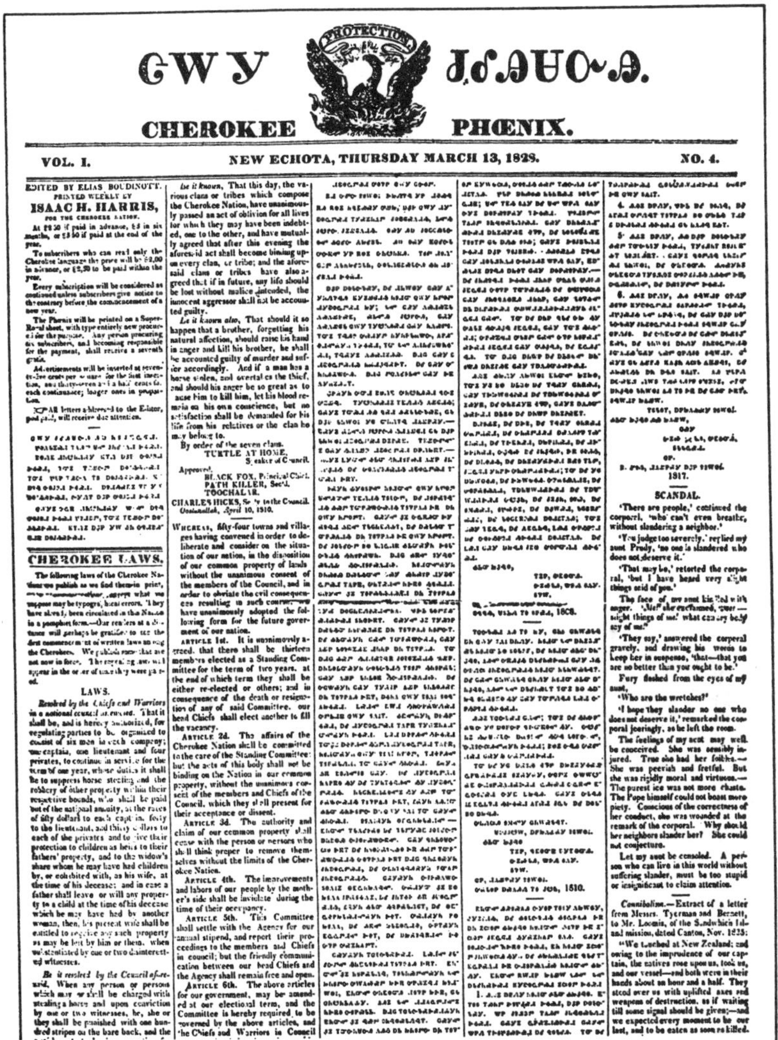
CHEROKEE PHOENIX.

VOL. I. NEW ECHOTA, THURSDAY MARCH 13, 1828. NO. 4.

Figure 8.3. *The Cherokee Phoenix* (1828), carried articles in both english and the Cherokee syllabary developed by Sequoyah. (Journalism History)

The *Cherokee Phoenix* was established by the Cherokee Nation near the current site of Calhoun, Georgia, and printed its first edition on February 21, 1828. It appeared weekly, with a few gaps, for 6 years until 1834, when it folded. Like *El Misisipí,* it was printed in a bilingual format, making use of both English and the 86-character Cherokee alphabet that had been introduced by Sequoyah (also known as George Gist) after 12 years of work in 1821.[14] James and Sharon Murphy write that the newspaper was started out of two needs. One was the desire of missionaries to use print media to spread Christianity among the Cherokees. The other was the desire of the leaders of the Cherokee Nation to unify Cherokees and others in support of the fight to keep their homelands.

The first editor was Cherokee school teacher Elias Boudinot, who also was clerk of the Cherokee National Council. To raise funds for the new newspaper he traveled along the East Coast speaking to philanthropic and religious groups. Financial support for the newspaper came both from Cherokee tribal leaders, who allocated $1,500 to help purchase a press and type before Boudinot began his fundraising trip, and from the American Board of Commissioners for Foreign Missions in New England, which helped support the casting of Sequoyah's alphabet into metal type. The missionary funds were requested by Samuel Worcester, a missionary among the Cherokees, who encouraged Boudinot's effort to start the first Native American newspaper. The Cherokees later repaid the missions board for its help.

Boudinot's vision, like that of the editors of *Freedom's Journal,* was of a newspaper that would accurately reflect the lives of his people and help mobilize public opinion in support of their struggle. In an 1826 speech titled "Address to Whites" at the First Presbyterian Church in Philadelphia he outlined the goals of the new newspaper as

> comprising a summary of religious and political events, etc., on the one hand; and on the other, exhibiting the feelings, dispositions, improvements, and prospects of the Indians: their traditions, their true character, as it once was, as it now is, and the ways and means most likely to throw the mantle of civilization over all tribes; and such other matters as will tend to diffuse proper and correct impressions in regard to their condition—such a paper could not fail to create much interest in the American Community, favorable to the aboriginies, and to have a powerful influence on the advancement of the Indians themselves.[15]

In its first issue the newspaper reprinted its prospectus prepared by Worcester that promised that, in addition to local news, the *Cherokee Phoenix* would report Cherokee laws and customs, cover their progress in education, religion, and culture, print news about other tribes, and "interesting articles calculated to promote Literature, Civilization, and Religion among the Cherokees."[16] Subscriptions came from as far away as Germany and the newspaper was circulated widely among the Cherokees, although sometimes only one copy was allocated for each village. In the fourth issue the newspaper carried the first written laws of the Cherokees, with Boudinot's comments that he hoped "Our readers will perhaps be gratified to see the first commencement of written laws among the Cherokees."[17] Although the newspaper printed articles in both languages, it was only on rare occasions that the same article was published in both languages. There were generally three columns in English for every two in Cherokee, because the structure of Sequoyah's alphabet devised characters for whole syllables and it took less space to write in Cherokee than in English.

Boudinot has been credited with building the *Cherokee Phoenix* "into a strong and loud voice of the Cherokee people as they struggled against increasingly insurmountable government opposition."[18] His voice was not always strident. In the first issue he promised the paper "will not return railing for railing, but consult mildness." But he made it clear that the newspaper would advocate the Cherokee position in those issues that brought them into conflict with the encroaching Whites and their governments. In the first issue he wrote:

> In regard the controversy with Georgia, and the present policy of the Central Government, in removing, and concentrating the Indians, out of the limits of any state, which, by the way, appears to be gaining strength, we will invariably and faithfully state the feelings of the majority of our people. Our views, as a people, on this subject, have been most sadly misrepresented. These views we do not wish to conceal, but are willing that the public should know what we think of this policy, which, in our opinion, if carried into effect, will prove pernicious to us."

At the end of the column he explained how he chose the name *Phoenix* for the newspaper and looked forward to a time when all tribes would rise up and put an end to both the physical oppression and negative language to which they had been subjected. He wrote:

> We would now commit our feeble efforts to the good will and indulgence of the public, praying that God will attend them with his blessings, and hoping for that happy period, when all the Indian tribes of America shall rise, Phoenix like, from their ashes, and when the terms "Indian depredation," "war whoop," "scalping knife" and the like, shall become obsolete, and for ever be "buried deep underground."[19]

As Murphy and Murphy point out, in subsequent issues Boudinot used the press to protest attempts by the state of Georgia to include the Cherokee Nation within its criminal laws and fought against federal appropriations to remove the Cherokees from their mineral-laden lands. But, like *Freedom's Journal*, it is unfair to describe the *Cherokee Phoenix* as a newspaper that was concerned solely with the struggles confronting the Cherokees. The newspaper also carried advertising for merchants, a boarding school, and other businesses catering to the needs of its readers. The newspaper also campaigned against alcoholism among the Cherokees and the slavery in which Blacks were held, although Cherokee law permitted the owning of slaves and had other provisions discriminating against Black slaves. The newspaper also ran advertisements by owners of runaway slaves and occasionally ran anecdotes in Black dialect.[20]

A year after it was founded the newspaper enlarged its title to become the *Cherokee Phoenix and Indian Advocate*, indicating its activist role in the Native American struggles. Over the years the editor and staff continued to protest encroachment of Cherokee legal and civil rights by Whites, including the harassment, arrests, and threats directed toward the newspaper's staff by Georgia officials. As the Cherokees came under intense pressure to move from their ancestral lands, the leaders of the nation itself became divided on the issue. Boudinot resigned the editorship in 1832, after he had been ordered by Cherokee Principal Chief John Ross not to publish reports of the division among the leaders. The new editor was Ross's brother-in-law, John Hicks, who continued to fight against the land grabbing and harassment confronting the Cherokees. But the newspaper appeared less regularly and finally ceased publication on May 31, 1834.

The *Cherokee Phoenix*, like the other Native American newspapers that were to follow it, found the bilingual format to be an effective way of communicating with both its Native American and immigrant audience. Although the bilingual format is diminishing among Native American newspapers today, it remained a characteristic of Native American publications for a number of years. Like the *Cherokee Phoenix*, many of the newspapers that followed devoted the majority of their space to news of specific interest to Native Americans, with less attention to national and international events without a specific impact on the Native American population. And, like the *Cherokee Phoenix*, those Native American newspapers that appear to have had the greatest success have been the tribal newspapers that have an affiliation and receive a portion of their financial support from a specific tribe.

The First Asian American Newspaper: The *Golden Hills' News* (1851?)

Although journalism historians point with certainty to *Freedom's Journal* as the first Black newspaper, *Cherokee Phoenix* as the first Native American newspaper and (with near certainty) to *El Misisipí* as the first Latino newspaper, it is with less confidence that the *Golden Hills' News* is identified as the first Asian American newspaper. There is little doubt that travelers and settlers from Asia were in the territories that now comprise the United States for a long time before what appears to be the first newspaper appeared. There are documented, though disputed, reports of Hui Shên, a Chinese Buddhist priest, sailing down the coast of what is now California following his arrival in what is now British Columbia, Canada, in 458 A.D., about a thousand years before Christopher Columbus first landed in the Americas. Spanish explorers in California reported finding the wreck of a ship that is believed to be of Asian construction on the California coast in 1774.[21] People from Asia have been reported steadily, but infrequently, in the United States since at least 1785, when several Chinese sailors became stranded in Baltimore.

Figure 8.4. *The Golden Hills' News* (1851?), apparently the first Asian American newspaper in the United States, used a bilingual front-page format with commercial notices in lithographed Chinese characters in the left-hand columns and a call for better treatment of Chinese immigrants in an English-language right-hand column, as this 1854 edition shows. (Journalism History)

The first enumeration of Chinese by the United States census was in 1820.[22]

But it was the need for cheap, hardworking labor in California, both before and during the Gold Rush, that brought the first in a series of waves of immigration from Asian countries to the United States. The *Alta California*, a leading English-language newspaper in San Francisco, made what one scholar has called "editorial humor" of the Chinese, including its own "Chinese letters" to ridicule Chinese literature. On a more serious and commercially lucrative side, English-language newspapers made use of lithography to insert Chinese characters into advertisements and in reports on the inscriptions on Chinese graves.[23] It is in the time, place, and context of the 1849 California Gold Rush that what is apparently the first Asian American newspaper is found.

Although there is some disagreement about the date of its founding, the first reported Asian American newspaper in the United States appears to have been a Chinese-language newspaper *Kim-Shan Jit San-Luk, The Golden Hills' News*, reported in some sources as beginning publication in San Francisco as early as 1851 and being printed thereafter on an irregular schedule. The newspaper took its title from the phrase *golden hills*, which was used by Chinese workers coming to California during the Gold Rush, and was a religious publication. Another early newspaper, the *Oriental*, is reported as having begun publication as a weekly in 1853 and also had a religious beginning. These founding dates were cited in a 1939 federal report on the history of foreign journalism in San Francisco,[24] but pioneer California editor Edward Kemble cited a founding date of 1854 for the *Golden Hills' News* and 1855 for the *Oriental* in his history of California newspapers written in 1858.[25]

But whatever its starting date, the *Golden Hills' News*, like the other newspapers that preceded it, was born in crisis. In this case it was the trauma faced by Chinese workers as they left their homeland, crossed an ocean, and came to the United States with hopes of making their fortune in the goldfields of California. Instead, they found a country that was not only vastly different than their own in language and culture, but often learned that they would have to do the hardest labor at little, or no, pay to repay the cost of their passage. Perhaps worst of all, they found themselves treated as outcasts in a state newly populated by immigrants; subject to legal, economic, and social discrimination in a strange land. Both the *Golden Hills' News* and the *Oriental* had their foundation among the Christian groups with missionaries in China and outposts in the Chinatown then developing in San Francisco. The groups offered support to Chinese immigrants in the hostile land, hoping to convert them to Christianity in the process.

In his history of the Chinese in the United States from 1850 to 1870, Gunther Barth notes that the first issue of the *Golden Hills' News*, which he cites as appearing in April 1854, stated the paper would appear twice weekly and that it was published by William Howard, with Chinese characters lithographed by F. Kuhl. But by July of that year it had begun weekly publication. In an article the day after the first edition appeared, the *San Francisco Herald* compared appearance of the typography in Chinese newspapers to a spider crawling out of an ink bottle and onto a white sheet of paper. The paper sold for 25 cents a copy, with a monthly subscription costing 75 cents. Charges for advertising were $1 for less than 25 characters, $2 for between 25 and 50, and 3 cents apiece for more than 50 characters. Barth describes most of the content as being in colloquial Cantonese, with most of the news coming from California and advertising coming from sales and auctions.[26] Like *El Misisipí* and the *Cherokee Phoenix*, the newspaper also used a bilingual format.

The front page of the May 27, 1854, edition features Chinese characters on about two thirds of the page on the left-hand side, with an English-language column apparently addressed to the White residents of San Francisco, on the right side. The Chinese characters reported commercial news and other business notices of interest to the paper's Asian American readers. The English column was apparently directed toward non-Asian Americans and argued for better treatment of the Chinese in California. The article noted that the Chinese were one of many groups coming to California and compared the treatment of Whites in China with the discrimination against Chinese in San Francisco:

> But the California picture is **unique**—their **tout ensamble** is the history of Civilization. The "Eastern States" have their Irish exodus, their German exodus, and hordes of Saxons, Danes, Celts, Gauls and Scandinavians, but we have **all** of these, and the most wonderful of all a

CHINESE EXODUS! The great wonder of the century is the astonishing flight of the hitherto immobile Chinamen across the Pacific ocean, to seek refuge and liberty in the bosom of "The Golden Hills."

The writer quoted missionaries in Shanghai who wrote that Americans could "wander unmolested" 40 miles into the Chinese interior and claimed that Chinese who saw Americans would "look up to them with profound respect." That behavior was compared with the treatment that Chinese immigrants were subjected to in San Francisco and made an appeal for better treatment of Chinese to the English-speaking readers:

"No Chinaman sneers at you in the streets; there is no hindrance whatever to your study of their character and habits; they always look at you with an expression of good will," says Bayard Taylor. Is it too much to ask of a Christian population "to do unto them," at least what it seems "they do to us," in their own land? Is it too much to ask of this Cosmopolitan state, in the veins of whose population flows the blood of a thousand tribes, to give freedom of growth and fair play to the Mongol element? Is it too much to ask of a Commercial People to give a generous aid and liberal encouragement to any means, that assist the Chinese to a knowledge of our laws and habits, and a sympathy with our interests? Surely not. Therefore Merchants, Manufacturers, Miners and Agriculturists, come forward as friends, not scorners of the Chinese, so that they may mingle in the march of the world and help to open for America an endless vista of future commerce.[27]

The English-language editorial was incorporated into the newspaper's format. Later issues continue to advocate the rights of Chinese in California and demonstrate the willingness of Chinese to take part in the traditions of their new country. Two July editorials were headed "Is There No Help for the Chinese in California" and "The Fourth of July and The Chinese Race." Barth writes that the English-language editorials set a precedent that was followed by other Chinese newspapers in California. It was primarily concerned with discrimination and other civil rights violations against the Chinese, while always pointing to evidence of their adaptation to the ways of the United States. The Chinese columns on the other hand continued to be filled with commercial notices and other business-related news.[28] By all accounts the *Golden Hills' News* did not publish for a lengthy period. Writing in 1858, Kemble concluded his three-line paragraph on the newspaper with the sentence, "It did not live long."[29]

Like the other racial publications discussed in this chapter, the *Golden Hills' News* established some precedents that have been followed in other Asian American newspapers. One was the use of a bilingual format, which continues in some periodicals today. Another was a column directed toward the English-speaking readers that argued for fairer treatment of the Chinese and pointed to the contributions they were making to the overall society. There are, no doubt, other precedents that will be discovered as students and scholars continue to study and analyze the history of the Asian American press in the United States.

Similarities in the Forgotten First Newspapers

The first Latino, Black, Native American, and Asian American newspapers in the United States are important for more than chronological reasons. Although it is important to establish and record the founding dates of the first media for these groups, it is even more interesting to examine the similarities among these different newspapers begun for different groups at different times and places.

One similarity has already been established, they were all founded in a period when the members of each group were facing a crisis of unusual stress or pain that was not being experienced by the majority population. But it is also interesting to note that three of the newspapers, *El Misisipí, Cherokee Phoenix,* and the *Golden Hills' News,* were also bilingual, using both their native language and the language of the majority population. Two of the periodicals, *Cherokee Phoenix* and the *Golden Hills' News,* were founded with the support of religious missionaries and a third, *Freedom's Journal,* was co-founded by a Black minister. All of the newspapers were especially attuned to the news and information needs of their target audience and, like media for these communities today, no doubt delivered both news and analysis that was unavailable in the mainstream press. For example, two newspapers, *Freedom's Journal* and *Cherokee Phoenix*, were established for the primary purpose of providing a voice that would be an alternative to the established press, and a third, the *Golden Hills' News*, appeared at a time when the mainstream media were playing an active role in ridiculing and disparaging members of that group. These three newspapers also all appeared in periods of time when the members of their audience were victims of legal discrimination, social subjugation, and violent oppression.

The racial press did not end with the founding of these four newspapers. In fact, each of these groups continues to have a broad range of newspapers, magazines, and broadcast stations targeted to them. Although many of these media have become increasingly commercial in their content and less fiery in their voices, these media have continued to fulfill the tradition of providing news, entertainment, and information that is an alternative to what is available in the media directed at the mainstream White audience.

This frustration with the mass audience press has long been felt and, in fact, was directed at the first mass circulation newspaper in the United States, the *New York Sun*. In the 1840s a Black man, Willis A. Hodges, took exception to editorials in the *Sun* opposing voting rights for Blacks. So he first tried the access approach, writing a reply to the editorial, which the newspaper published for a fee of $15. When the newspaper published his message, however, it was modified and carried as advertising. Hodges protested, but was advised "The *Sun* shines for all White men but not for Colored men." Told that the mass circulation newspaper would be closed to the views of Blacks, he started a Black newspaper, the *Ram's Horn*, in 1847.[30]

As long as there is free access to the establishment of print media in the United States, members of all races will be able to follow the avenue of Hodges and the founding editors of the first Latino, Black, Native American, and Asian American newspapers by starting publications for their own groups and presenting alternatives to the news and viewpoints expressed in the mainstream media.

◼◼◼

Notes

1. Edwin Emery and Michael Emery, *The Press and America*, Fifth Edition (Englewood Cliffs, NJ: Prentice Hall, 1984), p. 2. For further descriptions of communication in non-European cultures see Leonard W. Doob, *Communication in Africa* (New Haven, CT: Yale University Press, 1961); Irene Nicholson, *Mexican and Central American Mythology* (Paul Hamlyn Ltd., 1967); Robert T. Oliver, *Communication and Culture in Ancient India and China* (Syracuse, NY: Syracuse University Press, 1971); and Jacques Soustelle, *Daily Life of the Aztecs* (Stanford, CA: Stanford University Press, 1961).

2. Emery and Emery, *The Press and America*, p. 2.

3. James E. Murphy and Sharon M. Murphy, *Let My People Know* (Norman: University of Oklahoma Press, 1981), p. v.

4. Félix Gutiérrez and Ernesto Ballesteros, "The 1541 Earthquake: Dawn of Latin American Journalism," *Journalism History* (Vol. 6, No. 3, Autumn 1979). Also see Al Hester, "Newspapers and Newspaper Prototypes in Spanish America, 1541-1750," in the same issue.

5. Julio Jiménez Rueda, *Historia de la Cultura en México, El Virriento* (Mexico City: Editorial Cultura, 1950), p. 222, as quoted by Carlos Alvear Acevedo, *Breve Historia del Periodismo* (Mexico City: Editorial Jus, 1965), p. 79 (translation from Spanish by authors). For a description of *relaciones* in Spain see Henry F. Schulte, *The Spanish Press 1470-1966* (Urbana: University of Illinois Press, 1968), p. 72.

6. Alvear Acevedo, *Breve Historia del Periodismo*, p. 75.

7. Described in Emery and Emery, *The Press and America*, p. 16.

8. All quotes from *El Misisipí*, October 12, 1808, pp. 1-4. For a more complete translation of the issue see Félix Gutiérrez, "Spanish Language Media in the U.S.," *Caminos* (January 1984), pp. 10-12. See also Félix Gutiérrez, "Spanish-Language Media in America: Background Resources, History," *Journalism History* (Vol. 4, No. 2, Summer 1977), p. 37, and Raymond MacCurdy, *A History and Bibliography of Spanish Language Newspapers and Magazines in Louisiana, 1808-1949* (Albuquerque: University of New Mexico Press, 1951), pp. 8-9.

9. Walter C. Daniel, *Black Journals of the United States* (Westport, CT: Greenwood, 1982), p. 184.

10. Daniel, *Black Journals of the United States*, p. 184; and Kenneth D. Nordin, "In Search of Black Unity: An Interpretation of the Content and Function of 'Freedom's Journal,' " *Journalism History* (Vol. 4, No. 4, Winter 1977-1978), pp. 123-124.

11. Daniel, *Black Journals of the United States*, p. 185.

12. Lionel C. Barrow, Jr., " 'Our Own Cause': *Freedom's Journal* and the Beginnings of the Black Press," *Journalism History* (Vol. 4, No. 4, Winter 1977-1978), p. 122. Also Kenneth D. Nordin, "In Search of Black Unity," and Henk La Brie III, "Black Newspapers: The Roots Are 150 Years Deep," in the same issue.

13. Richard LaCourse, "An Indian Perspective—Native American Journalism: An Overview," *Journalism History* (Vol. 6, No. 2, Summer 1979), pp. 34-35.

14. See Murphy and Murphy, *Let My People Know*, pp. 21-33, for a description of the *Cherokee Phoenix*. See also Barbara F. Luebke, "Elias Boudinott, Indian Editor: Editorial Columns from *Cherokee Phoenix*," pp. 48-53, and Sam G. Riley, "A Note of Caution—The Indian's Own Prejudice, as Mirrored in the First Native American

Newspaper," pp. 44-47, both in *Journalism History* (Vol. 6, No. 2, Summer 1979). Elias Boudinot apparently shortened the spelling of his last name from Boudinott early in his career, but is referred to with both spellings in writings of the period and subsequent scholarly works.

15. Elias Boudinot, *An Address to the Whites: Delivered in the First Presbyterian Church on the 26th of May, 1826*, pp. 12-13, cited in Murphy and Murphy, *Let My People Know*, p. 24.

16. Murphy and Murphy, *Let My People Know*, p. 25.

17. "Cherokee Laws," *Cherokee Phoenix* (March 13, 1828), p. 1. Reprinted in *Journalism History* (Vol. 6, No. 2, Summer 1979), p. 46.

18. Luebke, "Elias Boudinot, Indian Editor," p. 48.

19. Luebke, "Elias Boudinot, Indian Editor," p. 51.

20. Riley, "A Note of Caution," p. 45.

21. Gladys C. Hansen and William F. Heintz, *The Chinese in California: A Brief Bibliographic History* (Richard Abel & Co., 1970), pp. 7-8.

22. Jack Chen, *The Chinese of America* (New York: Harper & Row, 1980), p. 3.

23. Gunther Barth, *Bitter Strength* (Cambridge, MA: Harvard University Press, 1971), p. 174.

24. Emerson Daggett, Ed., *History of Foreign Journalism in San Francisco*, Works Project Administration, 1939, as cited in Gladys C. Hansen and William F. Heintz, *The Chinese in California*, p. 45.

25. Edward C. Kemble, *A History of California Newspapers 1846-1858* (Talisman Press, 1962), pp. 117-119.

26. Barth, *Bitter Strength*, pp. 174-175.

27. "The Chinese Exodus," *Golden Hills' News*, May 27, 1854, p. 1. Translation of copy in Chinese by Stanley Rosen.

28. Barth, *Bitter Strength*, pp. 175-176.

29. Kemble, *A History of California Newspapers*, p. 117.

30. I. Garland Penn, *The Afro-American Press and Its Editors* (Willey & Co., 1891), pp. 61-65, as cited in Don Dodson and William A. Hachten, "Communication and Development: African and Afro-American Parallels," *Journalism Monographs* (No. 28, May 1973), p. 25.

Access

Developing a Multicultural Workforce

There is an old adage that says, "beauty is in the eye of the beholder."
As an observation on American popular media, it is equally appropriate to say that stereotypical, distorted images of non-Whites are
the visions of others. Media industry employment data clearly reveal
that non-Whites have little influence in determining how they are
represented. Resulting media images are, therefore, fashioned through
the eyes of White creators and decision makers.

People of color had been very aware, of course, of discriminatory
hiring practices in media professions and industries for generations.
Very little official attention, however, was focused on their employment in media prior to the civil rights movement in the 1960s. By
the late 1960s, U.S. government agencies had been formed to address
the question of fair employment practices in American business and
labor. Among those agencies were the Equal Employment Opportunity Commission (EEOC) and the U.S. Civil Rights Commission. Upon
publication of the Kerner Commission's strong indictment of mass
media culpability in perpetuating discrimination, both the EEOC
and Civil Rights Commission turned their attention to media hiring
practices. At the same time, the Kerner report stimulated some news
media professional associations to assess their hiring records. These
efforts can be summarized by looking at racial employment patterns
in the two major categories of entertainment and news.

198

Film and Television Entertainment Industries

Chapters 3 and 4 discussed racial portrayals in Hollywood movies and television and the roles in which the actors were employed. Here we discover the nature of the participation of people of color in behind-the-scenes stage crafts and in production management roles. In 1969 the EEOC held hearings in Los Angeles on minority employment in the film industry. The commission found Hollywood's non-White employment rates well below even the average for other industries that, themselves, had poor hiring records. Furthermore, the film industry data revealed discriminatory hiring practices in nearly every occupational category whether white collar or blue collar. The EEOC concluded:

> The motion picture industry reports approximately 19,000 employees, 13,000 of whom are white collar workers. But it is not the raw numbers of people employed that is significant, it is the fact that the industry plays a critical role in influencing public opinion and creating this country's image of itself. In order to portray accurately the nation's minority groups, the industry must employ minority personnel at all levels . . .
> The Equal Employment Opportunity Commission's analysis indicates that this is not happening.[1]

At that time a studio official who testified before the commission said that of 81 management-level personnel only 3 were people of color. Two were Latino, the single Black manager headed the janitorial department, and there were no Asian nor Native American managers. The studio executive also testified that his organization employed 184 workers classified as technicians. Of that number only 5 were non-Whites; 3 Latinos, 1 Black, and 1 Asian. Generally, in the late 1960s the non-White employment percentage among other industries in the Los Angeles metropolitan statistical area was twice that of the movie industry where they comprised approximately 40% of the Los Angeles metropolitan area population but made up only 3% of the movie industry labor force.

In 1977 the U.S. Civil Rights Commission conducted its investigation of the television entertainment industry and also convened a hearing in Los Angeles. Among those called to testify were officials of the various unions representing producers, directors, and writers as well as non-White craftsmen in the several theatrical trades. One witness, a member of the Cherokee nation, testified about how a trade union "lost" the job application of a highly skilled Native American worker. When a union official was confronted about the incident he replied, "No one tells us who we have to hire or anything of that matter. We decide that."[2] Other testimony revealed a union scheme systematically to phase out Blacks who attained union membership by seeking their suspension without due process hearings. In addition, experienced union members of color were overlooked for job promotion while young Whites, who were sons of union journeymen, obtained superior status directly out of high school without job experience. These examples of systematic discrimination and nepotism in the television industry were not countermanded by either network executives or union officials. The civil rights commission noted the television entertainment industry had not assumed equal employment opportunity responsibilities in hiring practices.

Data were compiled over a 3-year period (1974-1976) on union rosters representing the workers who produce the movies, situation comedies, and variety programs televised to millions of American viewers. Crafts represented in the trade union data included makeup artists, projectionists, prop workers, set designers, script supervisors, story analysts, and camera operators, among others. Keeping in mind that 8 years had elapsed since the EEOC had investigated the movie industry, the television trade union data presented at the 1977 hearing showed an average of only 8% non-White employment for the period. More revealing was the fact that not even one person of color obtained work during the 3 years as either a script supervisor or story analyst, according to data supplied to the U.S. Commission on Civil Rights. Although the industry was (as was American society in general) experiencing the waning years of emphasis on affirmative action, only 50% of non-Whites who applied for union rosters achieved their goal. Meanwhile, 62% of the White applicants were successful during the same period.

In August 1977 the civil rights commission published its findings on racial and female employment in television.[3] For historical perspective it must be noted that in 1969 the Federal Communications

Commission (FCC) had adopted equal employment opportunity guidelines prohibiting job discrimination by broadcast licensees. The implied penalty was loss of license. It was during this period that the term *two-fer* became part of the lexicon of American broadcasting. A "two-fer" was any woman employed in broadcasting who happened also to be non-White. Broadcast executives were able to list such women in their hiring statistics twice, once in the gender category and again in the ethnic category—a "two-for-one" employee. The tabulated result padded the actual affirmative action employment total. The use of two-fers and other manipulative measures created some unusual employment data reported by American broadcasters. In an attempt to make the hiring and placement of people of color in upper-level job categories seem more equitable, the industry reported an astonishing 45% increase in ethnic managers between 1971 and 1975. At the same time, however, the proportion of all employees in those job categories increased by only 13%. A close look at the broadcasters' figures also revealed a dramatic decline in the number of clerical and service jobs listed. These data prompted a public interest group to ask, "Do more executives need fewer clerks to serve them? Do larger staffs need less janitorial service?"[4] It was obvious that broadcasters had merely reclassified their non-White employees into upper job categories while keeping them on the same old jobs with the same low salaries. Most of these "managers," particularly in television, held jobs with such titles as "Community Relations Director" or "Manager of Community Affairs." Almost without exception even those persons (who were far removed from day-to-day programming decisions) reported to a White male department head.

Among the significant conclusions drawn in 1977 by the U.S. Commission on Civil Rights regarding the employment of non-Whites in television were:

- an underlying assumption by television executives that realistic representation of non-Whites would diminish the medium's ability to attract the largest possible audience
- that broadcasters misrepresented to the FCC the actual employment status of non-Whites and women via reports on FCC Form 395
- that people of color were not fully utilized at all levels of station management nor at all levels of local station operations

- that White males held the overwhelming majority of decision-making positions
- that non-Whites held subsidiary positions
- that increased multicultural visibility as on-air talent belied their lack of representation in managerial and other jobs off camera; in other words, people of color were merely "window dressing."

Employment conditions changed little in the 1980s. FCC statistics released in 1982 showed that non-Whites held about 17% of all jobs in broadcast television and about 14% in cable TV. Although the FCC reported the number of non-White "officials and managers" to be 9%, it still included in that category low authoritative positions such as promotion directors and research directors, jobs most frequently held by people of color.[5] Those figures included the small and slowly growing number of TV stations owned by people of color and that have largely non-White management staffs.

Another round of hearings descended upon Hollywood and the television industry on June 1, 1983, when the House Subcommittee on Telecommunications, Consumer Protection and Finance heard from a group of Black actors led by Sidney Poitier. Poitier, the first Black to win an Oscar for Best Actor, urged the committee to instigate a full-scale investigation of the "flagrant unfairness in the hiring practices of producers, the studios and the networks." Poitier's words seemed to echo the testimony of other witnesses who had appeared nearly 15 years earlier before another federal committee. But, by the 1990s EEOC employment data revealed that people of color had made significant strides in terms of share in the industry workforce. In 1991, the most recent year for which data are available, the total non-White percentage in the motion picture industry labor force had grown to more than 24% of about 42,000 employees (Table 9.1) from only 3% of approximately 19,000 workers in 1969. In 1991, people of color held 11% of jobs listed in the white-collar category of "officials and managers." The extent to which increased employment of non-Whites in the motion picture industry has impacted upon the quantity and quality of racial portrayals is a fertile topic for research as the medium approaches the 21st century. Demographic segmentation of the motion picture audience likely reflects economic motives rather than social concerns as the industry's driving force insofar as content and message are concerned.

TABLE 9.1 Non-White Employment in Motion Picture Labor Force, 1991

	Percentage of Total	Percentage Official/Managers	Percentage White Collar	Percentage Blue Collar
Blacks	11.0	5.1	8.0	11.9
Latinos	9.0	3.7	6.4	9.5
Asians	4.2	2.4	3.8	2.7
Native Americans	0.4	0.2	0.2	0.3
Totals	24.6	11.4	18.4	24.4

SOURCE: U.S. Equal Employment Opportunity Commission.

News Media

If employment opportunities for people of color in the motion picture entertainment industry increased substantially by the 1990s, professional journalism has progressed at less than half the pace. A 1992 study of journalists working for all forms of news organizations (daily and weekly newspapers, news services, magazines, radio and television stations) found non-Whites to comprise only 8.2% of the journalistic workforce.[6] The daily newspaper industry began to assess the racial composition of its labor force in the early 1970s. The American Society of Newspaper Editors (ASNE) reported that fewer than 1% of daily newspaper professionals were members of underrepresented racial groups when the decade of the 1970s began. In 1972 people of color comprised 1.6% of the total.

Interestingly, in the same year (1972) a Radio and Television News Directors Association (RTNDA) survey found that non-Whites held 14% of commercial television news jobs and 10% of those in radio news, figures that remained basically constant until the late 1980s. In 1988 RTNDA research revealed that television news hiring for non-Whites had increased to 16% but radio had slipped to only 8%. By 1992 the percentage of non-Whites in the television news workforce had grown to 18.5% and radio had reversed its decline with 11%.

The broadcasting industry initially moved much more quickly on the issue of multicultural hiring in news because radio and television frequencies are licensed by a government agency, the Federal Communications Commission. Newspapers, on the other hand, are

TABLE 9.2 Non-White Employment Rate at 5-Year Intervals in Daily
Newspapers, 1978-1993

Year	Non-White Percentage	Percentage Increase
1978	4.0	—
1983	5.6	1.6
1988	7.0	1.4
1993	9.8	2.8

SOURCE: Based on research data compiled by the American Society of Newspaper Editors.

private enterprises that had to be motivated by conscience, economics, or social pressure to improve their employment practices.

Although hiring of non-Whites in broadcast journalism lost mo-
mentum within 5 years after it began, the industry saw no such decline
in its drive for gender equality. The hiring of women and their
advancement up to decision-making ranks has far outstripped that
of people of color. For example, in 1972 only 4% of the nation's radio
news directors were women but by 1982 the figure had risen to 18%.
By 1992 female radio news directors comprised 29% of the total. In
contrast, people of color comprised only 4% of radio news directors
in 1982 and 8% in 1992. In 1972, only 57% of the nation's television
stations had at least one woman on the news staff but by 1982
virtually every station (97%) had at least one female journalist. By
comparison, non-Whites were in 60% of all TV newsrooms in 1972
but the figure had grown to only 72% by 1982 and 87.5% in 1992.

Daily newspapers lag behind radio and television news organizations in racial diversification of their workforce. By 1983 there was
only 5.6% non-White representation among the nearly 1,750 daily
newspapers in the nation. The newspaper industry experienced a
4-year decline in its multicultural employment growth rate from
1979 to 1983, according to the American Society of Newspaper Editors.
Economic reversals decreased the number of daily newspapers to
about 1,550 in 1993 and multiracial hiring did not reach the 10% level
until that year (Table 9.2). Yet, 1993 was also a year when half (51%)
of all daily newspapers in the United States still had no journalists
of color on their staffs.

A comparison of non-White journalist employment in newspapers, radio and television (Table 9.3) reveals television as the leader.
For perspective it is important to note that the 1990 U.S. Census

Bureau data showed people of color comprised about 25% of the nation's population and the number was growing rapidly. Against that criteria none of the news media industries has achieved statistical parity in minority hiring. The table shows that in 1992 Blacks found news media employment in greater numbers than Latino, Asian, or Native American journalists. The numerical ranking of the four ethnic groups has been constant since such records have been kept. Latinos, the second largest non-White group employed in news media professions, have narrowed the employment gap between them and Blacks, but Asian gains have been proportionally minimal. Native Americans have traditionally been the least represented of the four groups and their employment percentage remained virtually unchanged across all media in the decade between 1982 and 1992.

Table 9.4 provides a comparison of non-White news media employment by group in each medium for the years 1982 and 1992. Blacks, as noted earlier, were the most represented group in each medium, but Latinos made significant gains over the decade. The Latino share of the non-White employment data rose from 20% to 32% in television news and from 21% to 28% in radio news. Meanwhile, Asians increased their newsroom presence from 8% to 11% in television and from 3% to 19% in radio. Although Native Americans remained at 3% of non-White news employees in television, they nearly doubled their representation in radio from 6% to 11%.

It is important to note, once again, that non-Whites are still scarce in news department decision-making positions. Vernon Stone, research director for the Radio-Television News Directors Association, estimated that 2% of the nation's TV news directors were people of color in 1982 and had increased to only 8% by 1992. In 1992 approximately 7% of daily newspaper editorial supervisors were non-White.

Recruitment and Retention

Because the news professions are well aware of the shortage of non-White employees, the issue of their efforts to recruit and retain a more racially diverse workforce deserves attention. Until the mid-1980s some newspaper editors were openly hostile to the idea

TABLE 9.3 Non-White News Editorial Employment in White-Owned Daily Newspapers and Commercial Broadcasting Stations, 1992

News Medium	Estimated Total Employment	Percentage Blacks	Percentage Latinos	Percentage Asians	Percentage Native Americans	Total Percentage
Newspapers	54,530	4.8	2.6	1.7	0.3	9.4
Radio	15,670	4.7	3.2	2.2	0.6	11.3
Television	23,800	10.0	6.0	2.0	0.5	18.5

SOURCE: Based on research compiled by the American Society of Newspaper Editors and the Radio-Television News Directors Association.

TABLE 9.4 Percentage of Each Non-White Group of All Non-Whites Employed in White-Owned Daily Newspapers and Commercial Broadcasting Stations, 1982 and 1992

	Newspapers		*Radio*		*Television*	
	1982	*1992*	*1982*	*1992*	*1982*	*1992*
Blacks	56	51	70	42	69	54
Latinos	24	28	21	28	20	32
Asians	16	18	3	19	8	11
Native Americans	4	3	6	11	3	3

SOURCE: Based on research compiled by the American Society of Newspaper Editors and the Radio-Television News Directors Association.

of hiring non-White staff members and defended their absence from the newsroom. Among the reasons cited by such editors, who responded to the American Society of Newspaper Editors survey, was that they believed hiring people of color would lower the standards of their newspaper. "Generally, hiring minorities means reducing standards temporarily. Except for one reporter and one news editor, every minority person we've hired in 10 years was less qualified than a concurrently available White," said the editor of one of the largest Midwestern daily newspapers.[7] The discussion about qualifications of people of color to perform as journalists has been a sensitive one on a number of fronts. Even the Kerner report noted that news media officials complained that too few "qualified" minorities were available for hire. The implications raised the ire of some who observed that people of color have found success in fields ranging from medicine to engineering to law and the arts—and more—but somehow are not "qualified" to be writers, reporters, and editors for news media. On that issue one White newspaper editor agreed. "The business isn't magic. Mostly, it's trial-and-error training. If the word skills are adequate, any minority can be trained to do any newsroom task that any non-minority can do."[8] In 1982, *Columbia Journalism Review* reported that an angry exchange on the issue took place during a press coverage forum in New York City. In a confrontation reminiscent of Breed's study of newsroom policy (see Chapter 7 in this volume), WNBC-TV news correspondent Gabe Pressman responded to the charge of professional racism by invoking the importance of traditional standards of quality in reporting.

J. J. Gonzalez, then a reporter for WCBS-TV, rose from the audience to proclaim, "Who passes . . . judgment on competency? Come on, now! Don't tell me 'competency.' . . . When you get the competent person in, he is not allowed [to do the job]. So stop your bull!"[9]

By the 1990s, however, the debate over the notion that non-Whites were less qualified than Whites as journalists had subsided some- what in view of the overwhelming evidence of their success nation- wide. The emphasis turned instead to whether newsroom and other media efforts at multiracial inclusiveness was "politically correct" in a time when the terms *quota* and *affirmative action* were deemed passé. In the broadcasting and newspaper industries the gains that have been made must also be considered in view of the sagging U.S. economic fortunes of the early 1990s that forced staff layoffs and resulted in the closing of many newspapers and network television news bureaus. ASNE reported that newspapers hired about one- third fewer entry-level journalists in 1992 than in 1991. Thus, new hires of non-Whites reflect more significant ratios of entrance into journalism when compared to that of Whites.

Whereas the industry rationale for the dearth of non-Whites in the workforce had been, "we can't find any qualified," the issue into the 21st century appears to be, "we can't keep the qualified non-Whites we hire." The titles of the following studies and reports issued since 1990 are instructive: "Why Asian-American Journalists Leave Jour- nalism and Why They Stay" (Asian American Journalists Associa- tion, 1990), "Employee Departure Patterns in the Newspaper Indus- try" (Task Force on Minorities in the Newspaper Business, 1991), and "The Newsroom Barometer: Job Satisfaction and the Impact of Racial Diversity at U.S. Daily Newspapers" (Pease & Smith, 1991). In addition, a 1992 study of "The American Journalists in the 1990s" by Indiana University professors David Weaver and G. Cleveland Wilhoit, revealed "a serious problem of retention may be just over the horizon" and that "more than 20 percent of those [journalists] surveyed said they plan to leave the field in five years, double the figure of 1982-1983."[10] Although Weaver and Wilhoit's data include both White and non-White journalists' views of job satisfaction, it is clear that the news industry can ill afford any decrease in its very small pool of non-White professionals. One of the major reasons the percentage of non-White journalists has "treadmilled" since the 1970s is because of their departure rate from the profession. The study by Pease and Smith reveals the reasons underlying the exodus of people of color from newspaper staffs:

- 71% of non-White journalists said their papers cover issues of concern to their racial constituency marginally or poorly; 50% of White journalists agreed.
- Journalists of color (63%) were twice as likely as their White colleagues (31%) to believe that race plays a role in newsroom assignments, promotions, and advancement.
- 72% of non-Whites and 35% of Whites said newsroom managers and supervisors doubt the ability of journalists of color to perform their jobs adequately.

Pease and Smith conclude that, "These results paint a picture of newsrooms in which journalists of color feel themselves besieged because of their race. It's a picture few whites are aware of."[11] The issue of retention of non-White journalists is not new nor is it confined to newspapers. Randy Daniels, a Black journalist, left his job as a CBS correspondent in the 1980s after nearly 10 years because he saw no career advancement opportunities in the network:

> I met with every level of management at CBS News . . . over issues that specifically relate to Blacks and other minorities. . . . When it became clear to me that such meetings accomplished nothing, I chose to leave and work where my ideas were wanted and needed. . . . I have found my race an impediment to being assigned major stories across the entire spectrum of news.[12]

When viewed from the standpoint of responsibility for the education of journalists of color, the nation's secondary schools, colleges, and universities assume the spotlight. Educational institutions were asked by the Kerner Commission to develop training programs as early as the high school level with efforts to be "intensified at colleges." There have been obstacles, however, facing educators. For example, the small number of non-White students enrolled in journalism education programs partly reflects the historic discrimination against them in the news professions. As noted elsewhere in this book, the often negative and sporadic coverage of the non-White racial groups in American media has created a distrust and lack of media credibility among them. The result has been lessened interest in the field among college-bound high school students of color when compared to that of their White counterparts.

In 1992, non-White students comprised about 14% of the staffs of accredited college and university campus media, excluding those at historically Black institutions and the University of Hawaii where the student body is predominantly Asian.[13] This exceeds the percentage of non-Whites on professional newspaper staffs.

In 1978 the major academic journalism organization, the Association for Education in Journalism (now the Association for Education in Journalism and Mass Communication) adopted a "Resolution on Minorities." Eight years earlier AEJMC had created a Minorities and Communication division with a multiracial membership base, but by the time the resolution was adopted the division's membership was almost entirely comprised of academicians of color. In the 1990s, attendance at convention meetings of the Minorities and Communication (MAC) division began to reflect a broader racial spectrum, and in 1991 AEJMC established a Commission on the Status of Minorities. Efforts of the MAC division have focused on improving the cultural diversity of the journalism and mass communications curriculum and encouragement of research by and about people of color and their relationship to media.

Meanwhile, the organization charged with setting standards and certifying college journalism education programs is the Accrediting Council on Education in Journalism and Mass Communication (ACEJMC). ACEJMC utilizes 12 criteria—called standards—to measure the quality of a program. The most controversial of the criteria is Standard 12, the one that addresses issues of cultural diversity. Standard 12 requires accredited academic journalism units to develop and follow a plan for ensuring racial and gender inclusiveness. In 1994 about 95 journalism programs were accredited. Over the years Standard 12 has sparked controversy because many units have received accreditation despite not "being in compliance" with the criteria for hiring non-White faculty or enrolling students of color or for including multicultural issues in various courses in the curriculum. As for journalism faculties, it is estimated that nationally fewer than 4% of faculty members teaching journalism and mass communication courses are people of color.

Since the late 1960s there have been a number of training programs established by media organizations and professional groups to augment the journalism education establishment. Several of them owe their impetus to the Kerner Commission report. Perhaps most well known was the Summer Program for Minority Journalists. The program's history paralleled the interest level and commitment afforded the issue of multiracial inclusiveness by major media corporations and other interested parties. In the wake of the Kerner report the Ford Foundation supported creation of a training program at Columbia University briefly known as the Michelle Clark Program for Minority Journalists. The project trained and placed 70 people of color newspersons for print and broadcasting jobs from 1968 to 1974. When it lost its funding support in 1974 the program had been responsible for 20% of all journalists of color employed in daily newspapers nationally. Although the program was effective, the loss of financial support reflected the short-term commitment of the nation to the cause of news media integration. Fortunately, with seed money from the Gannett Foundation (now The Freedom Forum) the program was revived in Berkeley, California, as a newspaper-only training project under the auspices of the Institute for Journalism Education (IJE). IJE was formed by a dedicated interracial group of professionals to continue the struggle for racial parity in journalism. In 1978, IJE began a similar program to train minority editors at the University of Arizona also utilizing professionals as instructors. In 1993, IJE was renamed The Robert Maynard Institute for Journalism Education in memory of one of its founders, a Black journalist, editor, and publisher, who died earlier that year.

Several news organizations have instituted and maintained in-house training programs for aspiring journalists of color, but such efforts are few in number. Among the primarily newspaper-oriented programs are those sponsored by Capital Cities Communications, Gannett Newspapers, Knight-Ridder, and the Times-Mirror Co. Radio and television organizations, like many newspaper entities, have developed student internship and training programs for college students that in some instances may lead to permanent employment.

Analysis

The hiring records of the motion picture and television entertainment industries was found to be poor by federal agencies that conducted investigations during the late 1960s through the early 1980s. People of color continued to be scarce into the mid-1980s as workers in Hollywood trade unions. But by the 1990s their numbers had increased substantially to nearly approximate the percentage of non-Whites in the general population. Broadcasters, particularly in television, were the first to react to federal pressures because of the licensing power of the FCC. But, although their hiring rate initially exceeded that of companion media industries, broadcasters were caught cheating in reporting racial hiring statistics. One example was the ploy of counting non-White female employees twice, so-called two-fers, in an effort to pad hiring figures. In television, people of color were found primarily in visible "on-air" positions but were generally not found in decision-making management jobs.

Meanwhile in the nation's newsrooms, daily newspapers were the most grudging employers of people of color and maintained the lowest non-White employment rate of any media industry segment. In 1970 less than 1% of newspaper journalists were non-Whites and in 1985 the industry was still short of 6% and losing ground. Perhaps indicative of why daily newspapers lagged in this regard was the openly expressed attitude by some editors that they had neither the desire nor responsibility to integrate the profession. Broadcast industry hiring of journalists of color took a backseat to that of women in the late 1970s and 1980s. Coincidentally, as hiring of non-Whites slowed, White women were making rapid progress in assuming positions in both management and other job categories.

In the 1990s, the collegiate journalism education establishment, media organizations, and private institutions still scramble to provide opportunities for more people of color to enter the profession. But the slow rate of news media integration—with little penetration into power management levels—is a precursor to non-White attrition in the workforce. Meanwhile, journalists of color are leaving the profession over the lack of inclusiveness of perspective in news coverage and charging their superiors with a lack of respect for their skills. Predictably, the result is media product that continues to distort the reality of the United States' multiracial society.

Notes

1. U.S. Equal Employment Opportunity Commission, "Hearings Before the Equal Employment Opportunity Commission on Utilization of Minority and Women Workers in Certain Major Industries" (Los Angeles, March 12-14, 1969), p. 352.

2. U.S. Commission on Civil Rights, "Hearing Before the United States Commission on Civil Rights" (Los Angeles, March 16, 1977).

3. U.S. Commission on Civil Rights, "Window Dressing on the Set: Women and Minorities in Television" (August 1977).

4. Ralph Jennings and Veronica Jefferson, "Television Station Employment Practices: The Status of Minorities and Women, 1974," United Church of Christ, Office of Communications, New York (December 1975), p. 11.

5. Cynthia Alperowitz, "Fighting TV Stereotypes: An ACT Handbook," Action for Children's Television (Newtonville, MA, 1983).

6. David Weaver and G. Cleveland Wilhoit, *The American Journalist in the 1990s* (Arlington, VA: The Freedom Forum, November 1992).

7. American Society of Newspaper Editors, "Minorities and Newspapers: A Report by the Committee on Minorities" (Reston, VA, May 1982), p. 34.

8. American Society of Newspaper Editors, "Minorities and Newspapers," p. 35.

9. Michael Massing, "Blackout in Television," *Columbia Journalism Review* (November/December 1982), p. 38.

10. David Weaver and G. Cleveland Wilhoit, *The American Journalist*.

11. Ted Pease and J. Frazier Smith, *The Newsroom Barometer: Job Satisfaction and the Impact of Racial Diversity at U.S. Daily Newspapers* [Study] (Ohio University, Athens, 1991).

12. Michael Massing, "Blackout in Television," p. 39.

13. Kent State University School of Journalism and Mass Communication, "Third Census of Minorities in College Media" (Kent, OH, Kent State University, 1993).

Advocacy

Pressuring the Media to Change

The year was 1827 and the words appear in the first issue of *Freedom's Journal*, the first newspaper published by Black Americans:

> The peculiarities of this Journal, renders it important that we should advertise to the world our motives by which we are actuated, and the objects which we contemplate. . . . We wish to plead our own cause. . . . Too long has the publick been deceived by misrepresentations, in things which concern us dearly. . . . From the press and the pulpit we have suffered much by being incorrectly represented.[1]

Thus, from the beginning it was obvious that one of the primary objectives of the Black press was to protest and counter the negative and false reportage of the White press. We shall see that Blacks were not alone in exercising the option of "advocacy" of their own cause as a response to White media and, furthermore, that media advocacy by people of color has long-standing historical roots. But first, let us put the issue in perspective. We have established in previous chapters the nature of White-owned media and their treatment of other cultural groups. The social and cultural imperative that people of color communicate en masse is an issue of survival. Faced with Anglo-centric mass media tainted by racism and insensitive to their needs, non-Whites in the United States have three options: (a) they may develop and maintain their own alternative communications media; (b) they may seek access into mainstream media through employment; and (c) they may apply pressure techniques of various forms to effect changes in mainstream media content as it relates to them. These three options are related and have been utilized both independently and in combination with each other. For example, people of color who have obtained professional employment in White media often form organizations that work to change the portrayal or news coverage of non-White cultural groups. Or, a medium owned by people of color may protest inequities it finds in White media, as was the case with *Freedom's Journal*. We have discussed the first two options in Chapters 8 and 9. In this chapter we shall look at the advocacy option and complete the circle of media activism by non-Whites.

Nearly a century after the appearance of *Freedom's Journal*, the Black press was still publicly defending its constituency against the denigrating reporting of the White press. In 1919 the Black weekly *Wichita Protest* complained about the racial coverage of the Associated Press:

> Every newspaper editor of our group in the country knows that the Associated Press, the leading news distributing service of the country, has carried on a policy of discrimination in favor of the whites and against the blacks, and is doing it daily now. The Associated Negro Press is in receipt of correspondence from editors in various sections of the country decrying the way in which the Associated Press writes its stories of happenings where Colored people are affected.[2]

Even renowned Black spokesman Booker T. Washington spoke frequently of the poor coverage his speeches received from the White press. A Black journalist reported in 1916 Washington's lament that his successful speeches before large crowds, normally expected to receive front-page attention in the White press, would be relegated to the last page and given an inch or so of space. Instead, the front page would invariably be given to considerable reporting of a Black person involved in a minor criminal offense.[3]

There was advocacy for change from the earliest days of the motion picture industry. In 1911 the Spanish-language weekly *La Crònica* of Laredo, Texas, launched a campaign against the numerous movies shown throughout the state that denigrated both Mexicans and Native American Indians. The period marked the beginning of the heyday of Western movies. Movie screens were filled with images of "greasers" and "savage" Indians who were brought to justice by White cowboy heroes. Several prominent members of the Native American community wrote protest letters to the Bureau of Indian Affairs in Washington, D.C., over the images such movies projected of their people. *La Crònica* wrote:

> We are not surprised about the complaint of the North American Indians . . . because the Mexicans can make the same complaint . . . and other Latin races, who are generally the only and most defamed in these sensational American movies (such as are seen on the Texas border) . . . that serve only to show the level of culture of the learned makers of films, who have no more ingenuity except to think of scenes with many bullets, horses, 'cowboys' and then it's over.[4]

La Crònica proceeded to call for support from other Texas Mexican newspapers in urging an end to the offensive movies. Earlier the paper had addressed the negative effects such movies had upon its community.

> We judge these with much indignation and condemn them with all our energy . . . all exhibitions that make ridicule of the Mexican . . . because the showing of these facts are indelibly recorded in the minds of the children and this contributes very much to the development of the dislike with which other races see the Mexican race, who the film company has chosen to make fun of.[5]

In addition, the paper sought to persuade Texas theater owners not to acquire and show the films and to follow the lead of two Latinos who wrote letters to filmmakers to cancel further shipments to their theaters. *La Crònica* wrote that Latino families often reacted to negative stereotypes by leaving the theaters when they saw such portrayals and roles that "in reality [don't] fit us."[6] The paper noted that it would "with pleasure" publish the names of film companies that rejected movies denigrating Mexicans.

The first generation of Chinese immigrants who settled primarily in California were, for the most part, unsophisticated laborers whose immediate concern was survival in a new and hostile Anglo-Saxon world. Because they were not made to feel a part of American culture and because most were from the uneducated working class in China, aside from relatively mild protestations in the *Golden Hills' News* they did not often express displeasure of their treatment by Whites in written form. As small "Chinatown" enclaves developed in settlements in California and the Far West, the Chinese immigrants sought internal refuge and protection from the ravages of racism. They dared not, given their small numbers and immigrant status, publicly protest too vociferously against their hosts whose image of them as inferior precluded tolerance of criticism. The second wave of Chinese immigrants, however, included a number of representatives from China's upper classes. These people were educated and were not affected by the anti-Chinese immigration laws passed prior to 1900. They were diplomats, scholars, and prosperous merchants and despite their interest in promoting closer economic and political ties with the United States, some expressed disapproval of White racism against them in writing. One such writer was Wu Tingfang, a Chinese diplomat who lived in America for nearly a decade. Wu wrote his book "America Through the Spectacles of an Oriental Diplomat" in 1914. By that time Sax Rohmer's fictional and diabolical Chinese character, Dr. Fu Manchu, was 4 years old and the negative stereotype had found White Americans eager to adopt his imagery to existing racial prejudices against the Chinese. Ever the diplomat, Wu asked forgiveness if his "impartial and candid observations" should offend American readers:

> American readers will forgive me if they find some opinions they cannot endure. I assure them they were not formed hastily or unkindly. Indeed, I should not be a sincere friend were I to picture their country as a perfect paradise, or were I to gloss over what seem to me to be their defects.[7]

Despite this early warning in his book, Wu's criticisms were generally innocuous. He made it clear, however, that he opposed the racism against Blacks and Chinese he had observed in America. He tried to appeal to rationality among his White readers by arguing that they could not be racially superior to the Chinese, whose rich culture and intellectual history merited respect throughout the rest of the world.

There are numerous other incidents throughout American history in which people of color expressed their disfavor with White media as a means of advocating change in their treatment by them. Such activity has included every non-White cultural group and every form of mass communication media. The methods of advocacy have ranged from boycotts to letter-writing campaigns and from monitoring White media content to seeking legal redress of grievances, as well as other techniques.

Advocacy activists received a major boost when the Civil Rights Act was enacted in 1964. For the first time the weight of law added clout to media activists who sought change via employment in the media. Interestingly, it was often difficult to convince people of color that necessary changes could be made in media institutions by pursuing legal channels. The period of the late 1960s through the mid-1970s was marked by sit-in demonstrations, street rallies, marches, and picket lines. Many of those techniques had proven effective. The legal establishment, which included law enforcement agencies, prosecutors, lawyers, and judges, was seen by many non-Whites as a major contributor to the problems they were addressing. The suggestion that working through the legal system would result in the changes they sought was a difficult proposition to sell. Ultimately, however, the legal system paved the way for success in addressing the mass media issues of concern.

As we have noted elsewhere in this book, people of color were able to effect changes much more rapidly in broadcasting because Federal Communications Commission (FCC) employment guidelines for broadcast licensees are much more stringent than those of the Equal Employment Opportunities Commission, the federal body to which newspapers are answerable. In addition, other social, economic, and political forces began to bear upon mass media institutions. Although he was referring to the political process, futurist John Naisbitt captured the essence of why people of color were able to exert considerable leverage in the effort to improve their lot in media. The issue is related to racial pluralism and the trend toward decentralization in the United States. According to Naisbitt in his book, *Megatrends*:

> The key to decentralization of political power in the United States today is local action. Localized political power is not delegated from the federal level to the state, municipal, or neighborhood levels. Rather, it

stems from the initiatives taken by the state or neighborhood in the absence of an effective top-down solution. . . . Successful initiatives hammered out at the local level have staying power. Local solutions are resistant to top-down intervention and become models for others still grappling with the problems.[8]

How decentralization through technology and economics is generally affecting mass media in America is more thoroughly discussed in the next chapter. Here, we shall examine how multicultural advocates, working at the local level and using the force of law, began making an impact on mass media in the late 1960s. In some respects their successes are reminiscent of how the populist movement of the 1830s drastically altered communications media and entertainment in the United States, with the exception that meaningful change often had to be won in hard-fought courtroom battles.

Broadcasting

The advocacy story for non-Whites in broadcasting began with the United Church of Christ's Office of Communication. The United Church of Christ (UCC) had a long-standing interest in both civil rights and freedom of religious and other forms of expression. It committed its resources to such efforts in the United States and in various other nations. Generally, the organization, a coalition of Protestant denominations, has dedicated itself to the proposition that the communications media should operate under Judeo-Christian principles. It considers mass media to be a missionary sphere of interest. UCC's Office of Communication was the organizational arm assigned to the task of media advocacy. It was responsible for landmark legal decisions that changed the American broadcasting industry and its regulatory agency, the Federal Communications Commission (FCC), in ways even beyond the scope of racial concerns.

The first major case involved radio station WLBT in Jackson, Mississippi, in the 1960s. WLBT had incurred the wrath of Jackson's Black community for a number of years because of its discriminatory racial practices that included on-air references to Black people as "niggers" and refusal to carry a network show on race relations by

airing a sign that read, "Sorry, Cable Trouble" during the scheduled
time slot. Black people made up some 45% of the station's service
area audience. The station openly advocated racial segregation.
UCC became involved, among other reasons because it had a congre-
gation in near-by Tougaloo, Mississippi, and Blacks made up a significant portion of the membership. When WLBT began to attack
local civil rights activity in which church members were involved,
UCC took up the legal challenge of the station's right to hold an FCC
license by filing a petition to deny its renewal in 1964. Under the
social, political, and economic conditions of the time, local Blacks
faced reprisal and likely violence had they attempted to challenge
WLBT strictly as a local effort. The crux of the legal case was the FCC
requirement (established by the Communications Act of 1934) that
all licensees broadcast "in the public interest, convenience and
necessity." On the surface, it appeared that Black residents of Jackson and the UCC would have little trouble preventing WLBT from
retaining its license assuming their well-documented case was adequately presented. Unfortunately, although FCC rules allowed for
license challenges, only a minuscule fraction of license challenges
had ever been successfully upheld since the agency's inception. As
the subsequent legal developments showed, the FCC had evolved
into a protector of broadcasters' instead of the public's rights. When
the UCC and representatives of Jackson's Black community appeared before the FCC, the agency denied them "standing" to even
present their petition on grounds they had no "interest" (financial)
in the license renewal procedure. The FCC renewed WLBT's license
but the UCC filed suit in the U.S. Court of Appeals, which granted
standing to the complainants and ordered the FCC to hold a full
hearing of their case. The court maintained that members of WLBT's
audience most certainly had standing because as consumers they
had an interest in local broadcasting content over public airwaves.
In fact, the court's position was that the FCC could not do its job
without the assistance of the public in determining public interest.
Despite participation in the hearing process, the UCC was distressed
when the FCC granted a license renewal to WLBT on a 1-year pro-
bationary status.

Believing the FCC decision to be improper and unfair, the UCC
once again took the issue to the Court of Appeals and found relief.

In harsh language that took the FCC to task for its shoddy treatment of the petitioners, the court took matters into its own hands and denied WLBT the license. Significant also was the court's ruling that public petitioners should not bear the burden of proof in such cases but rather that the licensee must be able to show it handled its license privilege in a responsible manner. Moreover, the court ordered the denial on the grounds that the Fairness Doctrine had been violated and that WLBT practiced racial discrimination in programming and hiring—all extremely important issues for non-White groups. Another important right, the right of standing in FCC license hearings was, as noted, won in the initial phase of the case.

The UCC was also instrumental in a case involving Native American Indians in Rosebud, South Dakota.[9] Rosebud is a Sioux reservation whose inhabitants undertook a legal action against two South Dakota television stations, KELO and KPLO, that reached a combined 90% of the broadcast audience in the state during the 1950s and 1960s. KPLO became a virtual satellite to KELO, and by the mid-1960s was originating little or no local programming to serve the interests and needs of the Rosebud Sioux. The UCC assisted in filing a petition to deny license against KELO, which resulted in the negotiation of agreements with both stations. The agreements called for program changes and the employment of five Native Americans to full-time positions in broadcasting.

The concept of advocacy groups and the broadcast licensees they have challenged reaching agreement via negotiated settlement set the stage for the last major UCC-inspired milestone we shall consider. In a 1968 case involving local citizen's groups in Texarkana, Texas, with support from UCC, the license of KTAL television was challenged by a petition to deny its renewal. The station's owners negotiated a settlement that resulted in withdrawal of the petition. Part of the agreement called for reimbursement of legal expenses to UCC incurred during the process. The FCC, however, refused payment of the reimbursement, citing the possibility of encouraging frivolous lawsuits in the future and the potential for overpayment of such expenses. The FCC also feared the public interest merits of petition-to-deny cases could be overshadowed by the financial ramifications. Again, UCC took the issue before the appeals court and was granted a ruling that held negotiated reimbursements to be valid in instances where the petition-to-deny case is bona fide and the public interest has been served. The ruling gave advocacy groups added bargaining power (broadcasters have more at stake if they choose to draw out a proceeding in hope the citizens would exhaust their funds) and encouraged challenged licensees to negotiate settlements more quickly to avoid the more lengthy and expensive process of a fully litigated case.

A capsule review of the typical multicultural advocacy group (or other local citizen's group) procedure for prompting change in broadcasting was basically as follows. If it could be shown that racial discrimination existed in programming, employment or other areas detrimental to the public interest, a "petition to deny" the station's license renewal would be filed with the FCC. If the petition reached a hearing at the FCC, the licensee bore the burden of showing how its practices were, indeed, in the best interests of the community it served. That was because local citizens' groups had "standing" as interested parties to the license renewal process. If the citizens' advocacy group challenge was upheld, the broadcaster faced loss of its license or an arrangement could be made to ensure that the wrongs were rectified. If, however, the challenging group and the licensee negotiated a settlement prior to a hearing before the FCC, the challengers could withdraw the petition-to-deny action and seek reimbursement of legal expenses incurred. By the mid-1980s more than 100 such actions had been initiated, including some by other groups benefiting from precedents established by people of color. With deregulation and relaxation of enforcement, license challenges and other actions before the FCC were much less a factor in advocacy efforts in the late 1980s and 1990s. Nevertheless, FCC data revealed that in 1978 people of color owned about 0.5% of all commercial broadcast stations in the United States, but by 1994 the figure had increased to 3%.

Newspapers

Although newspapers operate under the less demanding guidelines of the Equal Employment Opportunities Commission and their response to grievances by people of color has been relatively slow, the advocacy movement has made inroads. Some of the credit must also go to the advocacy efforts directed toward broadcasting stations, because many of them are owned by large communications industry organizations with properties in print, broadcast, and other media. In 1980, for example, the Times-Mirror Company (owner of the *Los Angeles Times, Dallas Times-Herald,* and *Newsday,* among other newspapers) reached a negotiated settlement with the National Black Media Coalition (NBMC) over a purchase transaction of several broadcasting stations. The settlement not only addressed rectification of non-White employment and programming shortcomings existing in the broadcast operations Times-Mirror was purchasing, but included the appointment of a Black and a Latino to the company's board of directors. The company also agreed to provide scholarships for journalism and broadcasting students attending predominately Black colleges located near the newly acquired broadcast stations. In addition, several other employment and training programs were funded as a result of the agreement. (The agreement was made possible because citizen advocacy groups could also intervene when broadcast licenses were transferred, as in a change of ownership, as well as when licenses were considered for renewal.)

In the early 1980s two major events signaled the beginning of a more committed effort to increase multiculturalism in American newspaper staffs. Legal actions brought against the *New York Times* and the Associated Press forced the two news organizations to hire more people of color in the hope that more culturally sensitive coverage in the newspaper press would follow. That hope was founded on the premise that successful legal action—particularly when large, respected institutions were involved—would spur others because of the fear they, too, might be vulnerable to similar legal actions.

Individual activists also have aimed their efforts directly at newspapers and achieved some success in keeping the issue before the industry. Among the leaders who emerged in the mid-1970s to mid-1980s were Robert Maynard and his wife Nancy Hicks Maynard (instrumental in founding the Institute for Journalism Education, now known as The Robert Maynard Institute for Journalism Education, among other efforts); Jay T. Harris (who conducted demographic studies of employment in newspapers for the American Society of

Newspaper Editors from 1978 to 1983), Gerald Garcia (an executive with Gannett Newspapers), and Albert Fitzpatrick (an executive with Knight-Ridder Newspapers).

Perhaps most influential of all was a White executive, Gerald M. Sass of the Frank E. Gannett Newspaper Foundation (now The Freedom Forum), who was instrumental in the expenditure of more than $4 million in grants for multicultural programs in the newspaper industry between 1975 and 1985. Through the foundation Sass helped provide financial support to the Institute for Journalism Education, the California Chicano News Media Association, the Asian American Journalists Association, the Native American Journalists Association, the National Association of Black Journalists, and the National Association of Hispanic Journalists, among others.

The efforts of these and other advocates for multiculturalism in American daily newspapers were responsible for most of the progress that was made in the 1980s. They prompted the American Society of Newspaper Editors (ASNE) to adopt in 1978 the goal to have the nation's non-White newsroom population equal in percentage to that in the U.S. population by the year 2000. Although that goal is not likely to be met, ASNE has maintained an active institutional commitment to multiculturalism since 1977 through regional job fairs and an annual survey of newsroom employment. Into the mid-1990s the Newspaper Association of America (NAA) and the Associated Press Managing Editors (APME) are among the professional print media trade associations that maintain a profile of involvement in the move to multiculturalism. The Dow Jones Newspaper Fund has several programs for aspiring newspaper journalists of color including efforts aimed at high school students. It is among several corporate or private foundation sponsored endeavors focusing on various aspects of the issue on behalf of the newspaper industry.

The Multimedia Approach

A significant advocacy movement of the 1980s involved the resource of non-White professionals who succeeded in mainstream newspapers or electronic broadcast media but who were personally aware of, and keenly affected by, the biases that non-Whites encounter on the job. At the same time, they maintained a commitment to see other people of color join them in the profession. The result was the formation of national professional associations for journalists of color with membership categories open to practitioners in print and electronic media as well as related fields. Among them were the National Association of Black Journalists, the National Association of Hispanic Journalists, the Asian American Journalists Association, and the Native American Journalists Association. Each works separately but cooperatively to improve working conditions, increase job opportunities, and sponsor scholarships for promising students. The organizations hold national and regional conventions at which seminars and workshops are presented on issues relevant to news professionals of color. In 1994 the groups cosponsored the first national "Unity" conference in Atlanta, Georgia, where a multicultural gathering of more than 5,000 journalists convened to assess progress and strategize plans for the future as it relates to the role of people of color in communications media. The conference was covered nationally by the mainstream press throughout its 5-day span and was a visible demonstration of the positive impact multicultural advocates had made on media industries over the previous two decades.

As documented in previous chapters, anyone looking critically at film and television portrayals of people of color in the mid-1990s would still find ample cause for change. In addition, the employment of people of color in the various trades and crafts responsible for movies and entertainment television remains low. The number of strong, meaningful character roles and script plots is sporadic. That state of affairs is not for lack of multicultural activism among those who are part of the industry, however. Over the years people of color have organized caucuses in the Directors Guild, the Writers Guild, and the Screen Actors Guild. Professional actors and other artisans speak out frequently on the plight of non-White artists, but it is difficult to ascertain their effectiveness. Among the groups historically addressing these issues on the West Coast where they could apply direct pressure to Hollywood were The Media Forum, Nosotros, and Asian Americans for Fair Media. The question is whether conditions would be worse were it not for the efforts of those who speak out for multicultural inclusion and sensitivity in entertainment.

As technology brings new forms of communication into use there will be a need for advocacy voices in public policy to ensure that people of color—particularly those in lower income categories—are active participants in new information delivery systems.

Advocacy in Education

The Association for Education in Journalism and Mass Communication (AEJMC) is the primary organization representing college and university journalism and mass communication education in the United States. Nationally, some 90% of all full-time academic instructors in the discipline are White. In 1968, under the prodding of Lionel C. Barrow, Jr. (who had written an open letter to the organization's convention urging the journalism education establishment to end its de facto segregation against non-Whites), an ad hoc committee was formed by resolution to bring "minority group members into [the AEJ] pipeline."[10] A comprehensive set of multiculturally related goals was established by AEJMC (called the Association for Education in Journalism until 1982). Goals included raising of monies for 500 non-White student scholarships for 1969-1970 and the development of curriculum changes to reflect the contributions of non-White groups in America and media reporting of those contributions. In 1971 the association's Minorities and Communication division (MAC) was created. Barrow, who became dean of the school of communications at Howard University, was the division's first head. MAC's membership came to reflect multiculturalism and included a number of active White members. Increasingly over the years the division became the conscience of the larger body, and the ideals and goals under which MAC was founded became distant memories. The ambitious goals were never achieved but the attitude of the association paralleled that of American society when the initial rush of the civil rights movement had passed. Basically the association's members responded as if it were MAC's job alone to handle multicultural affairs. In 1978, 10 years after the creation of the ad hoc committee that lead to MAC's birth, AEJMC enacted another "Resolution on Minorities" but by 1985 much of its promise, too, was unfulfilled. In 1991 AEJMC elected its first non-White president when Tony Atwater of Rutgers University assumed the leadership mantle for a year. That same year, perhaps in recognition of the unremarkable progress of multiculturalism in the journalism/mass communications academy, AEJMC established a Commission on the Status of Minorities to place additional emphasis on the problem. Meanwhile, the Minorities and Communication division continued to press for a greater multicultural presence in journalism and mass communication education through curriculum pluralization, expanded research, and the maintenance and development of service programs.

In the mid-1980s, partly spurred by publication of the first edition of this book, a significant number of journalism and mass communication academic units began offering courses on the role of non-White groups in communications history and response to their treatment in the Anglocentric media. Other instructional materials, including textbook supplements and videotape presentations, were developed to meet the increased interest in the subject. The Accrediting Council on Education in Journalism and Mass Communication (ACEJMC) incorporated recognition of multicultural inclusion in faculty hiring and curriculum as part of accrediting standards. Despite the fact that the American journalism academy remained at least 90% White on the brink of the 21st century, there is no record of any college or university having lost its accreditation for lack of multicultural representation on its faculty, although a few have been afforded 1-year provisional accreditation to improve their record or lose accreditation. The number of non-White doctoral graduates in journalism and mass communication in the mid-1990s, however, remained less than a trickle for the "pipeline" mentioned in AEJ's 1968 "minorities" resolution.

Analysis

Throughout their experiences in American society peoples of color have expressed their discontent with the treatment they received from Anglocentric media industries. Non-Whites believed it was necessary to protect themselves from the harmful effects of the distorted portrayals and negative news reporting of American mass media. Their responses took several forms but the object was the same—they wanted to change the status quo that had offended and disturbed them. Each group developed advocates who fought for changes and reform of White media. With the passage of the Civil Rights Act in 1964, legal avenues were opened along which the advocacy activists could drive their point. Through the leverage provided by federal regulation of the broadcasting industry, major legal victories were won and some of the worst offenders were driven off the air. Meanwhile, the American free enterprise philosophy, which encouraged multiple business ownership and the development of conglomerates, ushered in the concept of cross-media ownership. Where broadcast licensees and newspaper groups shared common ownership, multicultural advocates had an opportunity to affect the slow-to-integrate newspaper industry.

Individual professional activists stimulated major White media organizations and trade associations to fund newspaper integration efforts. They served to "keep the industry's feet to the fire" on the issues of multicultural hiring, training, and coverage. Meanwhile, professional journalists of color, who had benefitted from the activists' efforts to open doors to employment, began forming their own organizations on the local, regional, and national levels that, in turn, became empowered institutional advocates for the entire communications spectrum. Although the film and entertainment television industries have multicultural advocacy groups as well as articulate spokespersons among Hollywood actors, little visible progress is apparent when the end products are considered. Technology and the trend toward specialized audience media may force changes in the industry as non-Whites continue to be desirable target audiences for economic reasons.

College and university educators, responsible for the training and ethical development of young mass media professionals, have been slow to meet the challenge of multiculturalism for an increasingly pluralistic American society. Although the Association for Education in Journalism and Mass Communication has had one African American president, its record shows little more than two resolutions, the creation of a "minorities" division, and a special commission since the issue emerged in the late 1960s. Despite the inclusion of multicultural requirements as criteria for the accreditation of journalism and mass communication programs in American colleges, the academic journalism and mass communication profession remained virtually all White into the mid-1990s and course offerings, for the most part, showed minimal progress toward multicultural inclusion in the curriculum.

Notes

1. "To Our Patrons," *Freedom's Journal* ([New York] March 16, 1827), p. 1.
2. Frederick G. Detweiler, *The Negro Press in the United States* (Chicago: University of Chicago Press, 1922), p. 149.
3. Detweiler, *The Negro Press in the United States*, p. 150.
4. Translation from Spanish cited in "Stereotyping and Chicano Resistance: An Historical Dimension," José E. Limon, *Aztlàn* (Vol. 4, No. 2, Fall 1973), p. 263.
5. Limon, "Stereotyping and Chicano Resistance," p. 263.
6. Limon, "Stereotyping and Chicano Resistance," p. 263.
7. Cited in Elaine H. Kim, *Asian American Literature* (Philadelphia: Temple University Press, 1982), p. 31.
8. John Naisbitt, *Megatrends* (New York: Warner Books, 1982), p. 112.
9. Emil Ward, "Advocating the Minority Interest: Actors and Cases," in Bernard Rubin, Ed., *Small Voices and Great Triumphs* (New York: Praeger, 1980), p. 250.
10. Lionel C. Barrow, Jr., *The Minorities and Communication Division—The Beginning,* a paper delivered before the Minorities and Communication Division, Association for Education in Journalism at the 63rd Annual AEJ Conference, Boston University, August 1980.

Conclusion

Class Communication
in Multicultural America

The 1990s have continued the evolution of communication media from mass communication in the years prior to the 1980s to class communication in the 1990s and beyond. Though some media, such as general circulation daily newspapers and prime-time network television, have continued to seek and attract mass audiences, they have experienced a steady decline in audience size and share when compared with media targeting desired classes of readers and viewers within the mass audience. General circulation newspapers have tried to keep the mass audience in their communities by targeting sections to certain classes of readers based on where they live, what their interests are, or what language they prefer. In their efforts to survive and thrive, newspapers strengthened these changes in the mid-1990s.

> In 1994, American newspapers worked perhaps more furiously than they ever have to reinvent themselves as a mass medium, but a mass medium that appeals to an increasingly divergent population and appeals individually to persons of any age, color, ethnic origin, sexual orientation or category yet to be defined,

reported an article in *Editor & Publisher*, the newspaper's trade magazine, in 1995.[1] Among the examples of the industry's efforts to attract desired classes of readers the article cited newspaper sections or articles in Spanish, Portuguese, and Creole produced by the *Miami Herald* and a section directed to Generation X readers in the Fort Lauderdale *Sun-Sentinel*.

Faced with steadily declining audience shares, prime-time network television programs were also increasingly geared to pull certain audience segments or build a large audience by having an ensemble cast or concurrent plots that each attract different classes of audience segments. Viewers were spending more time with television, but preferred to spend more of that time watching cable television, independent stations, or videocassettes. Television programs targeting racial and ethnic audiences that had long been overlooked by the networks were particularly popular and profitable.

"Quietly growing and prospering during the past year while the English-language networks experienced turmoil and uncertainty, the Spanish-language networks and the Hispanic television marketplace in general are in the midst of a boom," reported *Broadcasting & Cable* magazine in 1995. The magazine described the Univision network as being "atop an industry that, unlike its English-language counterparts, is on the grow, adding viewers and building viewer loyalty."[2]

Despite efforts to compete against media that attracted audience by race, culture, and class, by the mid-1990s both general circulation daily newspapers and prime-time evening network television programs continued to lose audiences to media that targeted different classes within the mass audience. In addition, the growth of racial and cultural diversity, the hiring progress and upward mobility of people of color spurred by pressures on the communication industry, the increased importance of racial and cultural audience segments to advertisers, and the potential for new media made possible by emerging communication technologies also combined to construct a media mosaic more racially diverse than in the past. As the last mass audience media of prime-time television and general circulation daily newspapers were losing audience the public in general was moving to more personal media in the form of multiple cable television channels, on-line computer services, multiscreen movie theaters, videocassettes, specialized magazines, and other forms of targeted media made possible by new technology.

Communication media had moved from the era of attracting the audience masses to targeting the audience classes, from mass communication to class communication, and from an approach of "one size fits all" to one of "we do it all for you." To gain and retain audiences in an increasingly competitive market, media managers found they needed to offer the public more of a choice and less of a chance that, when they turned on the television, went to the movies, or purchased a magazine, they would find something that they wanted. In the process, they found that people would pay for media content that was previously unavailable to them or that was previously subsidized by advertisers and received at little or no cost, such as on-line computer information services and pay channels on cable television.

The "pay to play" approach gained importance in the 1990s as electronic information services gained in popularity and consumers became accustomed to paying cable television charges and video-cassette rental fees for broadcast and movie content that had previously been available at little or no cost because of subsidizing in the form of advertising. This meant that in the future the public would probably have to pay for information and entertainment that was available for free or at a relatively low cost to earlier generations. As Nancy Hicks Maynard, former deputy publisher of the *Oakland Tribune*, said in a 1994 speech,

> In the new electronic environment, information products are priced for value. The most highly valued products are migrating away from subsidized and free information outlets and are moving toward paid media to command higher profits. General news is omnipresent. It has become a commodity that doesn't command high commercial value. On the other hand, specialty news does. Television sports is the best example. . . . Televised sports events are defecting from free network television to pay cable and pay-per-view delivery.[3]

Factors Forming the Future

As the United States moved into the 21st century, the development of class communication media and their relationship to racially diverse groups in the nation continued to change and was increasingly influenced by three major forces. These were not the only forces exerting influences in this arena; nor was their impact always predictable. But they exerted great influence on the ways in which media develop and interact with the racially and culturally diverse population of the United States. These forces are:

1. Growth of racial diversity in the United States
2. Technological advances in communication media
3. Targeting of audience segments by the media

In this chapter we analyze these forces in terms of their impact on racial diversity and the media. Information on some of these factors has already been covered in earlier chapters. Here we examine that information and its impact on the development of class communication media and its relationship to racial and cultural minorities in the United States.

Growth of Racial Diversity

As the data in the chapter on demographic trends demonstrate, since 1970 the United States has experienced its greatest population growth rate in the non-White populations. Lower median age; slightly larger anticipated family sizes; and continued immigration from Asia, the Caribbean, and Latin America all point to the development of a society in the United States in which racial minorities constitute a much larger percentage of the population than in the past. In some of the nation's largest cities it is already statistically incorrect to apply the term *minorities* to the non-White population, because non-Whites make up a majority of the people of those cities.

If current trends persist as forecast it is clear that the United States will continue to experience a greater growth rate in its non-White communities than in the White majority. Although it is impossible to predict exactly when the population lines will cross, it appears the United States will become a nation in which non-Whites comprise the majority of the population by the middle of the 21st century. As the racial makeup of the nation continues to change, the

Figure 11.1. Examples of magazines targeted to communities of color. *Hispanic Business* magazine covers business issues in the Latino community. *Indian Artist* is a magazine covering Native American arts and culture. *Filipinas* magazine covers Filipinos in the United States and around the world. *Emerge* is a monthly news magazine targeted to African Americans.

media and other institutions in the United States will have to respond to racial and cultural diversity to a greater extent than they
have in the past.

But projections of the available data also clearly indicate that
Whites will continue to be in the majority during the lifetime of most
people born in the 20th century. Even when they are outnumbered
by the collective strength of individual non-White groups, Whites
will continue to be the largest single racial group in the United States
for the foreseeable future. In many cities in which racial "minorities"
make up the majority, Whites are still the largest single racial group
and, in most cases, enjoy the largest share of economic and political
power. The numbers a racial group represents in the population of
a city, state, or nation does not directly translate to the amount of
power that group exercises, particularly in media ownership and
policy making for growth and pricing of new communication technologies. For all the growth of minorities in the past two decades,
in 1995 there was no metropolitan general circulation daily newspaper owned by a member of a racial minority group. The number
of major general audience media led by persons of color could be
counted on the fingers of both hands.

Finally, the growth in racial diversity will have an enduring impact
on the nation only if racial minorities retain their cultural identities
and remain "beyond the melting pot." Other groups have come to
the United States and, after a generation or two, blended into the
majority society both culturally and racially. Because of social and
legal barriers in the United States, non-Whites have not melted into
the mainstream society. In fact, for many years they had their integration severely restricted by laws limiting immigration, legislation
and court rulings curtailing their legal rights, as well as institutional
and personal acts of social and economic discrimination. Those
members of racial minority groups who have succeeded in penetrating predominately White educational institutions, professions, and
residential districts are still identifiable by physical characteristics
that distinguish them from the White majority. Retaining a cultural
identity does not mean that members of these groups must reject the
language and culture of the majority, but that they recognize that it
is not necessary to forget one language or culture in order to learn
and be successful in the ways of another. In so doing, they demonstrate

through their behavior that assimilation should not be the price for participation.

Some members of minority races have gained access through race-conscious admissions or hiring policies that since the late 1960s have placed a special priority in affording access to educational and employment opportunities to members of racial groups that have been victims of exclusion and discrimination. Although these members of the non-White population have achieved access to educational and professional arenas that were once closed to racial minorities, it is too early to predict if such advantaged minority persons will have the ability, or the desire, to shed the identity, culture, and, sometimes, language they share with others of their race. Intermarriage between members of different races is increasing and the number of persons of biracial parentage is growing. Given these factors, it is clear that the growing racial diversity of the United States will have a long-lasting impact on media and other institutions only if members of diverse racial and cultural groups continue to retain a higher degree of racial and cultural identity than the European immigrants who came to the United States in earlier decades. It is also clear that the comfortable racial and cultural categories will continue to be reexamined and adjusted to reflect the multicultural reality of the non-White population groups.

Technological Changes in Communication Media

Perhaps even more important than the racial changes taking place in the society of the United States are the worldwide changes in communication media triggered by technological advances. The past generation has witnessed fundamental changes in the technologies used in producing newspapers, television, radio, and video. Technical advances such as offset printing of daily newspapers in color, satellite transmission of cable television programs, stereo broadcasts on AM and FM radio, and the widespread use of videotape in entertainment and news programming have become commonplace only since the 1970s. Before 1970 the technologies needed to make them widely used were known only to relatively few persons with enough foresight to envision how they could be applied in the future. In addition, new technologies linked to computers, telephones, digital devices, satellites, and fiber optic lines have dramatically multiplied and personalized the media choices available to the public.

By the mid-1990s the changes wrought by these technological advances were taken as commonplace by most people living in the United States. At the same time, many persons in communities of color found themselves priced out of these technological advances or able to participate at only the most basic levels as the new technologies widened the gap between those who were information rich and those who were information poor. While children in affluent neighborhoods and schools did their homework on computers and used on-line services, lower income students were introduced to the new technologies by playing video games. The richer children used the media to create knowledge. The poorer were targets of media content developed by others.

As wide-ranging as these changes have been, they have merely set the stage for the technological and content changes that will continue the transformation of communication media in the near future. As the United States continues to become an information society, a society in which the collecting, processing, storing, and transmitting of information outstrips manufacturing or agriculture as the central economic activity, there will be continued growth in communication media and ways to make money from them. The movement of North American society into the information age has been greatly accelerated by technological advances at all steps of the information process. These new applications of technology have greatly broadened the range of communication media and the content they make available.[4]

In the 1980s a bewildering array of communication technologies were under development by large corporations and smaller entrepreneurs, with many devices being promoted as the communication technology that could dominate the others in the future.[5] But by the mid-1990s it was clear that no single technology or channel would dominate the communication media landscape of the future. Instead, people learned to pick and choose from different media, all of them affording a wider range of choices than before. In the past new technologies were billed as the key to the mass audience, but in the 1990s new media technologies and services were touted for their ability to pinpoint, target, and deliver information to targeted segments of the public and turn a profit at the same time. They made their money not from the mass audience, but by slicing, targeting, and reaching desired segments in the mass audience. These technological advances accelerated the media transition from mass communication to class communication.

Some of the technologies were completely new consumer applications: such as *cellular radio*, which offered enhanced communication for mobile telephones; *silent radio*, which transmits messages scrolling across receiving screens in public places; and *e-mail*, which permits two-way communication between persons via a central computer and personal terminals. Others were technological extensions of existing communication technologies that were already in place: such as *cable television*, which was extended into the suburbs and cities; *direct broadcast satellites*, which uses satellite transmission to beam television signals directly to homes; or *bilingual television*, which allows the audience to choose from between two audio signals for the same program. Still other new media were merely technological or regulatory changes that appeared to create new communication opportunities: such as *AM and VHF drop-in stations*, which used enhancements in telecommunications technology to allow licensing of additional radio and television stations in communities already given their quota of stations under earlier rules designed to prevent interference between stations; *videocassette recorders*, which allow the audience to record television programming and replay it in the future; and *low-power UHF stations*, which use an underutilized portion of the broadcast spectrum to allow licensing of television stations to a restricted geographic area.

These technologies afford new opportunities to racial minorities and other groups that have not enjoyed equal participation or service from existing communication media. But racial minorities will probably take part in the new technologies more as employees or users, rather than as owners or developers of the new media. This is because the major communication conglomerates have invested heavily in developing commercial applications of the new technologies. At the same time, the deregulatory attitude of the Federal Communications Commission and other federal and state agencies has allowed licenses for some new technologies to be auctioned off to the highest bidder, rather than allocated to the owner with the best ideas for using the public resource. In such an environment the advantage goes to larger corporations making money off the old technologies, such as print, movies, or broadcasting, to invest in the new technologies. Unsure about which technologies will become big moneymakers, major media corporations have spread their investments across several technologies that look promising and entered into shotgun marriages of convenience, forming partnerships between cable television systems and telephone companies, newspapers and computer software companies, and movie studios and television set manufacturers. If an investment in one technology or one marriage of convenience fails to pay off, such as CBS's investment in a cable arts channel or the joining forces of Bell Atlantic telephone company and TCI cable television, the conglomerates still have money invested in other technologies and marriages that may eventually produce profits.

But most minority investors have neither the seemingly infinite financial resources of large corporations, nor steady incomes generated by newspapers, movie studios, or broadcast stations making money off the technologies of the past. With less breadth of experience and expertise, it is difficult for them to capitalize on the new technologies at a competitive level with the major conglomerates and multinational corporations. Members of racial minority groups also have less financial resources to invest in developing commercial applications of the new technologies. For them the new technologies represent a one-shot, all-or-nothing, proposition. They can invest in a specific area, such as the low-power UHF television stations now airing Spanish-language programs provided by the Univision television network or cable television programming such as that distributed by Black Entertainment Television. Unlike the major corporations, they are unable to spread their limited capital and expertise across several new technologies.

In the 1970s it was hoped that government regulatory agencies, which license communication companies using the public's airwaves or receiving a monopoly franchise to serve a certain geographic area, would use their power to ensure that women and minorities would be owners and not just players in the new communication landscape. But the deregulatory attitude of government agencies in the 1980s and 1990s meant that the "free market" policies favoring larger corporations governed who would own and develop the new technologies. In 1995 a member of the Public Utilities Commission of California, the nation's most racially diverse state, was unable to mention a way in which minorities could become owners of new communication and information technologies regulated by the commission. He referred a question on ownership to an African American staff member, who said minorities could purchase long-distance telephone time from major corporations and then resell it to members of their own communities at a lower rate than they would be charged if they used the service directly.

Although the new technologies will continue to afford racial minorities new entry points into communication ownership, employment, and programming, people of color who enter the arena find themselves competing with major corporations. Like everything else in the free enterprise system, there are no guarantees of success. Members of racial minority groups will most likely continue to be the risk-takers who play at the greatest risk in the new technologies field. If their enterprise fails they will have to fold without being able to pick up profits from another investment or the proceeds of a previous venture. If their use of new technology succeeds they risk being taken over or copied by one of the major communication conglomerates.

But members of racial and cultural minority groups do have an advantage in their understanding of their communities that have not been well served by the communication media in the past. These gaps in telecommunication service provide the best entry point for people of color into the communications opportunities afforded by the new technologies. With a knowledge of racially and linguistically different communities, they can develop innovative uses of new technologies to serve segments of the audience that have been overlooked by the mass audience media.

In the past, minority entrepreneurs have succeeded by adapting "new" technologies such as printing and broadcasting to the unique social and economic structure of their communities. There is no reason for the future to be any different, particularly because the technologies vastly expand the opportunities for "narrowcasting" media content to specific audiences. As the range of outlets in radio, video, print, and other media continue to expand it will become increasingly important for the media to compete for audiences by narrowing both their content and appeal to attract specific segments of the mass audience, including members of racial and cultural minority groups. Thus, the movement to class communication can be to the advantage of media professionals who know and understand these communities.

Finally, the future of communication media will be determined more by content advances than by technological advances. With myriad choices, audiences will pay attention to the media that pay attention to them. Writers, editors, and producers with an ability to address the tastes and preferences of people in a multicultural audience will do more to shape the future of media than those who design the technologies to transmit those messages. The new media technologies are like plumbing. The engineers are the plumbers who will connect the pipes, but the media and information professionals will be the ones to decide what actually flows through the new communication technologies. And it is this content that will help determine which technologies prosper.

Continued Audience Segmentation and Targeting

Market segmentation, the strategy of dividing the potential consumers of a product into identifiable segments and then directing news, entertainment, and advertising through media that reach those audiences, has been an important advertising strategy since the then-new technology of television emerged as the most effective medium for reaching the mass audience in the early 1950s. Radio and magazines, which once delivered the mass audience to advertisers, were forced to survive by abandoning general audience content and, instead, targeting their media to specific segments within the mass audience. As a result, listeners turning the AM and FM radio dials in most cities will find that each station has a different programming format designed to attract a specific group of listeners. By the same token, a visit to the magazine section of a supermarket or convenience store reveals a plethora of magazines, all vying for the attention of potential readers with predefined interests. The only two mass audience magazines still surviving were begun as offshoots to other media: *Reader's Digest* and *TV Guide*.

Market segmentation is a consumer-driven sales approach in which corporations subdivide the total heterogeneous potential market for a product into smaller segments, each of which has its own homogeneous characteristics.[6] Audience segments are broken out a number of ways, by place of residence, socioeconomic status, sex, age, education, and race. Segmentation has become increasingly important for advertisers because they have found they can increase both their penetration of the audience and the sales of their products if they design advertisements geared to market segments and place them in print and broadcast media reaching those audience segments.

But more than population growth and technological advances, it is the economic mechanisms of support that control the development of media in the United States. Print and broadcast media are largely supported by advertising. When advertising is increased for a particular segment of the population, the media that reach and influence that segment gain increased advertising dollars. These dollars also make it more economically profitable for managers of existing media to consider changes to formats and content to try to attract that segment and the advertising dollars that will follow.

Media targeting communities of color have gained increased advertisement placements and profits because of this change in marketing strategy by major corporations and their advertising agencies. Because they often reach audience segments that are growing faster than the White majority, they will be even more important with advertisers in the future. Media directed to racially and culturally diverse groups will continue to grow as long as major corporations and advertising agencies take the mass audience and classify it into segments for advertising in media that penetrate and persuade those racial and cultural segments. This makes ownership of media directed toward racial and cultural minority groups more profitable and stimulates growth in these media, by both Whites and members of the targeted groups. For instance, by the mid-1990s nearly all major U.S. media corporations, including Times-Mirror, Knight-Ridder, Gannett, New York Times, NBC, Chicago Tribune, CNN, MTV, and HBO, had publications, programs, or channels directed toward Spanish-speaking audiences in the United States.[7] In the past these media had largely been owned by members of the Latino community.

Moving beyond advertising, the growth of the information society has meant that corporations and entrepreneurs have looked for audiences willing to pay for media content not available through the mass audience or advertiser-subsidized media. Thus, videocassette rentals of movies in Spanish and in languages of the countries of Asia and the Pacific Basin have become profitable, as are targeted television channels that are sometimes available only via cable television. This "pay to play" mentality moves minority-formatted media beyond advertiser support and into a dependence on the audience's ability to pay for the content.

The outlook for growth in media for racial and cultural minorities is further enhanced by the first two factors mentioned in this chapter: the growth of the United States as a racially diverse nation and the advances in communication technology. Together, these three factors point to a racially heterogeneous nation that can be divided and reached by a much wider array of communication technologies. Though such an outlook is favorable for the economic success of the minority-formatted media, it also represents a fundamental change in the role of the communication media as they relate to both the racial majority and the racial minorities in the United States.

Communication Media and the Segmented Society

The development of communication media in the United States for many decades was based on mass communication: content that overcame differences in sex, age, education, geography, race, and income in the audience and by delivering entertainment, news, and

Figure 11.2. *Indian Country Today* is a South Dakota-based national newspaper covering Native American issues in the United States. This edition includes four front-page stories by Washington correspondent Bunty Anquie.

advertising that would attract many and alienate only a few. But now the sales approach of editors, programmers, and advertisers is the opposite. Rather than wanting to address an undefined mass audience, advertisers prefer to classify the audience into subgroups and target their messages to specific audiences whose demographic profiles are known to them. They want to be able to tailor their advertising to men, women, specific age groups, the affluent, and other definable groups within the mass audience. As a result, the audience strategies of the media have changed. Media must attract the audience who can pay for the content and whom advertisers want to reach if they hope to reach that audience and sell space and time on their stations and publications. The commodity they sell to advertisers is not the amount of space or time for the advertising message, but the size and composition of the *audience* that will be exposed to the advertising message. In the old days they sold members of the audience based on their aggregate size, or mass. Today, they sell members of the audience based on their aggregate characteristics, or class.

Following the lead of the advertisers, the emphasis in media is now on market segmentation: the ability to classify audience segments, describe their demographic characteristics, and zero in on them through media content that will attract members of those classes. Rather than trying to blend all members of society into a mass audience melting pot, the advertisers have found they can have more impact with the advertising dollar if they can target their messages to specific audience segments and place advertising in media that reach that class of consumers.

Even mass audience media, such as general circulation newspapers and prime-time network television, are increasingly driven to draw specific audience segments in order to survive as effective audience and advertising vehicles. The television week and day are divided by programming designed to attract different audiences at different times of the day and different days of the week. Network prime-time television is often cited as the last mass audience medium in the United States. But prime-time television programs are increasingly dependent on the percentage of men, or women, or city dwellers, or young urban professionals in their audience. This is because figures from the A. C. Nielsen Co., which measures television audiences, showed that, on the average, prime-time network audiences dropped about 20 percentage points from the early 1980s to the early 1990s. In this period, more people were spending more time with their television sets, but they were watching cable television, independent stations, or videocassettes, not ABC, CBS, or NBC. Competition from the new Fox Television Network, Black Entertainment Television, and the Spanish-language Univision and Telemundo networks also drew from ABC, CBS, and NBC, particularly among African Americans and Latinos.

Facing a steadily declining audience, network television executives and programmers began the move from "mass appeal" to "class appeal" in the 1980s. They began to promote their audiences in terms of the demographic profiles of the people who did watch their programs and found that television programs had a better chance of staying on the air with moderate ratings if they pulled demographic groups advertisers wanted to reach into their audience. In 1985 the executive producer of the NBC program *Miami Vice*, whose audience ratings were in the bottom half of the Nielsen ratings when the program debuted in 1984, boasted "Our demos (demographics) are incredible."[8] This meant that the detective program, which incorporated a slick musical and video format, was successful in attracting a strong percentage of urban dwellers, under 35 years old; a group of affluent consumers that usually didn't watch television on *Miami Vice's* Friday night airtime. As a result, the program was attractive to advertisers wishing to reach that audience and was kept on the air for several seasons.

The emphasis on market segments and audience classifications has forced network executives to search for more refined ways of measuring and describing their audience. Raw numbers describing the size of the audience and percentage of viewers who are watching a particular program were sufficient when television was purely a mass audience medium. But the declining prime-time numbers, and the increased priority of advertisers on audience demographics, led television executives and audience measurement firms to experiment with more sophisticated devices and methodologies that could provide advertisers with what a *Daily Variety* reporter described as "more detailed demographic data that can tell them not just *which* households are watching a program in which they have purchased commercial time, but *who* is watching in that household."[9] Prodded by the entry into the United States of the British rating company AGB's people meters in the mid-1980s, the Nielsen rating company introduced its own people meter rating devices to identify each member of the household and ask each one to log-in when they begin watching television and log-out when they leave the room. In true "Big Brother" fashion, the people meter asks people to tell their television when they are watching. But, unlike the characters in George Orwell's novel, *1984*, the viewers are asked to verify their presence for the sake of audience demographics, not government control. The company also refined its survey sampling techniques to more accurately measure the viewing habits of African Americans and Latinos.

Daily newspapers, which serve a defined geographic area, were long thought to be somewhat immune to the move from mass communication to class communication, as long as their circulation figures could demonstrate that they attracted a certain percentage of the potential readers in their geographic area. Overall penetration of newspapers (the percentage of potential readers who actually read the newspaper), however, has declined steadily over the years. Newspaper advertisers also demand more demographic information on who is being exposed to their advertising messages. Newspaper executives have become increasingly concerned not only with the size, but the composition, of their readership. A key 1979 study financed by the American Newspaper Publishers Association led researchers to describe the newspaper audience not as a mass audience, but as an audience classified by numerous subsegments of the population.[10] Newspaper publishers are particularly concerned about younger, affluent readers between the ages of 18 and 34. Members of that age group are prime targets for advertisers looking for new customers; but they also read a newspaper less regularly than older, and less demographically desirable, members of the potential audience. In a 1984 article for the advertising trade magazine *Madison Avenue*, Janet Bamford commented on the importance of 18- to 34-year-old readers to newspapers and advertisers:

> But younger readers remain a desirable and lucrative audience for newspaper publishers. Advertisers want to reach them because they often have more disposable income than older adults, who may earn more, but who are also supporting a mortgage and children. Young

adults are willing to try new products, say marketers, and since they're often setting up housekeeping for the first time, they need just about everything.[11]

Newspapers have sharply increased their use of color and added special sections with emphasis on such topics as entertainment, health, sports, science, and business to draw younger readers and other more desirable audience segments. The use of special sections has been effective in attracting some younger readers and, at the same time, helping advertisers place their commercial messages next to editorial content that is targeted by topic to a specific audience segment. Most commercially successful newspapers are clearly divided each day into separate sections so the newspaper sections can be easily divided and distributed to members of the household that section should reach.

The current strategies of general circulation daily newspapers do not call for attracting the mass audience to every section of the newspaper. Just because a newspaper reaches a home does not mean each member of the household should read all of it. In fact, newspaper marketing departments and advertisers would prefer that different sections of the newspaper go to different members of the family with different demographic profiles. The old mass-audience magazines, such as *Life, Look, Colliers,* and *Saturday Evening Post,* operated under the editorial philosophy that when the magazine came into the home "nobody reads all of it, everybody reads some of it." Large newspapers today operate on a latter-day variant, with the advertising parceled out to specific sections that are supposed to subdivide the various demographic groups in the household.

But it is tough for newspapers to compete against electronic media such as television and computers for these audiences. Newspapers moved hesitantly into the electronic era in the early 1990s, first fighting the entry of cable television and telephone companies into electronic advertising and editorial content, and then launching their own electronic services as an adjunct to their newspapers. The issue facing newspaper executives in the mid-1990s was to take a look at the word *newspaper* and decide whether they saw themselves as being primarily in the *news* business or in the *paper* business. If they decided their basic product was the news they would move news to the audience through the medium that is most cost-effective and profitable, whether it be telephone lines, cable television lines, or television stations. If they decided their basic product was the paper, they would move news to the audience through home-delivered and street sales of newspapers and would try to make those newspapers as attractive and interesting as a paper medium can be.

Class communication and audience segmentation, because they are marketing tools, imply that the segments addressed are the ones that have the potential for returning advertising and sales dollars back to the advertisers and owners and, in the long run, will maintain a record of doing just that. It is not enough for an audience segment to be classified, measured, and addressed. Those who are in that group must also be attracted to the content and to the advertising of products that they purchase.

Race, Culture, and Class Communication

As advertising agencies continue to favor media that deliver the specific audience segments they want to reach, the societal role of the media has undergone a fundamental change. The communication media system once built a mass audience by looking for commonalities in a heterogeneous society. It focused on common ground and tried to overcome differences in society. It was the ladle that stirred the melting pot and refined or set aside those ingredients that did not mix, such as members of racial or cultural minority groups. But now the media seek, find, and reinforce the differences between groups in the society. The media are no longer mass media, but class media, classifying and playing to different segments of the audience and reinforcing differences between those groups to enhance the delivery of the advertising message.

Segmentation can be based on several criteria, such as geography, age groups, sex, and family life cycle.[12] In order for a portion of the audience to be segmented it must be:

1. identifiable,
2. measurable,

Figure 11.3. Asian American newspapers are often linked with publications in their homeland. This Western Edition of the Hong Kong-based *Tsing Tao Daily* offers news of the Western United States and advertisements for Northern California business seeking Chinese American clients.

3. accessible, and
4. substantial enough to be potentially profitable.

For many years minority audiences met the first three criteria, but were thought to be either too poor or too small to warrant attention by major advertisers. A 1981 marketing textbook by William and Isabella Cunningham cites segmentation based on race, religion, or national origin as possible segmentation bases in addition to the more commonly cited criteria:

> Ethnic and racial factors have been effectively used as a basis for segmenting markets. Although the U.S. is known as a great melting pot, certain groups have not been assimilated into society as quickly as others. In these situations, it has proven beneficial for firms to modify their product and promotion mix to fit the specific ethnic market.[13]

Print and broadcast media directed to racially and culturally diverse audiences have poured out surveys that argue that both the aggregate size and the collective wealth of their audiences can be translated into profits for corporations. In their desire to reach those audiences, advertising agencies have directed more and more dollars to those media and their audiences. Racial and cultural audiences meet the apparent criteria for segmentation, the minority media and their advertising agencies contend. They are identified, counted, and described by no less an authority than the U.S. Bureau of the Census. They are addressable through targeted media and, to the extent that large numbers of Latinos and Asians use languages other than English, they are unreachable through general audience media. Finally, because they are racially or culturally different from the White majority in the United States, they will carry a racial, if not cultural, identity with them for the rest of their lives.

From Mass Communication to Class Communication

Immigrants coming to the United States in the 19th and early 20th century were greeted by a plethora of newspapers in their first languages offering news from the old country and integrating them into American society. Later, radio and television served the same purpose. The role of the communication media was to build a mass audience based on commonalities. Differences between members or groups in the audience were overshadowed by the new interests and loyalties depicted and reinforced by the mass media of communication. Where the foreign language media existed, it mainly served first-generation arrivals and steadily declined in number and importance as the new arrivals and their children learned English and assimilated into the mainstream of mass society.

These media were transitional and generational, serving the first generation of immigrants and having less appeal for the second and third generation. The same was predicted for racial minority publications. In a 1954 book, one author predicted that the Spanish-language press would be extinct within 15 years. Instead, in 1970 *Editor & Publisher* reported on the continued health and expansion of Spanish-language newspapers.[14] Over the years the number of Black newspapers has declined, but the number of radio stations and magazines targeted to the Black population has increased. Media directed toward Asian Americans experienced a growth in the 1990s similar to the expansion years of Spanish-language media in the 1980s.

It could be said that these print and broadcast media directed toward racial minorities will go the way of the immigrant and foreign language media of the past; that they are a mere offshoot of the immigration from Asia and Latin America and the recent upward mobility of some Blacks. It could be argued that, as in the past, these media will serve only a transitional role in reaching racial minority audiences that are too small for the mainstream media. But such analogies would be short-sighted.

This is because references to European immigration and integration models of the past are inadequate for explaining the current demographic and communication trends in the United States. Since 1965, about 80% of the immigration to the United States has come from Asia and Latin America. These immigrants and their children are not just entering the United States at a different time and place. They are also encountering the communication media at a different stage of evolution. When the waves of European immigrants entered New York's Ellis Island, the communication media of the United

Figure 11.4. Newspapers for African Americans and other people of color have grown by covering news that is often unreported by the general audience media. This edition of the *Daily Oakland Post* in California reports about an unsung African American hero in the 1995 Oklahoma City federal building bombing.

States were truly the mass media. Their role was to address the new arrivals and the rest of society at the lowest common denominator, providing news and entertainment that would cut laterally through men and women, old and young, rich and poor, east and west, farmer and city dweller, and other social divisions by providing content that would attract many in the potential audience and alienate only a few. The audience of the masses was essential to the media because advertisers demanded that they attract a large and somewhat undifferentiated audience that could buy a wide range of products and services. But now, with class communication, the approach of the media to their audience is the opposite. The media and their advertisers now look for differences in the audiences and ways to reinforce those differences.

The impact of continued market segmentation on society is also affected by the advent of new technologies in the field of telecommunications. When television became widely available in the early 1950s it supplanted radio and magazines as the dominant mass audience medium when about 30% of the people in the United States had purchased receivers. But the new technologies now being developed are not being promoted as the new key to the mass audience, although all of them would like to maximize their penetration of the segment to which they are directed. Instead, they are billed as increasing the media's ability to address narrow audience segments that are not profitable for mass audience media. Therefore, it is possible that the new technology, when coupled with a market segmentation philosophy, will be able to serve racial and language minorities and still be profitable.

As a result, cable television (which exploded as a major communication force when it reached 30% of the television viewers in the United States in the mid-1980s) developed as a series of specialized channels offering a somewhat predictable fare of sports, movies, religion, or local programming. Like format radio that delivers a consistent sound to its audience, cable television stations are designed to provide a predictable blend of programming to those who tune in. The new technologies, which already are widening the array of media available, will be more quickly exploited if they are able to survive on a smaller audience base that responds to their advertising messages.

In order to do this they must generate more income from a smaller audience base, thus increasing the importance of requiring users to pay for information and entertainment. As the new electronic media have developed as "media for a fee" rather than "media for free," perceptive observers have warned that their low income status could leave many people of color off the information superhighway. In 1994, The Freedom Forum's senior vice president Gerald M. Sass warned those attending a National Association of Black Journalists dinner,

> We as a society are on the verge of launching the electronic version of "separate, but equal." The few available statistics suggest that the majority of users of key parts of the information superhighway are white and male. The issue is the same as 100 or 200 years ago. It's access to information.[15]

The most immediate implication of class communication in a racially diverse society is that minority groups will be more fully addressed than in a mass audience media system. A wider range of minority-formatted media will carry both advertising messages and content to groups that were previously thought to be too small or economically disadvantaged to merit serious attention. Racial and cultural groups will no longer have to depend on mass audience media that consider them only a secondary audience, if they consider them at all. To the extent that the segmented media provide entertainment and information content that serves the needs of these audiences, racial and cultural groups will benefit from this growth in media diversity.

But segmentation also means labels, labels that often mask the complexities of the people to whom they are applied. Just because a person is a member of a certain race, age, or sex does not mean that he or she thinks, lives, speaks, or consumes like other members of that group. Labels based on race, even though they may describe shared physical characteristics, do not adequately describe the complexity of Blacks, who are becoming increasingly polarized at the top and bottom of the economic ladder; Native Americans, who live in very different environments on a reservation or in a city; Latinos, who share a range of language ability and a variety of national backgrounds; and Asians, who—in addition to the differences that are similar to those of Latinos—do not share the same language. Each group is also divided by the geographic, educational, age, sex, and economic differences that divide members of all racial groups in the United States.

Media targeted to racial and cultural groups depending on market segmentation advertising act to identify characteristics that separate these groups from the majority and from each other, then reinforce those factors in their content and advertising. They also must prove that the audience they draw constitutes attractive potential consumers. Advertisers may want to target their advertising to media that reach only the affluent members of the racial group, or those in the age categories that buy their products. This means that the future of ethnic media could be dictated by their ability to attract the most lucrative segments of their racial group, not those in the greatest number or need.

Segmentation, because it is a marketing tool, will benefit those members of racial and cultural groups whose size makes them easily measured and reached, such as Blacks or Spanish-speaking Latinos. Racial groups that are smaller or harder to reach receive less attention, such as English-speaking Latinos and Native Americans in urban areas. Class communication does not mean that all racial and cultural groups will be addressed by the media, or addressed equally well. It merely means that those strata of the audience that the advertisers want to reach have a better chance of being courted by news and entertainment content than under the mass communication model.

Class Communication: Losing the Glue

But there are deeper implications to the classification and segmentation of racial and cultural groups in social fabric of the United States. Class communication can also mean that people of color become further separated, and possibly distanced, from the rest of society. Class communication points to a society in which people may be integrated in terms of the products they consume, but do not share a common culture based on the content of the entertainment or news media they use. Class communication means that society will no longer be as strongly bonded together by the media. This is a trend that affects all people in the United States who use the media, not only racial and cultural groups. The "Global Village" envisioned by communication theorist Marshall McLuhan in the 1960s is developing as a worldwide network in which people are not so much drawn together by a common media content they read, hear, or watch; but by the products they consume. We may all be members of the same village, but we are sitting at our own campfires.

Class communication through the media has even greater implications for society, and particularly the role of communication media in the society. For more than a century the mass communication media were the flexible "glue" that helped keep most of the society together. They built and developed a common culture, albeit commercial and superficial, that fed a similar diet of news and entertainment to people in different walks of life in different parts of the country. To be sure, this catering to the majority meant that certain segments of the population, such as racial and cultural minorities, were often either left out of the mainstream content or portrayed as seen through Anglo eyes. But the same media also served to transmit the culture and language of the dominant group to the new immigrants. Some of these immigrants, because of physical characteristics such as color or geographical proximity to their mother country, were outside of the melting pot. The media sometimes built common interests where they did not already exist, developing a surface culture or generating interest in events or personalities that were not of real importance to the readers, viewers, and listeners. And the emphasis on the lowest common denominator often meant that the mass media acted to lower public tastes, rather than elevate them.

But, the bottom line was that mass communication media sought and built an audience based on common interests, rather than differences. And out of this was forged the society that most Americans live in today. Now, with the emphasis on marketing and audience segmentation, the media play a very different role. The media, rather than trying to find commonalities among diverse groups in the mass audiences, classify the differences and ways to capitalize on those differences through content and advertising. The force in society that once acted to bring people together, now works to reinforce the differences that keep them apart.

Based on growth of numbers alone it would appear that both the mass audience media, which will need to attract an increasing share of a racially diverse population to claim it is truly mass media, and the media targeted to racial and cultural groups, which will have growing targets, will undergo cosmetic, if not basic, changes by the beginning of the 21st century. Mass audience news and entertainment media will have to include a more racially and culturally diverse cast of characters in a wider range of visible roles if they hope to attract shares of the growing ethnic groups. Personalities with crossover appeal to all races, such as Bill Cosby, will have the greatest opportunities for success. The media targeted toward racial and cultural audiences will most likely become more directed to specific strata within the market segment, such as Black teenagers or bilingual Latinos. As advances in technology make the media and information services more plentiful, they will become more targeted, which will benefit people of color and other segments of the population that are identifiable and potentially addressable.

The United States is not only becoming more racially and culturally diverse, but the divisions that have accompanied racial diversity are being reinforced by the communication media of the country. This division means that racial and cultural groups will be more fully served by an expanding communication media system than were racial minorities in the past. But it also means that the socialization function of media in developing and transmitting the common culture of the society will be less important.

Notes

1. Mark Fitzgerald, "All Things to All People," *Editor & Publisher* (January 7, 1995), pp. 11-14, 70.

2. For data and analyses of the impact of Latinos on broadcasting see "Hispanic Broadcasting & Cable," *Broadcasting & Cable* (January 9, 1995), pp. 40-52.

3. Nancy Hicks Maynard, *Managing the Future of News and Information*, Technology Paper, The Freedom Forum Media Studies Center, Columbia University, 1994.

4. For articles on new technologies and the need for content to communicate see *The Media Studies Journal* (Vol. 8, No. 1, Winter 1994), The Freedom Forum Media Studies Center, Columbia University. The theme of the issue is "The Race for Content."

5. For a brief description of the range of new technologies with implications for communications in the 1980s see chapter 13, "Mass Communication and New Technologies," in John R. Bittner, *Mass Communication: An Introduction* (Englewood Cliffs, NJ: Prentice Hall, 1983), pp. 312-360.

6. For general descriptions of market segmentation and market segmentation as applied to racial minorities see chap. 4, "Markets and People and Money," in William J. Stanton, *Fundamentals of Marketing* (New York: McGraw-Hill, 1981), pp. 65-86, and chap. 7, "Market Segmentation," in William H. Cunningham and Isabella Cunningham, *Marketing: A Managerial Approach* (Cincinnati, OH, South-Western Publishing, 1981), pp. 184-203.

7. See Melita Marie Garza, "Hola, América! Newsstand 2000," *The Media Studies Journal* (Vol. 8, No. 3, Summer 1994), pp. 153-161.

8. "Miami Vice: Pop and Cop," *Newsweek* (January 21, 1985), p. 67.

9. Mike Silverman, "Ratings Services Look for More Detailed Data via People Meters," *Daily Variety* (January 9, 1985), p. 4.

10. Ernest F. Larkin and Gerald L. Grotta, "A Market Segmentation Approach to Daily Newspaper Audience Studies," *Journalism Quarterly* (Vol. 56, No. 1, Spring 1979), pp. 31-37, 133.

11. Janet Bamford, "Wanted: Readers, 18-34, Affluent . . . ," *Madison Avenue* (May 1984), pp. 90-98.

12. Stanton, *Fundamentals of Marketing*, p. 78.

13. Cunningham and Cunningham, *Marketing*, p. 193.

14. See John H. Burma, *Spanish-Speaking Groups in the United States* (Durham, NC: Duke University Press, 1954), pp. 98-99, and Spyridon Granitsas, "Ethnic Press Alive and Well, 440 Published in the U.S.," *Editor & Publisher* (November 28, 1970), p. 12.

15. Gerald M. Sass, *Talking About Diversity: There's a Deadly Silence in Our Society*, Acceptance of the Ida B. Wells Award, National Association of Black Journalists National Convention, July 28, 1994. Reprinted by The Freedom Forum, Arlington, VA.

Suggested Readings

Allport, Gordon W. (1958). *The nature of prejudice.* Garden City, NY: Doubleday.

Almaguer, Tomàs. (1994). *Racial fault lines: The historical origins of White supremacy in California.* Berkeley: University of California Press.

American Management Association. (1987). *Successful marketing to U.S. Hispanics and Asians.* New York: AMA Membership Publications.

Bataille, Gretchen M., & Silet, Charles L. P. (Eds.). (1980). *The pretend Indians: Images in the movies.* Ames: Iowa State University Press.

Berkhofer, Robert F., Jr. (1978). *The White man's Indian: Images of the American Indian from Columbus to the present.* New York: Knopf.

Bogle, Donald. (1973). *Toms, coons, mulattoes, mammies, and bucks: An interpretive history of Blacks in American films.* New York: Viking.

Chen, Jack. (1980). *The Chinese of America.* New York: Harper & Row.

Cripps, Thomas. (1977). *Slow fade to Black: The Negro in American film, 1900-1942.* New York: Oxford University Press.

Dates, Jannette L., & Barlow, William. (Eds.). (1990). *Split image: African Americans in the mass media.* Washington, DC: Howard University Press.

Friar, Ralph, & Friar, Natasha. (1972). *The only good Indian . . . : The Hollywood gospel.* New York: Drama Book Specialists.

Gibson, D. Parke. (1979). *$70 billion in the Black.* New York: Macmillan.

Glazer, Nathan, & Moynihan, Daniel Patrick. (1963). *Beyond the melting pot.* Cambridge: MIT Press.

Greenberg, Bradley, Burgoon, Michael, Burgoon, Judee K., & Korzenny, Felipe. (1983). *Mexican Americans and the mass media.* Norwood, NJ: Ablex.

Guernica, Antonio. (1982). *Reaching the Hispanic market effectively*. New York: McGraw-Hill.

Horsman, Reginald. (1981). *Race and manifest destiny*. Cambridge, MA: Harvard University Press.

Hsu, Francis L. K. (1971). *The challenge of the American dream: The Chinese in the United States*. Belmont, CA: Wadsworth.

Kern-Foxworth, Marilyn. (1994). *Aunt Jemima, Uncle Ben, and Rastus: Blacks in advertising, yesterday, today and tomorrow*. Westport, CT: Greenwood Press.

MacDonald, J. Fred. (1983). *Blacks and White TV*. Chicago: Nelson-Hall.

Miller, Randall. (1980). *The kaleidoscopic lens: How Hollywood views ethnic groups*. Englewood, NJ: Ozer.

Murphy, James E., & Murphy, Sharon M. (1981). *Let my people know*. Norman: University of Oklahoma Press.

Pearce, Roy Harvey. (1965). *Savagism and civilization: A study of the Indian and the American mind*. Baltimore: Johns Hopkins University Press.

Ringer, Benjamin B. (1983). *"We the people" and others*. New York: Tavistock.

Robinson, Cecil. (1977). *Mexico and the Hispanic southwest in American literature*. Tucson: University of Arizona Press.

Rubin, Bernard. (Ed.). (1980). *Small voices and great trumpets: Minorities and the media*. New York: Praeger.

Shien-Woo Kung. (1962). *Chinese in American life: Some aspects of their history and contributions*. Seattle: University of Washington Press.

Suggs, Henry Lewis. (1983). *The Black press in the South, 1865-1979*. Westport, CT: Greenwood Press.

Toll, Robert C. (1982). *The entertainment machine*. New York: Oxford University Press.

Waters, Mary. (1990). *Ethnic options: Choosing identities in America*. Berkeley: University of California Press.

Wilson, Clint C., II. (1991). *Black journalists in paradox: Historical perspectives and current dilemmas*. Westport, CT: Greenwood Press.

Woll, Allen L. (1987). *Ethnic and racial images in American film and television: Historic essays and bibliography*. New York: Garland.

Wolseley, Roland E. (1990). *The Black press USA*. Ames: Iowa State University Press.

INDEX

About the Authors

Clint C. Wilson II is Associate Professor of Journalism at Howard University where he has served as Associate Dean and Department Chair in the School of Communications. Prior to joining the faculty at Howard University, he was Associate Professor of Journalism at the University of Southern California, where he was also director of the Media Institute for Minorities from 1980 to 1983. He is a professional journalist and editor in addition to being an educator. He has written professionally for the Associated Press, the *Los Angeles Times*, the *Pasadena* (CA) *Star-News*, the *Los Angeles Sentinel*, and the *Washington Post*, among others. He authored the book *Black Journalists in Paradox: Historical Perspectives and Current Dilemmas*, and he wrote a chapter for *Pluralizing Journalism Education: A Multicultural Handbook*. He has lectured extensively at colleges and universities across the United States and has received fellowships to the American Press Institute, The Freedom Forum Media Studies Center at Columbia University, and the Poynter Institute for Media Studies. His work on multiculturalism and the media has been published in such periodicals as *Columbia Journalism Review*, *Change* magazine, *Quill*, and *Journalism Educator*. He holds a doctorate in higher education administration and a master's degree in journalism from the University of Southern California, in addition to a bachelor's degree in journalism and public relations from California State University, Los Angeles.

Félix F. Gutiérrez is Vice President and Executive Director of The Freedom Forum Pacific Coast Center. Formerly a journalism professor at the University of Southern California (1979-1990) and California State University, Northridge (1974-1979), he also covered media issues on a weekly basis for the Los Angeles bureau of the Associated Press in the late 1980s. He is the author or coauthor of three books and more than 45 scholarly articles or book chapters on the media, nearly all focusing on racial diversity and the media. His education includes a doctorate (1976) and master's degree (1972) in communication from Stanford University, a master's from the Medill School of Journalism at Northwestern University, and a bachelor's degree in social studies from California State University, Los Angeles.

He is the first executive director of the California Chicano News Media Association (1978-1980), and a member of the boards of directors of the National Latino Communications Center and Hispanics in Philanthropy. He has been a scholar at the Tomás Rivera Center in Claremont, California and consultant on Latino media issues to a number of community, corporate, nonprofit, and government organizations.

He joined The Freedom Forum's predecessor, the Gannett Foundation, in January 1990 and was responsible for day-to-day administration of the organization's journalism education and professional grants and programs through October 1993. In November 1993 he moved from The Freedom Forum's World Center in Arlington, Virginia, to develop Freedom Forum efforts in the Western United States.